Q&A
Questions & Answers

Accountancy

BANKERS Q&A
Questions & Answers

Accountancy

Tony Sawyer & Ron Walk

First published in Great Britain 1984 by Financial Training Publications Limited, Avenue House, 131 Holland Park Avenue, London W11 4UT

© Tony Sawyer and Ron Walk

ISBN 0 906322 56 1

Typeset by LKM Typesetting Ltd, Paddock Wood, Nr Tonbridge
Printed by The Pitman Press, Bath

All rights reserved. No part of this book may be reproduced or transmitted in any form or by any means, electronic or mechanical, including photocopying, recording, or any information storage or retrieval system, without prior permission from the publisher.

Contents

Acknowledgement		vi
About the authors		vi
Introduction		vii
1	Elements of accountancy	1
2	Source and application of funds: SSAP 10	21
3	Interpretation of accounts	41
4	Budgeting	61
5	Cash budgets	113
6	Profit/cash/working capital	149
7	Share and business valuations	163
8	Liquidation	183
9	Reorganisation of capital	207
10	Group accounts	217
11	Taxation in company accounts: SSAPs 8 and 15	243
12	Published accounts	255
13	Current cost accounting: SSAP 16	287
14	Statements of Standard Accounting Practice	305
15	Capital project appraisal	321
Index		355

Acknowledgement

The authors and publishers wish to thank the Institute of Bankers for their kind permission to include selected past examination questions in this publication.

About the authors

Tony Sawyer is an Associate of the Institute of Bankers and also holds a Certificate of Education. After 12 years of experience with Lloyds Bank, he joined the accounting department of a West Midlands public company. He then trained as a teacher and has spent the last 6 years at City of Birmingham Polytechnic where he is a Senior Lecturer.

He is primarily responsible for Banking Courses but has also taught on degree and non-professional courses. He specialises in Financial Accounting and Practice of Banking.

Ron Walk is a Fellow of the Institute of Chartered Accountants qualifying in 1961. He also graduated as an external student of London University (BSc Econ).

He has wide experience of education, teaching over 20 years in universities, polytechnics, the private accountancy sector and has spent 2 years as the training manager at the Birmingham office of Peat Marwick and Mitchell.

He is currently a Senior Lecturer at City of Birmingham Polytechnic involved in both degree and professional courses where he specialises in Financial Management.

Introduction

This book has been written specifically for the Institute of Bankers, Stage 2 examination in Accountancy. It contains 100 questions together with model answers and the workings which are necessary to achieve those answers. The book is designed to help you practise answering examination standard questions and takes you through the various stages required to produce a good answer.

Most of the questions have been taken from past examination papers, the remainder have been formulated by the authors. All the answers have been written by the authors.

The structure of the book closely follows the syllabus. Each chapter has an introduction to the subject area and lists the main points required for study.

Chapter 1 is a revision chapter designed to refresh your memory of your previous Accountancy studies. Chapters 2-15 provide complete coverage of the syllabus.

You will find that the syllabus for this examination is demanding; financial information is of prime importance to lending bankers and thus fundamental to the profession.

The book is designed to be used in conjunction with whatever method of study you are currently pursuing and will provide you with essential practice at answering questions to test your understanding of the various topics contained in the syllabus.

1 Elements of accountancy

INTRODUCTION

This is a revision chapter concerned with the nature and preparation of accounting statements. It is vital to bankers firstly, because they are frequently required to prepare accounts, often in honorary positions, e.g., rotary clubs, Chambers of Commerce etc. Secondly because there is little likelihood of their being able to interpret and use accounting data unless they have a firm grasp of the principles and conventions upon which accounts are prepared.

PURPOSE

Accounts are produced to 'account' for the disposition and use of resources. They are submitted, at one level, to those who are responsible for the management and control of resources within an organisation. Managers and executives in their turn, have to account at a higher level to 'external' groups such as shareholders (or other proprietors) and loan creditors, and to provide financial information to employees, trades unions, government departments (e.g., Inland Revenue, Customs and Excise, Department of Trade, statistical office), customers, suppliers, potential investors, and the general public.

NATURE OF ACCOUNTS (STATEMENTS)

There are three major accounting statements which are closely related: balance sheet; profit and loss account; and source and application of funds.

Balance sheet (in the USA, the financial statement)

This is the basic accounting statement and is known as the financial statement since it summarises a firm's assets (resources owned or controlled) and forms of finance, which are of two types: capital, the proprietors' interest (or stake) in the assets; and liabilities, the finance provided by creditors, i.e., those to whom the firm owes money.

Since all of a firm's assets must have been financed by someone:

>   Assets = Finance = Capital + Liabilities

Any list of assets, liabilities and capital such as a balance sheet or financial statement must balance; the financial relationship is often expressed as:

   Capital = Assets less Liabilities

i.e., Capital = Net Assets.

Other expressions for capital, in this sense, are 'net worth' or 'wealth'. The purpose of business, and economic activity in general, is to create wealth for consumption by its creators. An increase in capital, i.e., an increase in the value of net assets generated by the use of those assets is known as profit — the expression 'surplus' is sometimes used as a more appropriate description.

   Profit (for a period) = Increase in Net Assets (generated during the period)

In the absence of proper records of financial activity an estimate of profit, and thus the tax payable on that profit, may be made by comparing the opening and closing capital balances.

As profit is an increase in capital, a loss is a decrease in capital, i.e., a loss is a loss of capital.

The form of a balance sheet

The major groupings on a balance sheet are:

(a) *Fixed assets*, i.e., assets which are intended to be kept in the business while they are useful, e.g., land, buildings, equipment, furniture and fittings, motor vehicles. They are generally valued at cost less depreciation. Depreciation is calculated to eliminate an asset's value from the balance sheet over its useful life.

(b) *Current assets*, i.e., assets which are held only temporarily since the firm's intention is to convert them into cash thus creating wealth; they are often referred to as circulating assets, since they are components of the business cycle, as illustrated:

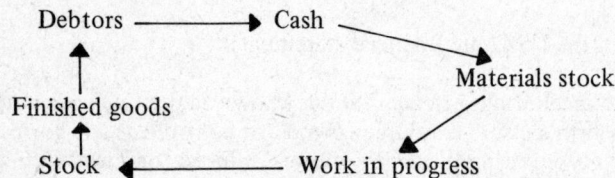

Since by convention profit is recognised and wealth created when the stock is sold, the larger the value of this circulating capital and the faster it is circulated, the greater will be the profit. Current assets are valued at cost until they are sold, thus becoming debtors, the valuation of which includes the profit.

Other current assets include short-term marketable investments and bills of exchange.

(i) Investments: although these are fixed assets in the sense that one does not intend to sell them, they represent capital invested outside the business and are shown separately on the balance sheet.

(ii) Intangible assets: i.e., untouchable or invisible assets. This group includes patent rights and trade marks, and goodwill. This latter asset only appears on a firm's balance sheet when it has purchased a business as a going concern, and has paid more for that business than the fair value of the individual or separable net assets.

(c) *Current liabilities:* this group includes those creditors which are repayable on demand or in the short term. Since the 1981 Companies Act requires a separate statement of liabilities payable in more than a year's time, the current period could well be a year.

The group includes:

(i) creditors and accruals;
(ii) taxation;
(iii) proposed dividends;
(iv) bills payable;
(v) bank overdraft.

Working capital or net current assets: Most UK companies deduct current liabilities from current assets to show on the balance sheet their working capital, i.e., the net current assets. An alternative, and more appropriate description is circulating capital.

(d) *Capital:* this section of the balance sheet includes, in the case of a company, the *share capital* introduced and the *reserves*, i.e., the profits retained in the business. Sole traders and partnerships do not as a rule bother to distinguish between the capital introduced and the profits retained.

Long-term liabilities or *loan capital:* these loans are usually at a fixed rate of interest and repayable at a fixed time, e.g., 10% debentures repayable 1.7.93.

Profit and loss account

In this statement a business explains how the profit has been made by comparing income (e.g., sales), with expenditure, suitably classified. Note that income creates assets and thus increases capital, while expenses consume assets and thus reduce capital.

(a) *The trading account* is the first part of a profit and loss account in which the cost of sales is deducted from the sales to show the gross (or basic) profit. The other expenses of the business, the overheads, are then listed under appropriate headings and deducted from the gross profit to show the net profit.

After taxation has been deducted from the firm's profit, the post-tax profit may be appropriated as dividends (payments to shareholders), transfer to specific reserves (i.e., profit retained for a particular purpose, or to comply with company law), or retained as a general reserve.

A reserve is simply retained profit.

(b) *A manufacturing account* is a sub-division of the trading account, in which a manufacturer summarises all the costs of manufacturing under the three headings of : materials, direct wages and overheads. The total of these three costs is required as an input to the cost of sales calculation.

Source and application of funds statement

This statement explains the movement of funds and the changes in the balance sheet structure from the beginning to the end of the year.

Since such statements are a popular examination question they will be dealt with separately — see Chapter 2.

QUESTIONS

1 S. GIBSON

The following is a list of assets and liabilities of a business owned by Mr S. Gibson, a manufacturer as at 30 September 1984:

	£
Stock of finished goods	1,000
Plant and machinery	21,440
Stock of raw materials	5,750
Mortgage on buildings	10,000
Cash at bank	660
Machine tools	1,900
Factory land and buildings	32,000
Lorries and delivery vans	9,500
Cash in hand	80
Owing to T. Jackson	2,130
Owed by D. Rigby	300

Required:

(a) Construct a balance sheet in vertical format to show Gibson's capital stake in the business.

(b) On 1 October the only transactions at the works are:

   (i) £50 of machine tools were bought by cheque; **and**
   (ii) £850 of raw materials were obtained on credit.

   How would the balance sheet alter? (Insert only the changes appropriate.)

(c) On 2 October the following occurred:

   (i) Rigby pays Mr Gibson but takes a 5% discount;

   (ii) one fifth of the finished goods were sold for cash to a Mr Churchill for £245;

   (iii) Mr Gibson drew motor expenses of £25 from petty cash.

   Again, insert the amendments to the balance sheet.

2 G. RICHARDS

The following balance sheet of G. Richards, an electrical retailer, was produced at 31 October 1983:

	Cost	Depreciation	Net
	£	£	£
Fixed assets			
Fixtures	1,000	400	600
Shop equipment	600	300	300
	1,600	700	900

Current assets			
Stocks		4,000	
Debtors		200	
		4,200	
Less: Current liabilities			
Creditors	2,200		
Overdraft	1,800		
		4,000	
Net current assets			200
			1,100
Capital			1,100

During the year to 31 October 1984, shop sales were £67,000, of which £500 was still outstanding at the year end. Purchases during the year were £49,000 including £1,900 due to creditors at the year end. Stock levels were maintained @ £4,000.

During the year the shop assistant's wages of £2,080 were paid in cash, as were all of the shop's running expenses of £4,400, and Mr Richards' drawings of £10,000.

Depreciation of fixed assets is at 10% by the straight-line method.

Required:

Produce Mr Richards' trading, and profit and loss account for the year ended 31 October 1984, and his balance sheet at that date.

3 S. HOUGH

Steve Hough is a carpenter who became self-employed on 1 September 1984. At that point his tools of trade were valued at £850, his motor vehicle was valued at £4,000, and he had £200 in cash.

During September the following transactions took place:

			£
September	2	Purchases: timber, etc.	124
	6	Work done (sales)	56
	7	Petrol	8
	9	Purchases: timber	62
	14	Work done (sales)	84
	16	Stationery	6
	17	Petrol	8
	20	Purchases: timber	33
	23	Postage stamps	2
	25	Work done (sales)	98
	27	Motor vehicle repair	17*
	28	Drawings	30

*This was the only transaction on credit (Hans' Garage), all the rest were for cash.

At 30 September his closing stock of materials was £125.

Required:

(a) Construct an opening balance sheet to show capital injected.

(b) Open ledger accounts for the balance sheet items. Take out a trial balance on 30 September 1984, and construct his trading and profit and loss account, and balance sheet as at 30 September 1984. (Ignore depreciation.)

4 J. BASS

The following list of balances was extracted from the books of J. Bass on 30 April 1984.

	£
Capital	3,350
Returns inward	10
Returns outward	10
Drawings	150
Sales	11,980
Sundry debtors	1,600
Sundry creditors	2,300
Cash in hand	40
Bank overdraft	250
Furniture	1,500
Furniture repairs	75
Carriage outwards	65
Wages	600
Purchases	11,000
Rent and rates	200
Advertising	150
General expenses	100
Stock at 1.4.84	2,400

Following the stocktake on the evening of 30 April 1984, stock in hand was valued at £2,700.

Required:

(a) Construct a trial balance to prove the accuracy of the above balances.

(b) Prepare final accounts in vertical form for the month ended 30 April 1984. (Ignore depreciation.)

5 LOWER TOWN TRADING CO LTD

The Lower Town Trading Co Ltd was founded on 1 January 1978 with an authorised share capital of £50,000 made up of ordinary shares of 25p each.

The following trial balance was extracted from their books on 31 December 1980:

	£	£
Share capital, fully paid and called up		20,000
10% debentures		10,000
Share premium account		5,000
Profit and loss account		5,000
Reserves		4,000
Debtors and creditors	8,500	7,000
Freehold premises (cost £24,000)	22,000	
Office furniture (cost £5,000)	3,500	
Stock at 1 January	9,500	
Salaries and wages	6,850	
Lighting and heating	500	
Rates	650	
Selling and distribution expenses	2,250	
Administration expenses	750	
Purchases and sales	22,500	44,500
Cash at bank	18,500	
	95,500	95,500

Additional information:

(a) Stock on hand at 31 December was valued at £9,300.

(b) Depreciation is to be provided on the straight-line method as follows:

    Freehold premises   5% p.a.
    Office furniture   10% p.a.

(c) There is an electricity bill for £50 outstanding.

(d) A full year's interest is due on the debentures.

(e) A provision for bad debts is to be created equal to 5% of debtors.

(f) Rates have been prepaid by £50.

(g) The directors propose that the profits be appropriated as follows:

    (i) in payment of final dividend of 20% on ordinary shares;
    (ii) the balance to be carried forward.

Required:

Prepare the trading, profit and loss account for the year 1980 and the balance sheet as at 31 December 1980.

6 A. WHEELER LTD

The following information was extracted from the accounts of A. Wheeler Ltd, manufacturer, as at 30 June 1984. Prepare their manufacturing, trading and profit and loss accounts for the year ended 30 June 1984. Insufficient information is available to prepare the balance sheet.

Show clearly within these accounts, the cost of materials used, prime cost, factory cost of goods completed, and cost of goods sold.

	£
Stocks at 1 July 1983	
Raw materials	6,500
Finished goods (at factory cost)	5,700
Purchases for year to 30 June 1984	
Raw materials	132,000
Other (indirect) factory materials	3,900
Fire insurance, 3/4 chargeable to factory, 1/4 to office	1,620
Direct wages	41,340
Factory fuel and power	4,100
Heat and light, 3/4 chargeable to factory, 1/4 to office	1,600
Rent and rates: factory	4,500
office	1,500
Factory salaries	7,000
Advertising	4,800
Office salaries	4,000
Provision for bad debts	220
Depreciation: factory machinery	6,000
office furniture	700
Sales	247,000
On 30 June 1984 stocks values are as follows:	
Raw materials at cost	8,500
Finished goods (at factory cost)	5,900

In addition you are given:

Prepayments at 30 June 1984: Fire insurance, factory £200 office £30.

The provision for bad debts to be increased to £320.

ANSWERS

1 S. GIBSON

(a) **Balance sheet as at 30 September 1984**

	£	£
Fixed assets		
Factory land and buildings		32,000
Plant and machinery		21,440
Lorries and delivery vans		9,500
Machine tools		1,900
		64,840
Current assets		
Stock of raw materials	5,750	
Stock of finished goods	1,000	
Debtor (Rigby)	300	
Bank	660	
Cash in hand	80	
	7,790	
Less: Current liabilities		
Creditor (Jackson)	(2,130)	
Net current assets		5,660
		70,500
Less: Mortgage loan		(10,000)
		60,500
Capital (stake of proprietor)		60,500

(b) 1 October 1984

	£
	+ 50 b(i)
	+ 850 b(ii)
	− 50 b(i)
	+ 850 b(ii)
	No change

(c) 2 October 1984

	£
	− 200 c(ii)
	− 300 c(i)
	+ 285 c(i)
	+ 245 c(ii)
	− 25 c(iii)
	− 15 c(i)
	+ 45 c(ii)
	− 25 c(iii)

Tutorial note

This question illustrates that all business transactions can be recorded in balance sheets. Since 'assets less liabilities equals capital', profit is reflected only in the capital changes.

Balance sheets, however, are not produced every day due to the sheer volume of transactions, the majority of which have an insignificant effect on capital. In practice firms merely keep a detailed record of their income and expenditure, and receipts and payments of cash. Periodically income and expenditure are compared to provide the profit figure, which will equal the change in capital per the balance sheets at the beginning and end of the period.

2 G. RICHARDS

Trading, and profit and loss account for the year ended 31.10.84

	£	£
Sales		67,000
Less: Opening stocks	4,000	
Purchases	49,000	
Closing stocks	(4,000)	
Cost of sales		49,000
Gross profit		18,000
Less: Shop assistant's wages	2,080	
Running expenses	4,400	
Depreciation of fixtures	100	
Depreciation of equipment	60	
		6,640
Net profit		11,360

Balance sheet as at 31.10.84

Fixed assets	Cost £	Depreciation £	Net £
Fixtures	1,000	500	500
Shop equipment	600	360	240
	1,600	860	740

Current assets			
Stocks		4,000	
Debtors		500	
		4,500	
Less: Current liabilities			
Creditors	1,900		
Overdraft (the balancing figure)	880		
		2,780	
			1,720
			2,460
Capital			1,100
Net profit for year			11,360
Less: Drawings			(10,000)
			2,460

Tutorial notes

(a) These two statements have been produced in standard form, in the case of the balance sheet summarising assets, liabilities and capital under appropriate headings.

The trading and profit and loss account summarises the income and expenditure, in the first place to show the gross (or basic) profit, and secondly, by deducting the overheads, to show the net profit.

(b) The drawings (withdrawals of capital) do not appear in the profit and loss account proper, since they are not expenses of the business.

(c) The final balance at the bank, £880, can be proved as follows:

Total bank account

RECEIPTS	£	PAYMENTS	£
Last year's debtors settled in full	200	Opening overdraft	1,800
Cash from sales this year		Shop assistant's wages	2,080
(i.e., £67,000 less £500)	66,500	Running expenses	4,400
Therefore, closing overdraft	880	Drawings	10,000
		Last year's creditors paid	2,200
		Stock purchases this year	
		(i.e., £49,000 less £1,900)	47,100
	67,580		67,580

3 S. HOUGH

(a) **Balance sheet as at 1 September 1984**

	£
Fixed assets	
Motor vehicle	4,000
Tools of trade	850
	4,850
Current assets	
Cash in hand	200
	5,050
Capital injected	5,050

(b)

Motor vehicle A/C		Tools of trade A/C	
	£		£
1.9 Balance	4,000	1.9 Balance	850

Cash in hand A/C

RECEIPTS	£	PAYMENTS	£
1.9 Balance	200	2.9 Purchases	124
6.9 Work done	56	7.9 Petrol	8
14.9 Work done	84	9.9 Purchases	62
25.9 Work done	98	16.9 Stationery	6
		17.9 Petrol	8
		20.9 Purchases	33
		23.9 Postages	2
		28.9 Drawing	30
		30.9 Balance	165
	438		438

Purchases A/C

	£
2.9 Cash	124
9.9 Cash	62
20.9 Cash	33
	219

Work done (sales) A/C

	£
6.9 Cash	56
14.9 Cash	84
25.9 Cash	98
	238

Capital A/C

	£
1.9 Balance	5,050

Petrol A/C

	£
7.9 Cash	8
17.9 Cash	8
	16

Stationery A/C

	£
16.9 Cash	6

Postages A/C

	£
23.9 Cash	2

Motor vehicle repair A/C

	£
27.9 Hans' Garage	17

Hans Garage A/C

	£
27.9 Motor vehicle repair	17

Drawings A/C

	£
28.9 Cash	30

Trial balance at 30.9.84

	Dr £	Cr £
Motor vehicle	4,000	
Tools of trade	850	
Cash in hand	165	
Capital		5,050
Petrol	16	
Purchases	219	
Work done		238
Stationery	6	
Postages	2	
Motor vehicle repair	17	
Creditor		17
Drawings	30	
	5,305	5,305
Closing stocks	125	125
	5,430	5,430

Trading, and profit and loss account for September 1984

	£	£
Work done		238
Less: Opening stocks	Nil	
Purchases	219	
Closing stocks	(125)	
Cost of sales		94
Gross profit		144
Less: Overheads:		
Petrol	16	
Stationery	6	
Postages	2	
Motor vehicle repairs	17	
		41
Net profit		103

Balance sheet as at 30 September 1984

	£	£
Fixed assets		
Motor vehicle		4,000
Tools of trade		850
		4,850
Current assets		
Stocks	125	
Cash in hand	165	
	290	
Less: Current liabilities		
Creditor	17	
		273
		5,123
Capital		5,050
Add: Net profit for month		103
Less: Drawings		(30)
		5,123

Tutorial notes

(a) In a double-entry accounting system, assets are recorded as debit balances, and liabilities and capital as credit balances.

Since revenue and profit increase capital, they are recorded as credits. Expenses and losses, on the other hand, reduce capital, and are therefore recorded as debits.

To summarise:

Assets
Expenses } are debit balances
Losses

Liabilities
Revenue
Profits } are credit balances
Capital

(b) Since all financial transactions have two aspects, one recorded as a debit, and the other as a credit, a list of the results of recorded transactions (a trial balance) will have an equal amount of debit balances and credit balances.

A trial balance is produced: (i) to prove the accuracy of the double-entry system; and (ii) as a convenient store of financial data from which final accounts (trading, profit and loss, and balance sheet) may be prepared.

(c) The closing stock is introduced to the system by debiting a stock account (an asset) and crediting the trading account to adjust the purchases to the cost of sales (the cost of the goods consumed).

4 J. BASS

(a) Trial balance at 30.4.84

	Dr	Cr
Capital		3,350
Returns inward	10	
Returns outward		10
Drawings	150	
Sales		11,980
Sundry debtors	1,600	
Sundry creditors		2,300
Cash in hand	40	
Bank overdraft		250
Furniture	1,500	
Furniture repairs	75	
Carriage outwards	65	
Wages	600	
Purchases	11,000	
Rent and rates	200	
Advertising	150	
General expenses	100	
Stock at 1.4.84	2,400	
(note 1)	17,890	17,890
Closing stock (note 2)	2,700	2,700
	20,590	20,590

Notes

(1) The trial balance, a list of all the balances, proves the accuracy of the double-entry accounting; the total was £17,890.

(2) The closing stock has been introduced to the trial balance (a debit and a credit) for illustration purposes only.

(b) **Trading, and profit and loss account for the month ended 30.4.84**

	£	£
Sales		11,980
Less: Returns inward		10
		11,970
Less: Opening stock	2,400	
Purchases	11,000	
Less: Returns outward	10	
	10,990	
Less: Closing stock	(2,700)	
Cost of sales		10,690
Gross profit		1,280
Less: overheads:		
Wages	600	
Furniture repairs	75	
Carriage outwards	65	
Rent and rates	200	
Advertising	150	
General expenses	100	
		1,190
Net profit		90

Balance sheet as at 30.4.84

	£	£
Fixed assets		
Furniture		1,500
Current assets		
Stocks	2,700	
Debtors	1,600	
Cash	40	
	4,340	
Less: Current liabilities		
Creditors	2,300	
Overdraft	250	
	2,550	
Net current assets		1,790
		3,290
Capital		3,350
Add: Net profit for April		90
Less: Drawings		(150)
		3,290

5 LOWER TOWN TRADING CO LTD

Trading and profit and loss account for the year ended 31.12.80

	£	£
Sales		44,500
Less: Opening stocks	9,500	
Purchases	22,500	
Closing stocks	(9,300)	
Cost of sales		22,700
Gross profit		21,800
Less: Overheads:		
Salaries and wages	6,850	
Lighting and heating (£500 + £50)	550	
Rates (£650 − £50)	600	
Selling and distribution expenses	2,250	
Administration expenses	750	
Depreciation of freehold premises	1,200	
Depreciation of office furniture	500	
Bad debts	425	
Debenture interest	1,000	
		14,125
Net profit		7,675
Less: Dividend on ordinary shares		4,000
Retained profit		3,675
Add: Profit and loss account balance 1.1.80		5,000
Profit and loss account 31.12.80		8,675

Balance sheet as at 31.12.80

	Cost £	Depreciation £	Net £
Fixed assets			
Freehold premises	24,000	3,200	20,800
Office furniture	5,000	2,000	3,000
	29,000	5,200	23,800
Current assets			
Stocks		9,300	
Debtors	8,500		
Less: Provision for bad debts	425		
		8,075	
Prepayments		50	
Bank		18,500	
		35,925	

	£	£	£
Less: Current liabilities			
Creditors	7,000		
Accruals: Dividend	4,000		
Electricity	50		
Debenture interest	1,000	12,050	
Net current assets			23,875
			47,675
Less: 5% debentures			10,000
			37,675
Capital			
Authorised 200,000 ordinary 25p shares			50,000
Issued 80,000 ordinary 25p shares fully paid			20,000
Reserves: Share premium	5,000		
Revenue reserves	4,000		
Profit and loss account	8,675		17,675
			37,675

6 A. WHEELER LTD

Manufacturing, trading and profit and loss account for the year ended 30 June 1984

		£	£	£
Sales				247,000
Less: Manufacturing costs:				
Stocks of raw materials 1.7.83		6,500		
Purchases of raw materials		132,000		
Stocks of raw materials 30.6.84		(8,500)		
Raw materials consumed		130,000		
Direct wages		41,340		
Prime cost		171,340		
Add: Factory overheads:	£			
Factory materials	3,900			
Fuel as power	4,100			
Heat and light	1,200			
Fire insurance	1,015			
Rent and rates	4,500			
Factory salaries	7,000			
Depreciation of machinery	6,000	27,715		
Production cost			199,055	
Add: Stocks of finished goods 1.7.83			5,700	
Deduct: Stocks of finished goods 30.6.84			(5,900)	
Cost of sales				198,855
Gross profit				48,145

		£	£
Gross profit brought forward			48,145
Less: Administration and selling overheads:			
Heat and light		400	
Fire insurance		375	
Rent and rates		1,500	
Advertising		4,800	
Office salaries		4,000	
Bad debts		100	
Depreciation of furniture		700	11,875
Net profit before tax			36,270

2 Source and application of funds: SSAP 10

INTRODUCTION

Funds statements are the most important historic accounting statement from a banker's point of view because they are concerned with the actual generation and disposition of cash.

Until the 1970s, the established balance sheet and profit and loss account, with supporting ratios, were considered adequate statements of business affairs. With the wider spread of company shareholdings among those with little or no understanding of accounts, and the impact of serious inflation making profit measurement less reliable, a simpler and more direct statement was considered necessary. The purpose of a source and application of funds statement is to explain how the closing balance sheet is related to the opening balance sheet, particularly in respect of cash and other liquid assets, i.e., it purports to state where a company has obtained its money from and what it has done with it. Rather than including details of income and expenditure, the statement starts with the profit figure per the profit and loss account.

After considerable experimentation, the Accounting Standards Committee produced the following format, which should be used when a statement of source and application of funds is required.

STATEMENT OF SOURCE AND APPLICATION OF FUNDS FOR THE YEAR ENDED...............

	£	£
Sources:		
Profit, before taxation	XXX,XXX	
Add: Items not involving the movement of funds, e.g., depreciation	X,XXX	
Funds from trading		XX,XXX
Issue of shares		XX,XXX
Issue of debentures, and other capital issues		XX,XXX
Sale of fixed assets		X,XXX
Sale of long-term investments		XXX
		XXX,XXX

Applications:	£	£
Purchase of fixed assets	XX,XXX	
Purchase of investments	X,XXX	
Repayment of share capital	XXX	
Repayment of loans	X,XXX	
Payment of tax	XXX	
Payment of dividends	XXX	XXX,XXX
		XXX,XXX

Increase/Decrease in working capital:		
Stock changes		XX,XXX
Debtors changes		XXX,XXX
Creditors changes		(X,XXX)
		XXX,XXX

Increase/Decrease in net liquid assets:		
Bank balances	XX,XXX	
Cash balances	X,XXX	
Short-term marketable investments	(XX,XXX)	
		XX,XXX
		XXX,XXX

The following points should be noted:

(a) The majority of the figures for this statement can be calculated by simple subtraction of the items in the opening balance sheet from the corresponding items in the closing balance sheet.

(b) Since the main function is to explain changes in liquid resources, such items should appear at the end of the statement.

SUGGESTED METHOD FOR ANSWERING THE QUESTION

Memorise and construct a 'gapped' funds flow statement layout. Consider completing the lower section on working capital first, which gives the answer to the top section and is therefore a very helpful guide.

Difficulty in the top section centres mainly around:

(a) Obtaining exact *cash* movements for sale and purchase of fixed assets. Remember that a 'profit' on sale is not really profit but an understatement of depreciation over the years the asset has been held. A loss is the converse.

(b) Obtaining net profit for the year, which usually means working an appropriation account in reverse order.

QUESTIONS

1 BOSWELL LTD

The balance sheets of Boswell Ltd at 31 March 1982, and 31 March 1983, appear below.

	31 March 1982 £	31 March 1983 £		31 March 1982 £	31 March 1983 £
Issued share capital	30,000	40,000	Freehold property at cost	25,000	25,000
Profit and loss account	27,000	23,000	Equipment (see note)	18,000	22,200
Corporation tax due:			Stock in trade	16,400	17,800
			Debtors	13,600	14,000
1 January 1983	6,000	–	Bank	2,000	1,000
1 January 1984	–	4,000			
Creditors	12,000	13,000			
	75,000	80,000		75,000	80,000

Note: Equipment movements during the year ended 31 March 1983, were:

	Cost £	Depreciation £	Net £
Balance at 31 March 1982	30,000	12,000	18,000
Additions during year	9,000		
Depreciation provided during year		3,800	
	39,000	15,800	
Disposals during year	4,000	3,000	
Balance at 31 March 1983	35,000	12,800	22,200

The company's summarised profit calculation for the year ended 31 March 1983, revealed:

	£	£
Sales		100,000
Gain on sale of equipment		400
		100,400
Less: Cost of goods and trading expenses	86,600	
Depreciation	3,800	
		90,400
Net profit		10,000
Corporation tax on profits of the year		4,000
Retained profit of the year		6,000

During the year ended 31 March 1983, Boswell Ltd made a bonus issue of 10,000 £1 ordinary shares by capitalisation from the profit and loss account.

Required:

A flow of funds statement for Boswell Ltd revealing the sources and applications of working capital during the year ended 31 March 1983.

20 marks

2   RETAIL LTD

Simon is puzzled by the accounts of Retail Ltd. He says:

> I have calculated the company's funds generated from operations by adding back depreciation to net profit. The amounts came to £29,000 in 1975 and £35,000 in 1976 but, despite modest dividends and fixed assets acquisitions, the company started 1975 with a bank balance of £5,000 and finished 1976 with an overdraft of £13,000. Why?

You are provided with the following figures for Retail Ltd:

Balance sheets at 31 December	1974 £000	1975 £000	1976 £000
Issued share capital	100	100	100
Reserves	33	42	58
Proposed dividends	8	10	8
Trade creditors	28	36	39
Bank overdraft	–	5	13
	169	193	218
Fixed assets at cost, at beginning of year	126	137	149
Additions during year	11	12	13
	137	149	162
Less: Depreciation	38	48	59
	99	101	103
Stocks	25	32	35
Trade debtors	40	60	80
Bank	5	–	–
	169	193	218

Profit statements for years ended 31 December		1975		1976
	£000	£000	£000	£000
Sales: For cash		200		150
On credit		300		400
		500		550
Deductions:				
Opening stock	25		32	
Purchases	357		388	
	382		420	
Less: Closing stock	32		35	
Cost of goods sold	350		385	
Sundry expenses	121		130	
Depreciation	10		11	
		481		526
Net profit		19		24
Proposed dividends		10		8
Retained profit		9		16

It can be assumed that all sundry expenses were paid in the year in which they were incurred and that trade creditors relate only to purchased goods.

Required:

(a) Numerical statements showing the *cash* receipts and payments which explain the changes in the bank account of Retail Ltd in 1975 and 1976, so far as the information available permits.

(b) Brief comments, for Simon's benefit, on the statements you have prepared.

Ignore taxation.

20 marks

3   BIX LTD

Balance sheets as at		31.3.82		31.3.83
Fixed assets	£000	£000	£000	£000
Freeholds		180		270
Plant at cost	300		610	
Less: Accumulated depreciation	90		194	
		210		416
		390		686
Trade investment		16		Nil

Current assets		£000	£000		£000	£000
Stock		103			101	
Debtors		85			100	
Bank		31			7	
		219			208	
Less: Current liabilities	£000			£000		
Creditors	39			22		
Proposed dividend	40			50		
Corporation tax	26			32		
		105			104	
			114			104
			520			790
Capital						
£1 ordinary shares			400			550
Revaluation reserve (freehold)			Nil			90
Profit and loss account			70			100
Shareholders funds			470			740
Loans: 8% debenture			50			50
			520			790

Notes

(1) Profit and loss account for 1983 was:

	£000
Net profit	112
Less: Corporation tax	32
	80
Less: Proposed dividend	50
Retained profit for year	30

(2) Plant which had cost £45,000 some years ago and had a written-down value of £6,000, was sold during the year for £8,000.

(3) The trade investments were sold for £19,000.

Following production of the accounts for 1983, the managing director has enquired of his financial director as follows:

How is it, following a record year with net profit at £112,000, that bank balances have fallen so dramatically? With turnover planned to rise by 40% next year, will we have enough cash in the bank to finance expenses?

Required:

To produce a statement explaining why bank balances have not kept in line with profit.

20 marks

4 GREEN LTD

The directors of Green Ltd are reviewing the company's financial requirements for the year to 31 August 1980.

The summarised balance sheet of Green Ltd at 31 August 1979 showed:

	£		£	£
Ordinary share capital	40,000	Goodwill		6,000
Profit and loss account	36,200	Freehold warehouse		26,000
Trade creditors	19,800	Fittings and equip-		
Bank overdraft	3,000	ment at cost	20,000	
		Less depreciation	8,500	
				11,500
		Stock in trade		23,000
		Trade debtors		32,500
	99,000			99,000

The company's plans are based upon the following expectations for the year to 31 August 1980.

Issue for cash of 10,000 £1 ordinary shares at a premium of 50p per share in October 1979.

New equipment will be purchased for £7,000 cash on 1 September 1979. Goodwill will be written down by £3,000.

Stock in trade at the end of the year will be £29,000.

The following trading transactions etc. will occur at an even rate throughout the year:

	£
Sales	240,000
Purchases	186,000
General expenses	35,000
Directors' salaries	8,000

The period of credit allowed to customers will be 2 calendar months and the period of credit taken from suppliers will be 1½ calendar months. All amounts (including debtors and creditors outstanding at 31 August 1979) will be paid in full at the end of the credit periods. No amounts for general expenses or directors' salaries will be outstanding at the end of the year.

Depreciation on all equipment held at the end of the year will be provided at the rate of 10% p.a. (on cost).

Required:

(a) A statement of the estimated sources and applications of funds of Green Ltd for the year ending 31 August 1980. Ignore taxation.

(b) A statement showing how the following alternative assumptions would affect the cash available to the company at 31 August 1980, compared with the previously estimated position:

(Specify your answer in each case as either *increase* £ . . . or *decrease* £ . . . or *no change*. Comments on your answers are not required.)

- (i) Freehold shop revalued in accounts at £34,000.
- (ii) Period of credit allowed to customers 1½ months.
- (iii) Period of credit taken from suppliers 1 month.
- (iv) Depreciation provided for year increased to 15% on cost.
- (v) Remainder of goodwill written off.

30 marks

5 COHEN LTD

The following balance sheet has been prepared for Cohen Ltd at 31 December 1979:

Balance sheet at 31 December 1979

	£	£		£	£
Ordinary share capital (£1 shares)		800,000	Freehold property at cost		400,000
10% redeemable preference share capital		300,000	Plant and machinery at cost	1,446,600	
Reserves		625,500	Less: Depreciation	617,900	
		1,725,500			828,700
			Investment at cost		230,000
12% debentures, 1990		500,000	Current assets		
			Stock	1,063,700	
Current liabilities	£		Debtors	682,300	
Trade creditors	476,200				1,746,000
Taxation due 30.9.80	196,000				
Dividend	60,000				
Bank overdraft	247,000				
		979,200			
		3,204,700			3,204,700

The directors of Cohen Ltd are concerned about the fact that the present overdraft is close to the facility allowed by the company's bank. The financial director has prepared the following estimated statement of funds for 1980.

Estimated statement of funds for 1980

	£	£
Sources:		
Profit before taxation		437,100
Add: Items not involving the outflow of funds:		
Loss on sale of plant (note 1)		3,500
Depreciation		247,600
Funds generated by trading activities		688,200
Funds from other sources:		
Sale of investments (note 2)		175,000
Sale of plant (note 1)		2,000
Ordinary share capital (note 3)		240,000
		1,105,200
Applications:		
Dividend paid: ordinary shares	60,000	
preference shares	15,000	
Redemption of preference shares (note 4)	300,000	
Taxation paid	196,000	
Purchase of plant and machinery	206,500	777,500
		327,700
Changes in working capital items:		
Increase in trade creditors	(43,400)	
Increase in debtors	59,700	
Increase in stock	103,500	
Increase in net liquid funds	207,900	327,700

Notes on the above accounts

(1) Plant which had cost the company £25,000 some years ago will be sold for £2,000.

(2) This represents the proceeds arising from the sale of 20,000 shares which had cost the company £7.00 each in 1970.

(3) As the result of the share issue the company's authorised and issued ordinary share capital will consist of one million ordinary shares of £1 each.

(4) Preference share capital is to be redeemed at par value on 1 July 1980.

(5) The freehold property is to be revalued during 1980; it is expected that a firm of professional valuers will place a figure of approximately £660,000 on the property and this revised figure will be written into the books.

(6) Tax payable on the estimated profits for 1980, including the capital gain on the sale of investments will be £203,800 and the directors propose to pay a final dividend of 10p on each ordinary share.

Required:

The estimated balance sheet of Cohen Ltd at 31 December 1980, presented in vertical format and taking account of the above information. You should show clearly how the figure for reserves appearing in the forecast balance sheet has been calculated.

Ignore advance corporation tax.

30 marks

ANSWERS

1 BOSWELL LTD

Source and application of funds statement for the year ended 31.3.83

	£	£
Sources:		
Net profit on trading (W1)		10,000
Add: Depreciation for year	3,800	
Less: Profit on sale of equipment	400	3,400
Funds from trading		13,400
Other sources:		
Sale of equipment (W2)		1,400
		14,800
Less: Applications:		
Tax paid	6,000	
Purchase of equipment	9,000	
		15,000
Net decrease		200
Represented by a decrease in working capital:		
Increase in stock		1,400
Increase in debtors		400
Increase in creditors		(1,000)
		800
Decrease in bank		(1,000)
		(200)

Workings

1 Profit, taken from profit statement

The profit and loss account change from £27,000 to £23,000 is explained as follows:

	£
Balance at 31.3.82	27,000
Add: Retained profit	6,000
	33,000
Less: Profit capitalised as bonus shares (see tutorial note)	10,000
	23,000

2   Proceeds of sale of equipment

Disposal Account

	£		£
Cost of asset	4,000	Depreciation	3,000
Profit on sale	400	Therefore, cash	1,400
	4,400		4,400

or, written-down value:

	£
Cost	4,000
Less: Depreciation	3,000
	1,000
Profit	400
Therefore, cash received	1,400

Tutorial notes

(a) The profit on sale of equipment is really an over-provision for depreciation and serves to reduce the depreciation for the year to £3,400.

(b) The bonus issue slightly changes the capital structure of the company but does not provide additional funds. It does not, therefore, appear in the sources statement.

(c) The tax paid is simply the creditor appearing in the opening balance sheet.

2 RETAIL LTD

(a) Cash receipts and payments

			1975			1976
			£000			£000
Receipts:						
Sales: Cash			200			150
Credit		300			400	
Add: Debtors at beginning		40			60	
Less: Debtors at end		(60)	280		(80)	380
			480			530
Payments:						
Purchases on credit	357			388		
Add: Creditors at beginning	28			36		
Less: Creditors at end	(36)	349		(39)	385	
Expenses		121			130	
		470			515	
Dividend		8			10	
Purchase of fixed assets		12			13	
		490	490		538	538
Reduction in cash			10			8

(b) These statements have summarised the movements of cash into and out of the business, illustrating the differences between sales and receipts and between expenses and payments.

It can be seen that although the credit sales in 1975 were £300,000, £60,000 of those sales were not received until 1976, and that £40,000 of the 1974 sales was received in 1975, producing a cash flow of £280,000 for credit sales. Similarly, the 1975 purchases (all on credit) were £357,000, but the cash movement in 1975 in respect of purchases was £349,000.

Besides the payments of trading expenses which are set against income to calculate profit, there have been capital items, dividends, and purchases of fixed assets, which do not reduce the profit but have been met out of the cash flow on trading.

These comments can be summarised as follows:

		1975 £000		1976 £000
Trading receipts		480		530
Trading payments		470		515
Cash flow on trading		10		15
Purchase of fixed assets	12		13	
Payment of dividends	8	20	10	23
Reduction in cash balance		10		8

Tutorial note

If a source and application of funds statement had been required, we would have started with the profit figures £19,000 and £24,000 and worked through to the cash reductions by considering changes in all the balance sheet items, including stock.

3 BIX LTD

Source and application of funds statement for year ended 31.3.83

	£000	£000
Sources:		
Net profit		109
Add: Depreciation for year		143
Less: Profit on sale of assets		(2)
Funds from operations		250
Other sources:		
Investment sold		19
Shares issued		150
Plant sold		8
		427
Less: Applications:		
Plant bought	355	
Dividends paid	40	
Tax paid	26	
		421
		6

Represented by increase in working capital:	£000
Stocks decrease	(2)
Debtors increase	15
Creditors decrease	17
	30
Bank decreases	(24)
	6

Workings

Plant account

	£000		£000
Opening balance	300	Sales	45
Therefore, purchases	355	Closing balance	610

Accumulated depreciation on plant account

	£000		£000
Sales	39	Opening balance	90
Closing balance	194	Therefore, depreciation for year	143

Sale of plant account

	£000		£000
Cost account	45	Accumulated depreciation	39
Therefore, 'profit'	2	Cash on sale	8

4 GREEN LTD

(a) **Source and application of funds statement for the year ended 31.8.80**

	£
Sources:	
Profit on trading (W1)	14,300
Add: Depreciation	2,700
	17,000
Issue of shares (10,000 × £1.50)	15,000
	32,000
Less: Applications:	
Purchase of fixed assets	7,000
	25,000

Increase in working capital (W2):

	£
Stock increase: £29,000 − £23,000	6,000
Debtors increase: £40,000 − £32,500	7,500
Creditors increase: £23,250 − £19,800	(3,450)
	10,050
Bank increase: £11,950 − £3,000	14,950
	25,000

(b) (i) No change
    (ii) Increase £10,000
    (iii) Decrease £7,750
    (iv) No change
    (v) No change

Workings

1   Profit on trading, year ended 31.8.80:

		£	£
Sales			240,000
Stock at 31.8.79		23,000	
Purchases		186,000	
		209,000	
Stock at 31.8.80		29,000	180,000
			60,000
Expenses		35,000	
Salaries		8,000	
Depreciation:	£20,000		
	£ 7,000		
	10% × £27,000	2,700	45,700
Profit on trading			14,300
Goodwill written off			3,000
			11,300
Balance at 31.8.79			36,200
			47,500

35

2   Balance sheet at 31.8.80:

	£			£
Share capital (£40,000 + £10,000)	50,000	Goodwill (£6,000 − £3,000)		3,000
Premium £10,000 × 0.5	5,000	Warehouse		26,000
Profit and loss account	47,500	Equipment	£27,000	
	102,500	Depreciation: (£8,500 + £2,700)	£11,200	15,800
Creditors £186,000 × (1½/12)	23,250	Stock		29,000
		Debtors £240,000 × (2/12)		40,000
				113,800
		Bank balancing figure		11,950
	125,750			125,750

5 COHEN LTD

Estimated balance sheet at 31.12.80

	£	£
Freehold property, as revalued (£400,000 + £260,000)		660,000
Plant and machinery at cost (W1)	1,628,100	
Less: Depreciation (W1)	846,000	782,100
		1,442,100
Investments at cost (W2)		90,000
Current assets		
Stock (£1,063,700 + £103,500)	1,167,200	
Debtors (£682,300 + £59,700)	742,000	
	1,909,200	
Less: Current liabilities	£	
Creditors (£476,200 + £43,400)	519,600	
Taxation	203,800	
Proposed dividends	100,000	
Bank overdraft (£247,000 − £207,900)	39,100	862,500
		1,046,700
		2,578,800
Ordinary share capital		1,000,000
Share premium account (W3)	40,000	
Capital redemption reserve (W4)	60,000	
Revaluation reserve	260,000	360,000
General reserves (W5)		718,800
		2,078,800
12% debentures		500,000
		2,578,800

Workings

1 Plant and machinery at cost: Provision for depreciation:

	£		£
Balance at 31.12.79	1,446,600		617,900
Less: Sales	25,000	(W6)	19,500
	1,421,600		598,400
Additions	206,500	Depreciation for year	247,600
Balance at 31.12.80	1,628,100		846,000

2 Investments at cost:

	£	£
Balance at 31.12.79		230,000
Less: Sales	175,000	
Profit on sale	35,000	140,000 (20,000 × £7)
Balance at 31.12.80		90,000

3 Share premium:

		£
Proceeds of issue		240,000
Nominal value of shares issued	1,000,000	
	− 800,000	200,000
		40,000

4 Capital redemption reserve:

	£
Cost of redemption of preference shares	300,000
Less: Amount provided by new issue	240,000
Distributable profit to be capitalised for Companies Acts 1948 and 1981	60,000

5 General reserves:

	£	£	£
Balance at 31.12.79			625,500
Profit for year		437,100	
Add: Profit on sale of investment (see note 2)		35,000	
		472,100	
Less: Dividends:	£		
Preference (paid)	15,000		
1,000,000 × 10p ordinary (proposed)	100,000		
Tax	203,800		
Capital redemption reserve (W4)	60,000	378,800	93,300
			718,800

6   Depreciation of machinery sold:

	£
Sale proceeds	2,000
Loss on sale	3,500
Written-down value when sold	5,500
Cost	25,000
Depreciation to date of sale	19,500

Tutorial notes

Those adept at double-entry book-keeping may have tackled this complex question as follows:

W1   Plant and machinery account

	£		£
Balance at 31.12.79	1,446,600	Disposal account	25,000
Cash	206,500	Therefore balance at 31.12.80	1,628,100
	1,653,100		1,653,100

Depreciation account

	£		£
Disposal (W6)	19,500	Balance at 31.12.79	617,900
Balance at 31.12.80	846,000	Depreciation for year	247,600
	865,500		865,500

W2   Investments account

	£			£
Balance at 31.12.79	230,000	Cash*	140,000	
Profit	35,000		35,000	175,000
		Balance at 31.12.80		90,000
	265,000			265,000

*Investments costing £140,000 (i.e., 20,000 × £7) were sold for £175,000.

W6 Machinery disposal account

	£		£
Asset cost	25,000	Cash	2,000
		Loss	3,500
		Therefore, depreciation	19,500
	25,000		25,000

W3 In this country any value received for the issue of shares, in excess of their nominal value, must be credited to a share premium account, the uses of which are strictly limited. Since 200,000 × £1 shares (1,000,000 − 800,000) had been issued for £240,000, they had been issued at a premium of £40,000.

W4 Company law requires shares redeemed out of profits to be replaced by a capital (i.e., non-distributable) reserve known as a capital redemption reserve.

W5 Profit and loss account

	£		£
Preference dividend paid	15,000	Profit for year	437,100
Ordinary dividend proposed	100,000	Profit on sale of investments	35,000
Taxation	203,800		
Capital reserve (W4)	60,000		472,100
Balance c/f	718,800	Balance b/f	625,500
	1,097,600		1,097,600

3 Interpretation of accounts

INTRODUCTION

This is a very important area since the ability to understand and interpret accounting data is the foundation upon which most lending and investment decisions are based. Clearly one set of accounts is not adequate to provide evidence of the trends and thus lending bankers will usually require to see at least the last three years' accounts.

The term interpretation of accounts encompasses the techniques of analysis employed by users to establish the meaning and significance of financial statements. One of these techniques is that of ratio analysis, which is used extensively not only in analysis and appraisal but also in planning and control.

A firm's most significant ratios relate to performance, activity, stability and growth.

PERFORMANCE RATIOS

The basic measure of business performance, known as the primary ratio, is the return on capital employed, i.e.

$$\frac{\text{Profit}}{\text{Capital}}$$

To be of any real significance the ratio must relate the appropriate profit figure to the relevent capital. The three major return ratios are:

(a) Return on equity = $\dfrac{\text{Profit after tax}}{\text{(Equity) Shareholders' funds}}$

(b) Return on long-term capital = $\dfrac{\text{Profit before interest and tax}}{\text{Shareholders' funds + Loan capital}}$

(c) Return on assets = $\dfrac{\text{Profit before interest and tax}}{\text{Total assets}}$

SECONDARY RATIOS

(a) Profit margin = $\dfrac{\text{Profit}}{\text{Sales}}$ measures 'profitability'

(b) Capital turnover = $\dfrac{\text{Sales}}{\text{Capital}}$ measures 'activity'

Note that the product of the two secondary ratios is the primary ratio, i.e., the Primary ratio can be factorised into two components as follows:

$$\frac{\text{Profit}}{\text{Capital}} = \frac{\text{Profit}}{\text{Sales}} \times \frac{\text{Sales}}{\text{Capital}}$$

Profitability

The major ratios in this category can be calculated from a profit and loss account.

(a) The net profit margin (%) = $\dfrac{\text{Profit}}{\text{Sales}}$

(b) The gross profit % = $\dfrac{\text{Gross profit}}{\text{Sales}}$

Gross profit = Sales less cost of sales; the cost of sales includes all the costs of putting the goods into a saleable state.

(c) The profit/volume ratio (P/V ratio) = $\dfrac{\text{Contribution}}{\text{Sales}}$

Contribution (or direct profit) = Sales less variable costs.
Variable costs vary directly with output (sales).

A product's contribution, towards fixed expenses and profit, is its selling price less the variable cost.

To break even, i.e., for income just to cover expenses, the contribution must equal fixed overheads.

For example, a department's fixed overheads are £20,000 p.a. It sells a standard product, with a variable cost of £6, for £10. To break even it must sell 5,000 units, i.e., 20,000/(10 – 6).

Activity

These ratios are concerned with the use a company makes of its assets. They comprise an element from the profit and loss account and an element from the balance sheet. They may be expressed as an asset being turned over so many times a year, or as the asset representing so many days credit (or holding).

The major ratios and periods in this category are:

(a) Asset turnover (or utilisation) ratio = $\dfrac{\text{Sales}}{\text{Assets}}$

(b) (i) Stock turn (or turnover) = $\dfrac{\text{Cost of sales}}{\text{Average stock for year}}$

(ii) Stock life = $\dfrac{\text{Average stock}}{\text{Cost of sales}} \times 12$ months or 365 days

(c) Credit taken by debtors = $\dfrac{\text{Debtors}}{\text{Sales}} \times 12$ months or 365 days

(d) Credit allowed by creditors = $\dfrac{\text{Trade creditors}}{\text{Purchases}} \times 12$ months or 365 days

(e) Cash operating cycle

A firm's cash operating cycle is the interval between payment for goods and the receipt of cash for those goods when sold. It is calculated as follows (referring to the ratios above):

Stock life	b(ii)
Add: Credit allowed to debtors	c
	b(ii) + c
Less: Credit late from creditors	d
	b(ii) + c − d

STABILITY

Solvency (safety) ratios

(a) Current ratio = $\dfrac{\text{Current assets}}{\text{Current liabilities}}$

Since the current assets are the cash-producing assets, the current ratio or working capital ratio measures basic solvency.

(b) Liquidity ratio = $\dfrac{\text{Cash + near cash assets}}{\text{Current liabilities}}$

Note that stock is excluded from this ratio, since stock must be sold, thus becoming a debtor, before producing cash.

These two solvency ratios relate to short-term stability, and are concerned with the components of working capital. Financial strength and long-term stability are more related to fixed assets, particularly their ability to generate cash flows which do not fluctuate too widely, and which are adequate to meet the claims on them, i.e., the cash flows must be adequate to meet interest payments on short and long-term debt, to satisfy the reasonable demands of shareholders, to provide capital for growth, and to replace capital eroded by inflation.

Ratios concerned with long-term financial strength and stability

(a) Proprietorship ratio = $\dfrac{\text{Equity}}{\text{Total finance}} = \dfrac{\text{Share capital + reserves}}{\text{Total liabilities and capital}}$

Since one would expect a company's shareholders to have the majority stake in the assets it employs, the ratio is usually greater than 50%.

(b) A related ratio is the

Asset cover = $\dfrac{\text{Equity or shareholders' funds}}{\text{Assets}}$

This is of particular importance in relation to the fixed assets.

(c) Gearing (leverage): this is the general expression for the relationship between the fixed interest capital and the equity capital, and is modified to meet the analyst's requirements, e.g., inclusion of the bank overdraft with loan capital.

Gearing ratio = $\dfrac{\text{Loan capital}}{\text{Equity capital}}$

Note that preference share capital is included with the loan capital.

In general, the higher the gearing the greater the financial risk, since the fixed charge for interest, which as an expense must be paid, takes a larger proportion of variable profits. The greater the variability, due to business risk, the greater chance that profits will not even cover interest payments.

GROWTH AND STRENGTH (INVESTMENT RATIOS)

A company's ability to grow is directly related to its ability to generate cash flow in excess of that which is required to service its loan and equity capital, i.e., to provide a relatively safe return to its investors. Even in small companies there may be a distinction between the managers (the directors) and the shareholders (the proprietors).

Yields

(a) Dividend Yield = $\dfrac{\text{Current dividend}}{\text{Price*, ex div.}}$

(b) Earnings yield = $\dfrac{\text{Earnings}}{\text{Price, ex div.}}$

Earnings are the profits for the period available for ordinary shareholders.

(c) Dividend cover = $\dfrac{\text{Profits}}{\text{Dividends}}$

(d) Price/earnings (P/E) ratio = $\dfrac{\text{Price}}{\text{Earnings}}$

i.e., the inverse of the earnings yield.

*Share prices are usually quoted cum div.; to calculate an ex div. price simply deduct the dividend.

SUGGESTED METHOD FOR ANSWERING THE QUESTION

Consider the relationship between appropriate sections of the accounts under the headings of:

(a) performance;
(b) activity; and
(c) stability.

After a little practice the significant ratios will be easily memorised and their information analysed.

QUESTIONS

1 A LTD AND B LTD

The following information is provided relating to the affairs of two companies engaged in similar trading activities:

	A Ltd	B Ltd
Ordinary share capital	£800,000	£500,000
15% debentures	£200,000	£500,000

Each company earned a trading profit before finance charges of £110,000 in year 1 and £190,000 in year 2.

Corporation tax is charged at 50% on the trading profits after finance charges have been deducted.

The company pays out as dividends its entire after-tax profits.

Required:

(a) Summary profit and loss accounts, dealing with the results of each of the two companies' activities during year 1 and year 2, so far as the information given above permits.

(b) Calculations of after-tax profits, expressed as percentages of ordinary share capital for each company in respect of both year 1 and year 2.

(c) A discussion of the returns earned for shareholders over the two-year period.

20 marks

2 GRASSINGTON LTD

The following forecasts are provided in respect of Grassington Ltd, a company trading in a single product, for 1984:

	£000
Sales	2,700
Purchases	1,800
Cost of goods sold	1,830
Average trade debtors outstanding	300
Average trade creditors outstanding	160
Average stocks held	305

All purchases and sales are made on credit, and trading transactions are expected to occur at an even rate throughout the year.

Required:

(a) Calculations of the rate of payment of creditors, the rate of collection of debtors and the rate of stock turnover. *9 marks*

(b) A calculation of the expected cash operating cycle (i.e., the time lag between making payment to suppliers and collecting cash from customers in respect of goods purchased and sold) for 1984. *5 marks*

(c) Using the information provided, explain any one method by which the directors *might* achieve a reduction of £20,000 in the company's bank overdraft requirement at 31 December 1984, and demonstrate the effect on the cash operating cycle. *6 marks*

Note: Assume a 360 day year for the purpose of your calculations.

Total 20 marks

3 GREYWELL PLC AND KENDALL PLC

Greywell plc and Kendall plc trade in the same industry but in different geographical locations. The following data are taken from the 1982 annual accounts:

	Greywell £000	Kendall £000
Turnover	40,000	60,000
Total operating expenses	36,000	55,000
Average total assets during 1982	30,000	25,000

Required:

(a) Calculate the rate of return on total assets (profit as a percentage of total assets) for each company. *4 marks*

(b) Analyse the rates of return in part (a) into the net profit percentage and the ratio of turnover to total assets. *6 marks*

(c) Comment on the relative performance of the two companies in so far as the information permits. Indicate what additional information you would require to decide which company is the better proposition from the viewpoint of:

　(i) potential shareholders; and
　(ii) potential loan creditors. *10 marks*

Note: ignore taxation.

Total 20 marks

4 AIX LTD

The following are the summarised revenue accounts and balance sheets of Aix Ltd.

Revenue accounts for years ended 31 December:

	1978 £000	1978 £000	1979 £000	1979 £000
Sales		800		1,100
Less: Opening stock	110		130	
Costs of production	500		700	
Closing stock	(130)		(170)	
Cost of goods sold	480		660	
Running expenses (including interest charges)	260	740	362	1,022
Net profit		60		78
Proposed dividend		–		40
Retained profit		60		38

Balance sheets as at 31 December:

	1978 £000	1979 £000
Ordinary share capital	200	200
Retained profit	100	138
12% debentures, issued 1 January 1979	–	200
Bank overdraft	10	–
Dividends	–	40
Creditors	110	120
	420	698
Fixed assets	170	338
Stock	130	170
Debtors	120	160
Bank	–	30
	420	698

No dividends were paid during either 1978 or 1979.

Required:

(a) A calculation of the following accounting ratios and percentages for 1978 and 1979 presented in the following tabular format:

	1978	1979
Liquid ratio		
Average rate of stock turnover		
Net profit as a percentage of sales		
Earnings as a percentage of long-term capital employed		
Net earnings for ordinary shareholders as a percentage of equity		
Ratio of sales to long-term capital employed		

For the purpose of your calculations equity and long-term capital employed are to be included at their estimated figures at 30 June in each year, assuming no seasonal variations in the level of business activity.

(b) Comments on the implications of the differences between the above ratios and percentages between the two years.

Note: ignore taxation. *20 marks*

5 PUMPS LTD AND SHOES LTD

Pumps Ltd and Shoes Ltd are two independent companies which have no connection with each other, except that both companies are currently negotiating borrowing arrangements with Dogger Bank.

The following are summaries of balance sheets at 30 June 1981, and revenue accounts for the year ended 30 June 1981:

Balance sheets	Pumps Ltd £000	Shoes Ltd £000
Issued ordinary shares	75	15
Issued preference shares	10	—
Revenue reserves	20	30
8% debentures (secured on freehold property)	30	25
Trade creditors	45	30
Bank overdraft	20	—
	200	100
Freehold property, at cost	30	45
Equipment, etc., less depreciation	40	15
Stocks		
Finished goods	30	25
Raw materials and work in progress	40	—
Trade debtors	60	5
Bank	—	10
	200	100

Revenue accounts	£000	£000	£000	£000
Sales: Cash		–		170
Credit		240		30
		240		200
Purchases*	120		150	
Wages, expenses, etc.	100		35	
Depreciation	10		5	
		230		190
Net profit (retained)		10		10

*There were no increases or decreases in stocks for either company during the year.

Pumps Ltd manufactures components for central heating equipment; Shoes Ltd is a footwear retailer.

Required:

A succinct statement, from the viewpoint of Dogger Bank's assessment of the *financial stability* of the two companies, of:

(a) three ways in which Pumps Ltd seems to be *stronger* than Shoes Ltd;
(b) three ways in which Pumps Ltd seems to be *weaker* than Shoes Ltd.

Note: Ignore taxation. *20 marks*

6 MANUFACTURER LTD AND BANK LTD

Manufacturer Ltd and Bank Ltd are two independent companies which have no financial connection with each other.

The following are summaries of balance sheets at 31 December 1974, and excerpts from the companies' profit and loss accounts for the year ended 31 December 1974:

	Manufacturer Ltd £000	Bank Ltd £000
Issued share capital	13,000	2,000
Revenue reserves	7,000	5,200
10% debentures	29,000	800
Current taxation	1,000	1,000
Trade creditors	43,000	–
Overdraft	7,000	–
Current and deposit accounts	–	91,000
	100,000	100,000

	£000	£000
Fixed assets, less depreciation	39,000	4,000
Goodwill	6,000	–
Unquoted investments	1,000	9,000
Advances	–	59,000
Stock in trade	17,000	–
Trade debtors	37,000	–
Cash and liquid assets	–	28,000
	100,000	100,000
Net profit before taxation	1,800	1,600
after charging depreciation of	1,200	100

The companies' businesses are entirely concerned with the activities which their names suggest.

Required:

(a) A list comparing, in numerical terms, *six* aspects from the accounts which you consider reveal the most important differences or similarities between the two companies. Use ratios where appropriate.

(b) A brief discussion of your figures in part (a), with particular regard to the apparent financial stability of the two companies. and the usefulness or limitations of the comparisons you have made.

20 marks

ANSWERS

1 A LTD AND B LTD

(a) Summarised profit and loss accounts

	Year 1	Year 2
A Ltd	£	£
Trading profit	110,000	190,000
Less: Debenture interest	30,000	30,000
	80,000	160,000
Corporation tax at 50%	40,000	80,000
Profit for year	40,000	80,000
Dividends	(5%) 40,000	(10%) 80,000
Profit for year retained	Nil	Nil
B Ltd		
Trading profit	110,000	190,000
Less: Debenture interest	75,000	75,000
	35,000	115,000
Corporation tax at 50%	17,500	57,500
	17,500	57,500
Dividends	(3.5%) 17,500	(11.5%) 57,500
Profit for year retained	Nil	Nil

(b)
A Ltd	5%	10%
B Ltd	3.5%	11.5%

(c) These two companies are identical in terms of capital employed and profit. The returns to the shareholders differ because of the differences in the companies' capital structures, i.e., the discussion is about gearing (or leverage). A Ltd is a low-geared company, 1:4; B Ltd is highly geared, 1:1 (see tutorial note).

Gearing is a measure of the sensitivity of equity profits (earnings for ordinary shareholders) to company profits. Changes in profits have proportionally greater effect on the earnings and dividends of the high-geared company than on those of a low-geared company. The pre-tax profits of both companies have increased by 73% (80/110), whereas the equity earnings of A Ltd have doubled (5% up to 10%), and those of B Ltd have more than trebled (3.5% to 11.5%).

Although the profits have increased, the same fixed amount, £30,000 for A Ltd and £75,000 for B Ltd, is paid to the loan creditors, leaving a proportionately higher amount for the shareholders. In year 1, the relatively low profits are apportioned:

	A	%	B	%
Debenture-holders	30	27	75.0	68
Tax	40	36.5	17.5	16
Shareholders	40	36.5	17.5	16
	110	100	110	100

Whereas in year 2, relatively higher profits are apportioned:

	A	%	B	%
Debenture-holders	30	16	75.0	39.0
Tax	80	42	57.5	30.5
Shareholders	80	42	57.5	30.5
	190	100	190	100

In year 1, 68% of B's operating profit is distributed as a fixed charge, whereas in year 2, this has fallen to only 39%. For the low-geared company, A Ltd, the corresponding figure are 27% falling to 16%.

Gearing also affects the proportion of profits being paid as tax. The high-geared company, making large interest payments which are allowable for tax, pays relatively less tax than the low-geared company paying larger dividends which are not allowable for tax.

Tutorial note

There are a number of measures of gearing. The one used here, probably the most popular, is:

$$\frac{\text{Loan capital} + \text{Preference share capital}}{\text{Equity capital}}$$

A Ltd $\dfrac{200}{800} = 1:4$ B Ltd $\dfrac{500}{500} = 1:1$

The answer has considered the nominal value of the capital, whereas the real gearing upon which much financial theory is based considers the market value.

2 GRASSINGTON LTD:

(a) Rate of payment of creditors:

$$\frac{160}{1,800} \times 360 = 32 \text{ days or } 11.25 \text{ times/year}$$

Rate of collection of debtors:

$$\frac{300}{2,700} \times 360 = 40 \text{ days or } 9 \text{ times/year}$$

Rate of stock turnover:

$$\frac{305}{1,830} \times 360 = 60 \text{ days or } 6 \text{ times/year}$$

(b) Expected cash operating cycle:

	Days
Holding stock	60
Add: Credit allowed to customers	40
	100
Less: Credit allowed by suppliers	32
	68

(c) The average working capital to be financed is:

	£000
Stock	305
Debtors	300
	605
Creditors	160
	445

Part of this has probably been financed by fixed capital (equity or loan capital). The figure can be reduced by reducing stock, reducing debtors or increasing creditors. Reduction of debtors by £20,000 requires a reduction of 6.7% (20/300), that is, approximately 3 days, and probably can only be achieved by measures affecting the profit, e.g. allowing discount which is not effective, or reducing the price which is not necessary. Increasing the creditors by £20,000, i.e., 12½% (20/160), means taking 4 days longer to pay. This is possible, but probably the present 32 days is already 2 days longer than the invoice terms of 30 days, and extending it further could destroy the relationship with suppliers, whose goodwill is required in times of shortage or in any serious attempt to reduce stockholding.

The reduction of stock by £20,000 has no effect on debtors or creditors in the long term, and requires only internal changes.

The stockholding period will be reduced by approximately 4 days, i.e., (20/305) × 60 days. To achieve the improvement in stock turn requires careful and well thought out stock control procedures including a consideration of the possible loss of sales because the firm is reducing stock availability.

The effect on the cash operating cycle will be to reduce it by four days, as calculated above.

3 GREYWELL PLC AND KENDALL PLC

(a)

	Greywell plc	Kendall plc
Rate of return on assets, i.e. $\dfrac{\text{Profit}}{\text{Assets}}$	$\dfrac{4{,}000}{30{,}000} = 13.3\%$	$\dfrac{5{,}000}{25{,}000} = 20\%$

(b)

	Greywell plc	Kendall plc
Profit %, i.e. $\dfrac{\text{Profit}}{\text{Sales}}$	$\dfrac{4{,}000}{40{,}000} = 10\%$	$\dfrac{5{,}000}{60{,}000} = 8.3\%$
Asset turnover, i.e. $\dfrac{\text{Sales}}{\text{Assets}}$	$\dfrac{40{,}000}{30{,}000} = 1.33$ times	$\dfrac{60{,}000}{25{,}000} = 2.4$ times

(c) These three ratios provide a crude summary of a company's performance. They are related in that the return on assets employed calculated in (a) is the product of the profit margin and the asset turnover, the two ratios calculated in (b). This relationship can be illustrated by the following:

$$\frac{P}{A} = \frac{P}{S} \times \frac{S}{A}$$

where the sales or turnover cancels out.

This simple analysis is at the apex of a pyramid of ratios used by many organisations to investigate their strengths and weaknesses relative to other organisations in the same industry.

Comparing the two companies

	Return on assets $\left(\dfrac{P}{A}\right)$	Profit % $\left(\dfrac{P}{S}\right)$	Asset turnover $\left(\dfrac{S}{A}\right)$
Greywell plc	13.3%	10%	1.33 times
Kendall plc	20%	8.3%	2.4 times

Although Greywell, with a profit margin of 10%, appears to perform better than its rival (8.3%) in the area of profitability, Kendall's return on assets (20%) is significantly higher than its rival's (13.3%) as is its asset turnover at 2.4 times (compared with 1.33 times).

Profit margin is the least significant measure of performance, since it may be the result of higher prices, which can be eroded by competition, rather than lower cost per unit.

While return on assets is still the major measure of performance — it is known as the primary ratio — the asset turnover or asset utilisation ratio is probably the most significant since it is a better measure of business activity, the purpose of which is to use resources (assets) to create resources, which are sold to its customers.

From the point of view of potential investors, shareholders and loan creditors, the overall performance is important, but of equal importance is the apportionment of the profit between the two types of finance (loan or equity). They will, therefore, need information about the gearing, i.e., the relationship between equity and loan capital and the relationship between profits and fixed interest payments.

The potential loan creditor will also require information about security in terms of asset cover and priority of payment in the event of liquidation. For similar loans to similar companies there is not likely to be much variation in the return (or yield) to the lender.

The potential shareholder is interested in future dividends and gains as well as the current yield and will need information about the share price, and recent movements as well as the earnings or profits attributable to his share — the earnings per share — so that the relevant comparisons can be made against other similar investments, in terms of P/E ratio and yield.

4   AIX LTD

(a)

	1978		1979	
Liquid ratio	(120/120)	1:1	(190/160)	1.19:1
Average rate of stock turnover	$\dfrac{480}{(110+130)/2}$	4 times p.a.	$\dfrac{660}{(130+170)/2}$	4.4 times p.a
Net profit/Sales	(60/800)	7.5%	(78/1,100)	7.1%
Earnings/Long-term capital employed*	$\dfrac{60}{300-(60/2)}$	22%	$\dfrac{78+24}{300+\dfrac{78}{2}+200}$	18.9%
Equity earnings/ Equity*	$\dfrac{60}{300-(60/2)}$	22%	$\dfrac{78}{300+39}$	23%
Sales/Long-term capital employed*	(800/270)	2.96:1	(1,100/539)	2.04:1

*The calculations of equity and long-term capital employed, as defined in the question, are:

	30.6.78 £000			30.6.79 £000
Ordinary share capital		200		200
Retained profit, 31.12.78	100		100	
Less: ½ × 60	30	Add: ½ × 78	39	139
		70		
Equity at 30 June		270		339
Add: loan capital employed throughout 1979				200
Long-term capital employed at 30 June				539

Since the figure of £539,000 includes loan capital, the profit figure with which it is compared should be the profit before deducting interest of £24,000. Thus the return on long-term capital employed for 1979 is:

$$(78 + 24)/539 = 102/539 = 18.9\%$$

(b) The **liquid ratio** (the quick ratio or acid test) at 1:1 is satisfactory in itself, but has risen by 19% due partly to the substantial borrowing, which could have been, say, £30,000 to £40,000 less, without causing real problems.

The **stock turn** has improved by 10% indicating better use of capital tied up in that asset, though possibly at the cost of increasing expenses related to stock, e.g., more frequent machine set-up costs, with shorter production runs, to reduce stockholding costs.

The **profit** % has fallen from 7.5% to 7.1%. This is apparently due to the internal charge of £24,000, since the cost of goods sold remains at 60% of sales, (480/800 in 1978 and 660/1,100 in 1979) and the running expenses, excluding interest, have fallen from 32.5% of sales in 1978 (260/800) to 30.7 % in 1979 ((362 − 24)/1,100). Further analysis requires more data, e.g., the amount of interest on the bank overdraft included in the 1978 figures.

The **earnings/long-term capital** has declined from 22% to 18.9%. This is the product of the profit margin, which has declined (see above) and the asset turnover, which has also declined from 2.96 to 2.04, as discussed below.

The **return on equity** (earnings for shareholders/equity) has increased from 22% in 1978 to 23% in 1979. This is a direct result of the gearing, i.e., the introduction of long-term debt to the company's capital structure; the long-term capital at 31.12.78 was £300,000 equity which changed to £500,000 on 1.1.79, comprising £300,000 equity and £200,000 debt, i.e., quite high gearing.

The **asset turnover** has fallen substantially, i.e., from 2.96 to 2.04, and is probably the most disappointing aspect of the expansion. The stock turn has improved as noted above, but the turnover of fixed assets has declined considerably. In 1978 the ratio was 4.7 (800/170); in 1979 it was only 3.2 (1,100/338). However, fixed assets are relatively long-term investments and one year is too short a period to make a fair judgment, particularly as the investment was so large, amounting to a doubling of the fixed assets, which so far has only produced a 40% increase in sales.

5   PUMPS LTD AND SHOES LTD

Financial stability may be considered from a number of general aspects, including liquidity, solvency, profitability, activity, cash flow, and a number of specific aspects, including gearing, security and control.

(a)   Pumps Ltd appears to be stronger in terms of liquidity, but the ratios are not strictly comparable since their financial activities are dissimilar (e.g., Shoes Ltd makes predominantly cash sales). Similarly, Pumps Ltd, with a significantly higher current ratio, appears to be stronger in terms of solvency, but again the ratios are not really comparable, since Shoes Ltd, without large debtors to be funded, could well be 'safe' with a much lower ratio. More specifically, from the point of view of a financier, including the bank, Pumps Ltd is stronger in that it is more low-geared and the charged assets are only 15% of total assets compared with Shoes Ltd's 25%, at least in terms of book value.

(b)   In terms of performance (profitability and activity) which generates the cash for long-term stability, Pumps Ltd seems weaker than Shoes Ltd. Whether the weakness stems from weak credit control (debtors take three months to pay), or poor stock turn and fixed asset utilisation, could only be established by comparison with similar companies.

There is inadequate information to produce cash flow statements, but Pumps Ltd's cash flow is likely to suffer from its seasonal trade relative to Shoes Ltd. From a lender's point of view, the company's assets are more specific to the trade and, therefore, less marketable than the general assets of Shoes Ltd.

Neither company appears to be paying a dividend. Pumps Ltd apparently is not even paying its preference dividend, presumably, because payment would increase the overdraft. The extent of this weakness depends on the shareholders (e.g., are the shareholders also directors?).

Calculations

	Pumps Ltd		Shoes Ltd	
Liquidity ratio	(60/65)	0.92:1	(15/30)	0.5:1
Current ratio	(130/65)	2:1	(40/30)	1.33:1
Return on capital employed (shareholders)	(10/105)	9.5%	(10/45)	22%

	Pumps Ltd		Shoes Ltd	
Profit margin	(10/240)	4.2%	(10/200)	5%
Capital turnover	(240/105)	2.3 times	(200/45)	4.4 times
Stock turnover (a)	((120 + ?)/70) –		(150/25)	6 times
Gearing ratio (b)	(40/95)	5:12	(25/45)	5:9

Tutorial notes

(a) The stock turnover ratio for Pumps Ltd cannot be calculated from the data given; the wages and expenses attributable to the cost of sales is not known.

(b) In calculating gearing ratios, preference shares (although share capital) are included with the loan capital since the preference dividend must be paid in priority to equity dividends.

6 MANUFACTURER LTD AND BANK LTD

(a) Since these two companies are similar only in terms of total assets (and total finance) and the nature of the assets are so different, the following table illustrates six important differences:

		Manufacturer Ltd		Bank Ltd	
(i)	Size (£ million):				
	Long-term capital	49		8	
	Nominal share capital	13		2	
	Physical real assets	56		4	
(ii)	Capital structure (gearing ratio)	(29/20)	1.45:1	(800/7,200)	1:9
(iii)	Performance				
	Return on long-term capital (note 1)	(1,800 + 2,900)/49,000	9.6%	(1,600 + 80)/8,000	21%
	Return on equity (note 2)	(800/20,000)	4%	(600/7,200)	8.33%
	Effective tax rate (note 3)	(1,000/1,800)	55%	(1,000/1,600)	62.5%
(iv)	Solvency (current ratio)	(54/50)	1.08:1	(87/91)	0.96:1
(v)	Liquidity (liquid ratio)	(37/50)	0.74:1	(87/91)	0.96:1
(vi)	Security (shareholders stake)	(20/100)	20%	(7.2/100)	7.2%

Notes

(1) In order that a comparison of returns on long-term capital may be meaningful between companies with different capital structures, the profit **before** interest and taxation is used in the calculation, e.g. Manufacturer Ltd's profit before interest and tax was £1,800,000 + (10% × £29,000,000) = £4,700,000.

(2) Since shareholders are paid dividends out of a taxed fund of profits, the appropriate calculation is based on the profit after tax, e.g., Manufacturer Ltd's post-tax profit for the year was £1,800,000 − £1,000,000 tax = £800,000; and for Bank Ltd it was £1,600,000 − £1,000,000 tax = £600,000. The current tax per the balance sheet is based on the current year's profit and is payable normally nine months after the year end.

(3) The effective rate of tax usually differs from the actual rate (52% 1983/84) because capital allowances differ from the depreciation charge in the profit and loss account − see the chapter on company taxation.

(b) Manufacturer Ltd is a very much larger company than Bank Ltd; in terms of nominal share capital, and probably number of shares, it is 6½ times as large; in terms of long-term capital, more than 6 times as large, and in terms of physical real assets much larger.

The larger company has substantial gearing (whereas Bank Ltd is almost ungeared) and is currently suffering the penalty of high gearing, in that low profitability (9.6% return) leaves little profit for the shareholders (4%).

Possibly low profitability over a number of years accounted for the poor solvency and liquidity ratios. Combined with the apparent need to replace fixed assets (the low depreciation charge of £1,200,000 relative to a book value of £40,200,000 before this year's depreciation suggests either inadequate provisions or old assets, whose relative inefficiency may contribute to the poor performance), Manufacturer Ltd's financial stability is questionable. The shareholders' stake of 20% does not even cover the fixed assets.

The nature of Bank Ltd's activities makes most ratio comparisons with the manufacturing company invidious. The liquidity ratio (the same as the solvency ratio), may be considered weak. However, the fact that up to £59 million is a contra item in advances and current accounts, and the statistical improbability of any significant part of current and deposit accounts becoming a drain on bank and liquid assets, indicates that 0.95 is relatively safe.

4 Budgeting

INTRODUCTION

This is undoubtedly the most important section of the syllabus both from a practical banking point of view and examination frequency. All decisions, including lending decisions, are based upon projections of business activity (income and related expenditure) and the consequent ability of the enterprise to repay its loans and service its debt. Also all business control systems are based upon plans (i.e., budgets) and performance based on those plans.

Financial planning and control are effected through budgets. The major or master budgets with which you must be fully conversant are the trading and profit and loss accounts for future years, and the related balance sheets.

THE PROFIT AND LOSS ACCOUNT

The major determinants of the profit and loss account are the sales (or output) and the firm's 'cost behaviour' or cost structure. Over a period as long as a year — the normal period of a profit and loss account — costs can be treated as being either fixed or variable. The majority of costs are said to be semi-variable and can be considered as comprising a fixed and a variable element. Be quite clear about the following distinction:

Variable costs **vary** directly with **output**
Fixed costs **do not vary** with **output**

Although fixed expenses do not vary with output, they do change, generally by a fixed amount, due to external factors (e.g., inflation) or internal factors (e.g., additional salaries or additional depreciation, and other expenses which may have an effect on output, but which are not directly related to it).

To produce a budget, therefore, you must be able to establish a firm's cost structure from its most recent accounts and apply it, with appropriate modification, to the budgeted output.

THE BALANCE SHEET

The balance sheet in a year's time will be today's balance sheet modified by the year's financial transactions as summarised in the budgeted profit and loss account, together with capital transactions, e.g., any purchase or sale of fixed assets during the year, etc. To establish the effect on the forecast balance sheet it is necessary to establish the present relationship between balance sheet items and the profit and loss account. These relationships, possibly modified by company policy, can thus be applied to the profit and loss account to indicate the shape of the balance sheet, which will be made to balance by inserting the missing component, the bank balance.

Keep clearly in your mind the most significant relationships between balance sheet items and profit and loss account items, which are:

Stock is related to the **cost of sales** by the **stock turn**
Debtors are related to **sales** by the **period of credit** allowed to customers
Trade creditors are related to **purchases** by the **period of credit** allowed by suppliers.

Cost of sales = Sales less gross profit*

Purchases = Cost of sales + closing stock − Opening stock

*Gross profit is usually a fixed percentage of sales, since the cost of sales usually comprises only variable costs. If the cost of sales includes fixed overheads, the gross profit % would be replaced by the P/V (profit/volume) ratio, which is the

$$\frac{\text{Contribution}}{\text{Sales}}, \text{ since}$$

Contribution = Sales less variable costs.

SUGGESTED METHOD FOR ANSWERING THE QUESTION

Question 1 to 9 and 16 are budgets using ratios which must first be determined from the historic data presented, e.g., last year's accounts.

Having produced a budgeted trading and profit and loss account from the information supplied you are to proceed to the budgeted balance sheet using the ratios calculated. There is often one missing figure in the budgeted balance sheet which has to be 'forced out' — the bank balance — this is the subject of the question.

Questions 10 to 14 are budgets prepared using the given cost behaviour of the business, i.e., fixed costs and variable costs etc. Sometimes this has to be estimated, but usually it is given. Procedure then becomes: establish variable costs relationship to sales. Establish the 'contribution' and apply this towards payment of fixed expenses, after the payment of which profit is made.

QUESTIONS

1 DEF LTD

A company is preparing budgets for its 1985 operations and has made the following estimates:

(a) Trade creditors will decrease by £17,000.

(b) Stock will increase by £65,000.

(c) Debtors: opening balance £212,000; end of year balance £232,000; (after writing off £3,000 bad debts).

(d) Liability for operating cost creditors will increase by £4,000.

(e) Payments in advance will fall by £4,000.

(f) Ordinary shares for £150,000 cash will be issued.

(g) £50,000 will be paid to shareholders in 1985 for a dividend owing at 1 January 1985 out of 1984 profits. No dividend is expected to be recommended for payment out of 1985 profits.

(h) Plant costing £130,000 will be bought.

(i) During 1985 corporation tax of £115,000 due on 1984 profits will be paid. The tax due on 1985 estimated profits will be owing as at 31 December 1985.

(j) Debenture capital of £20,000 will be repaid at the beginning of 1985.

(k) The cash bank balance at 31 December 1984 is £55,000.

The budgeted income account for 1985 is:

	£
Sales less returns	1,450,000
Cost of sales	1,026,000
Gross profit	424,000
Operating costs (including depreciation, £16,000)	168,000
	256,000
Corporation tax	110,000
Net income before dividends on shares	146,000

Required:

On the assumption that all budget estimates are realised, make a calculation of the bank balance as at 31 December 1985. *20 marks*

2 DISCOUNT LTD

A summarised balance sheet for Discount Ltd at 31 March 1982, is shown below:

	£			£
Issued share capital	25,000	Freehold premises		19,200
Less: Profit and loss account (loss)	1,300	Fixtures and fittings	£8,000	
		Less: Depreciation	200	
	23,700			7,800
Creditors	16,800	Stock in trade		13,900
Bank overdraft	5,600	Debtors		5,200
	46,100			46,100

The company, which has been trading for only a few months, is reviewing its past experience and determining its future financial requirements.

For the coming year to 31 March 1983, the company expects that for every £1,000 of sales it makes, it will incur cost of goods of £800 (i.e., there is a 20% gross profit margin on sales). Expense payments for the year, all of which will remain fixed irrespective of the level of sales, are:

	£
Rent	7,000
Wages	14,000
Administration, bank interest, etc.	8,000

Depreciation on fixtures and fittings is to be provided at the rate of 12½% p.a.

The period of credit taken from suppliers will be 1½ calendar months. Cash sales will make up 64% of total sales; payment for the remaining 36% of sales will be received one month after the date of sale.

These trading transactions will take place at an even rate during the year to 31 March 1983. All amounts due (including debtors and creditors outstanding at 31 March 1982) will be paid in full at the end of the relevant credit periods, and no amounts for rent, wages, administration, interest, etc., will be outstanding at the end of the year.

Stock in trade at 31 March 1983, will be 10% of the cost of goods sold during the year.

Ignore taxation, dividends, and any fluctuations in bank interest.

Required:

(a) A calculation of the sales which Discount Ltd would have to make in the year to 31 March 1983, *in order to break even* (i.e., make neither profit nor loss) during that year.

(b) A balance sheet for Discount Ltd at 31 March 1983, consistent with the information provided and with the requirement in (a) above.

(c) A flow of funds statement (statement of sources and applications of funds) for the year ending 31 March 1983, consistent with (a) and (b) above.

30 marks

3 HENRY

Henry plans to start a wholesale business on 1 January 1985. On that date he will introduce £10,000 capital, which will be paid into a business bank account, and he will immediately make cash purchases of £6,000 equipment and £3,100 stock in trade. In 1985 he will keep his stock of goods replenished at £3,100.

Henry expects that he will receive a credit period of five weeks from his suppliers (apart from the initial cash purchase of goods) and that all his customers will take a credit period of eight weeks. He expects to earn a gross profit margin of 40% on selling price of all sales. The gross profit margin is stated before charging the following costs, which will remain fixed irrespective of the level of sales:

Estimates for year ending 31 December 1985:

	£
Wages	5,000
Rent	4,000
Sundry expenses	4,000
Depreciation	600

Wages, rent, and sundry expenses will be paid as they are incurred. It can be assumed that all transactions involving credit will take place at an even rate throughout a year of *50 weeks* (for ease of calculation).

Henry asks his bank to provide a temporary overdraft to finance his working capital requirements. He explains:

> I estimate that I will make a net profit of £2,400 during the year. I shall withdraw only £1,400 for my own needs during the year, so the retained profit of £1,000 will be ample to ensure that there is no overdraft outstanding at the end of the year.

Required:

(a) A calculation of the sales Henry would have to make in 1985 in order to achieve the net profit of £2,400 which he expects.

(b) Henry's balance sheet at 31 December 1985, assuming that he makes a net profit of £2,400 during 1985, of which he withdraws £1,400.

(c) A numerical statement summarising the funds flows which caused the change in Henry's bank account from the opening balance of £10,000 to the position at 31 December 1985 shown in your answer to part (b).

(d) A calculation of the sales Henry would have to make in 1985 in order to have a nil bank balance at 31 December 1985. Assume that Henry withdraws £1,400 from net profit, as before.

Note: Ignore taxation and bank interest.

30 marks

4 BAIN LTD

The balance sheet of Bain Ltd at 30 June 1983, and the company's profit statement for the year ended 30 June 1983, are shown below.

Balance sheet

	£		£
Issued capital	30,000	Equipment at cost	48,000
Revenue reserves	22,000	Less: Depreciation	12,000
Trade creditors	6,000		
Bank overdraft	8,000		36,000
		Stock in trade	9,000
		Trade debtors	21,000
	66,000		66,000

Profit statement

		£
Sales		120,000
Less:		
Cost of goods sold	72,000	
Wages	18,000	
Sundry expenses	12,000	
Rent	7,000	
Depreciation	4,000	
		113,000
Net profit		7,000
Directors' remuneration		5,000
Retained profit		2,000

One of the directors of Bain Ltd in discussing the company's trading estimates and borrowing requirements for the year to 30 June 1984, makes the following statement to the company's bank manager:

> We expect that our retained profit in 1984 will be £5,000, after paying the same directors' remuneration as in 1983. Add back the 'non-cash' depreciation charge of £4,000 and that gives us an estimated 'cash flow' of £9,000. Since we do not propose to make any outlays on fixed assets during the year, and our stock in trade is not expected to increase, we should have a favourable bank balance of £1,000 in the balance sheet at 30 June 1984.

The bank manager is sceptical of the estimated effect on the bank account and asks you to prepare some calculations for the year to 30 June 1984.

Assume:

(i) The company will not acquire any additional fixed assets and stock in trade at 30 June 1984 will be £9,000; the company will not pay a dividend or raise any new long-term capital.

(ii) Cost of goods sold, wages and sundry expenses are variable costs which will bear the same direct proportion to sales in 1984 as in 1983.

(iii) Trade creditors and trade debtors in the balance sheet at 30 June 1984, will increase or decrease proportionately with sales — and the same proportions will apply as in 1983.

(iv) There will be no wages, sundry expenses, rent or directors' remuneration unpaid at 30 June 1984.

Required:

(a) Calculations showing the sales which, on the basis of the above assumptions, would be required to produce retained profit of £5,000 for the year ending 30 June 1984.

(b) The estimated balance sheet for the year ended 30 June 1984, consistent with the sales calculated above and with the assumptions stated in the question.

(c) Calculations of the sales which would in fact be required to give Bain Ltd a bank balance of £1,000 at 30 June 1984, on the basis of the stated assumptions.

Note: Ignore taxation and bank interest.

30 marks

5 GRIFFIN LTD

William, who has been in business for many years, has decided to set up a new company called Griffin Ltd in Exmorth. William plans that his company should take over some fixed assets from an existing business for £40,000 and stock for £15,000; none of the other assets or liabilities of the former concern is to be acquired.

The company will begin trading on 1 January 1985 and William, who has expert knowledge in these matters, expects sales at an even rate amounting to £150,000 during the first year of business. The gross profit margin will be 20% on sales, and William expects his stock to turn over six times during 1985, based on the average of opening and closing stocks. It is intended to allow debtors 72 days credit, and suppliers are expected to allow 45 days for the payment of amounts due to them. Expenses, other than depreciation, debited to the profit and loss account will amount to £15,000. Depreciation is to be charged at 10% on the cost of fixed assets.

The bank have agreed to provide certain limited overdraft facilities for the new venture. The borrowing limit will be set so that William's current assets will be double his current liabilities at 31 December 1984. It will be necessary for William to arrange sufficient share capital to ensure compliance with this condition.

Required:

(a) The estimated balance sheet of Griffin Ltd at 31 December 1985, showing clearly the share capital, which would have to be raised at the outset, and a bank overdraft consistent with the information given above.

(b) A calculation of the revised figure for stock at 31 December 1985, assuming that the bank introduces an alternative requirement that the liquid ratio (ratio of debtors to current liabilities) at 31 December 1985 should be at least 1.2:1, and that the company decides to achieve this by increasing the rate of stock turnover.

Note: Ignore taxation and interest on the bank overdraft. All sales and purchases are to be on credit. Assume a 360-day year throughout.

20 marks

6 CROWTON LTD

Two customers of Solid Bank are planning to establish a new company, Crowton Ltd on 1 January 1977. The company will commence trading on that date, and its estimated trading transactions for the year ended 31 December 1977 are:

	£
Purchases	36,000
Wages and expenses	20,000
Sales	60,000

These transactions are expected to take place at an even rate throughout the year. Wages and expenses will be paid immediately they are incurred, and it is estimated that at 31 December 1977 payments will be outstanding for two months' purchases and two months' sales.

In addition, the company will buy fixed assets for £20,000 and opening stock in trade for £5,000 on 1 January 1977; these items will remain at the same amounts at the end of the accounting year.

Crowton Ltd will raise finance by the issue of 10% debentures at par on 1 January 1977. The lenders require that the company shall have a share capital which is at least twice the amount of the debentures; they also require that net profit *before* charging interest must cover the annual interest on the debentures at least five times. Net profit after charging interest will be retained by the company.

The proposed directors of Crowton Ltd have decided that the company should have a current ratio of 3.0 on 31 December 1977.

The company will issue the *minimum* share capital consistent with the above estimates.

Assume a bank balance or bank overdraft of an amount consistent with the information given and, in the event of an overdraft, ignore bank interest.

Required:

The estimated balance sheet of Crowton Ltd at 31 December 1977.

Note: Ignore taxation.

20 marks

7 MARTIN

Martin plans to establish a retail business which will commence trading on 1 July 1977. Estimated trading transactions for the year ended 30 June 1978, are as follows:

	£
Purchases	90,000
Wages and sundry expenses	72,000
Sales	180,000

These transactions are expected to take place at an even rate throughout the year. Martin estimates that he will take one month's credit on purchases. that he will pay all wages and sundry expenses in the month in which they are incurred, but that his customers will take two months' credit on all the sales he makes.

In addition to these transactions, Martin will purchase fixed assets for £36,000 and an opening stock in trade of £12,000 on 1 July 1977. The stock in trade will be maintained at the same level throughout the year.

Martin will raise some finance by a long-term loan from Annabel at 15% per year. Annabel insists that Martin's expected profit for the year ending 30 June 1978, *before* charging interest or drawings cover the amount of interest at least six times. Martin will borrow the maximum permissible amount on 1 July 1977. The amount borrowed will remain unchanged throughout Martin's financial year, and he will pay the full year's interest on 30 June 1978.

After paying interest on the long-term debt, Martin will withdraw £2,000 for his own use on 30 June 1978; the remaining profit will be retained in the business.

Martin has decided that the current assets should be three times current liabilities at 30 June 1978. Martin will introduce cash into the business on 1 July 1977 to provide the necessary capital consistent with the above estimates.

It can be assumed that at all relevant times the business will have a bank balance or bank overdraft consistent with the information provided.

Required:

(a) Martin's estimated balance sheet at 30 June 1978.

(b) A calculation of the *lowest* level of the current ratio during the year, and the *month* in which it will occur.

Note: Ignore taxation and depreciation.

30 marks

8 SPANNER LTD

The summarised balance sheet of Spanner Ltd at 31 March 1977, and the company's summarised profit statement for the year ended 31 March 1977, are shown below.

Balance sheet

	£		£	£
Issued share capital	50,000	Fixed assets	75,000	
Reserves	22,000	Less: Accumulated		
Trade creditors	11,000	depreciation	25,000	
Bank overdraft	9,000			50,000
		Stock in trade		13,000
		Trade debtors		29,000
	92,000			92,000

Profit statement

	£	£
Sales		200,000
Less: Cost of goods sold	120,000	
Depreciation	6,000	
Other expenses	66,000	
		192,000
Net profit retained		8,000

Spanner Ltd will purchase additional fixed assets for £13,000 cash during the coming year to March 1978. The company intends to obtain some of the necessary finance by controlling working capital more effectively.

In the year to 31 March 1978, the company plans to reduce its holding of stock in trade to an average level of 30 days' supply (based on cost of goods sold). In addition, the company plans to collect trade debtors in 45 days, on average. The average period of trade credit taken by the company will remain unchanged (except for requirement (c), below).

Spanner Ltd is a wholesaling company, which acquires finished goods for resale and does not undertake manufacturing activities. It is to be assumed that the company will operate at the same level of trading transactions in the year ended 31 March 1978 as in the preceding year, with the same level of prices and costs; depreciation will be £6,000 as before. There will be no transactions other than those indicated by the information above.

The company's balance sheet at 31 March 1977, does not include any expense creditors, accruals or prepayments, nor will there be any such items in the balance sheet at 31 March 1978.

Assume a year of 360 days throughout.

Required:

(a) Estimated balance sheet of Spanner Ltd at 31 March 1978.

(b) A calculation of the amount of cash that would have been made available by the estimated changes in the levels of stock in trade and debtors.

(c) A calculation of the bank overdraft or bank balance the company would have at 31 March 1978, if it were to pay its creditors in *15 days* (on average), with all other assumptions remaining unchanged.

Note: Ignore taxation.

20 marks

9 KENDAL LTD

The summarised balance sheet of Kendal Ltd, a well established private company which has banked with you for many years, contained the following information:

Summarised balance sheet at 31 March 1984

	£000		£000
Share capital	1,000	Fixed assets at cost	920
Profit and loss account	205	Less: Accumulated depreciation	170
	1,205		750
Trade creditors	200	Temporary investments at cost	70
Corporation tax due		Stocks	350
1 January 1985	120	Trade debtors	320
		Bank balance	35
	1,525		1,525

The company's managing director, who is also the major shareholder, believes that there is a strong demand for the products Kendal supplies, and he intends to expand the level of activities by renting additional premises and acquiring new plant. He is attempting to assess the financial implications of his plans and he approaches you for advice. He provides you with the following forecasts and information:

(i) Plant will be purchased in May 1984 at a cost of £270,000 and, from 1 June onwards, the level of business activity will be 50% above the previous level. The rate of stock turnover and the period of credit obtained from suppliers are expected to remain unchanged, but the period of credit allowed to customers will increase, on average, by 25%.

(ii) The following are extracts from the company's forecast profit and loss account for the year to 31 March 1985, which takes account of the plans and assumptions made in (i) above.

Profit and loss account extracts, year to 31 March 1985

	£000	£000
Operating profit before charging depreciation:		
April-May		60
June-March		450
		510
Less: Depreciation	130	
Corporation tax on profit from operations	180	310
		200
Add: Gain arising on sale of the company's temporary investments, in May, net of a tax charge of £16,000		24
		224

Required:

(a) The forecast balance sheet at 31 March 1985 (a bank balance or bank overdraft may be inserted as the balancing item). *12 marks*

(b) An assessment of the financial implications of the proposals for expansion. The assessment should include calculations of relevant 'solvency' ratios and an indication, so far as the information permits, of the overdraft requirement on 1 June 1984 assuming that the bank agrees to help to finance the project. For this purpose, you may assume that the increase in the working capital requirement occurs on 1 June 1984. *18 marks*

Notes

(1) Ignore interest payable on any bank overdraft.
(2) A year consists of twelve calendar months of equal duration.
(3) There are no seasonal fluctuations in the level of trading activity.

Total 30 marks

10 BASKETWEAVERS LTD

The cost incurred by Basketweavers Ltd in the years ended 31 December 1981 and 31 December 1982, are shown below:

	1981	1982
	£	£
Materials	18,000	22,500
Wages for direct labour	20,000	25,000
Rent of workshops	6,000	6,000
Fixed manufacturing expenses	11,500	11,500
	55,500	65,000

The baskets woven and sold in each year were:

	1981	1982
Number of baskets woven	20,000	25,000
Number of baskets sold	20,000	18,000

In both 1981 and 1982 all sales were made at a constant price of £3 per basket.

There were no stocks of finished baskets at 1 January 1981, nor were there any stocks of raw materials or work in progress at the beginning or end of either 1981 or 1982.

Required:

(a) Calculate the net profit of Basketweavers Ltd for the years 1981 and 1982. Stock in trade is to be valued at cost, including all overheads.

(b) Examine and explain fully the difference between the net profit achieved by Basketweavers in 1982 and the net profit of 1981.

Note: Ignore taxation.

20 marks

11 RADIOS LTD

Radios Ltd commenced business on 1 January 1983. In the years 1983 and 1984 the company's production and sales were:

	1983	1984
Number of radios manufactured	11,000	10,000
Number of radios sold	9,000	11,000

In both years all sales were made at a constant price of £10 per radio. The company's manufacturing costs in the years 1983 and 1984 were:

	1983	1984
	£	£
Raw materials	14,300	13,000
Other variable costs	18,700	17,000
Fixed manufacturing costs	68,200	68,200

There were no stocks of raw materials or work in progress at the relevant balance sheet dates.

Required:

(a) Calculations revealing the net profit of Radios Ltd for the years 1983 and 1984. Finished goods are to be valued at full cost, including manufacturing overheads.

(b) A clear explanation (supported by figures) of the difference in net profit of the company in the two years.

Note: Ignore taxation.

20 marks

12 SEESAW LTD

A new company, Seesaw Ltd, is being established for the manufacture of a patented product. The directors of the company are faced with a choice between two different methods of production:

Option A

The company would buy components which would be assembled and then sold by Seesaw Ltd. Estimated costs would be:

Fixed costs	£80,000 per year
Variable costs	£34 per unit

The company's estimated opening balance sheet under this option would be:

	£		£
Share capital	200,000	Premises and equipment	150,000
		Net current assets	50,000
	200,000		200,000

Option B

Seesaw Ltd would acquire additional equipment, which would allow certain manufacturing operations in the company's own premises. Estimated costs would be:

Fixed costs	£185,000 per year
Variable costs	£20 per unit

The company's estimated opening balance sheet under this option would be:

	£		£
Share capital	200,000	Premises and equipment	250,000
10% debentures	100,000	Net current assets	50,000
	300,000		300,000

(Interest on the debentures has been included in the fixed costs for this option.)

The maximum feasible production capacity under either option would be 10,000 units per year. The company intends to sell its product at £50 per unit irrespective of the level of sales achieved.

Required:

A clear analysis of the financial implications of the two alternatives (so far as the information permits) with appropriate calculations and/or diagrams.

Note: Ignore taxation.

20 marks

13 CAVALINO LTD

Cavalino Ltd has been in existence for a number of years. The directors are examining the possibility of using certain premises which the company owns (and which have recently become vacant owing to de-stocking) to manufacture a new product, designated Blanc. Two alternative methods of producing Blanc are under consideration.

Method I

This would involve the acquisition of plant costing £100,000. The labour cost per unit manufactured would be £4.50 and the material cost per unit £2.50. General expenses which would remain unchanged for output up to 50,000 units, would be £40,000 p.a.

Method II

This would involve the acquisition of plant costing £300,000. The labour cost per unit manufactured would be £1.50 and the material cost per unit £2.50. General expenses which would remain unchanged for output up to 50,000 units, would be £68,000 p.a.

Under either method the plant would be expected to last five years, and 70% of its cost would be covered by a loan from one of the company's directors. An appropriate allowance for interest payable to the director under either method is included in the figures for general expenses.

The company would need to acquire an initial stock of raw materials, sufficient to manufacture 4,000 units, for cash. Subsequent purchases would be made monthly to replace items used up and a month's credit would be allowed by suppliers, i.e., stocks, other than the initial purchase, would be financed by suppliers. Two months' credit would be allowed to customers on sales. The company's bank has agreed to provide overdraft facilities to finance the project for one year only.

Blanc would sell for £12 per unit and, according to one of the directors who has experience with this type of product, annual sales of 30,000 units should be possible.

For the purpose of assessing the two alternatives, the directors intend to apply two criteria:

(i) that the project should yield a target profit of at least £40,000;
(ii) that the bank overdraft should be repaid by the end of the year.

Required:

(a) Calculations of the level of sales required in year 1, under each of the two methods, in order to:

    (i) break even (i.e., where total revenues equal total costs);
    (ii) yield the target profit of £40,000;
    (iii) enable the bank overdraft to be repaid.

(b) A discussion of the two alternative methods, based on the results of your calculations under (a) above, and any other information you consider relevant.

Notes

1   Ignore the time value of money.
2   All sales will be made on credit.
3   Ignore interest on bank overdraft.

30 marks

14   ALUMINEX LTD

Ken Dowden and his two brothers are the three directors of a small company, Aluminex Ltd, which manufactures aluminium widgets. The company has banked with you for a number of years and is financially sound. The summarised final accounts for 1982 are set out below:

Summarised profit and loss account for 1982

	£	£
Turnover (100,000 units at £5 each)		500,000
Less: Variable costs	300,000	
Depreciation	20,000	
Other fixed costs	120,000	440,000
Net profit		60,000

Summarised balance sheet at 31 December 1982

	£
Fixed assets at cost	200,000
Less: Accumulated depreciation	80,000
	120,000
Working capital	200,000
Bank deposit account	25,000
	345,000

	£
Financed by:	
Share capital	200,000
Retained profits	145,000
	345,000

It is expected that during 1983 production costs for the existing level of activity will remain unchanged; the selling price is also expected to remain the same. In 1982 the company worked a day shift only, and existing plant was used to its full capacity. There is a heavy demand for the company's product and the three directors are planning to increase the level of activity. Ken Dowden's brothers believe that it will be possible to sell another 50,000 widgets, without reducing the sales price, but Ken believes that an increase of 30,000 is a more realistic estimate. Two alternative proposals for increasing the level of output are under consideration:

I   Work an evening shift. This would enable the company to produce additional output of up to 50,000 units. The variable cost per unit would be 50% higher than the rate for the day shift, the depreciation charge would remain unchanged and other fixed costs would increase by £2,000.

II   Purchase additional plant costing £120,000, with a capacity of 50,000 units. The plant would be depreciated on the straight-line basis over 10 years, assuming a nil residual value. The variable cost per unit and annual depreciation charge on the existing plant would remain unchanged but other fixed costs would increase by £40,000.

Under either alternative, working capital requirements would increase proportionately with the level of activity. The balance on the bank deposit account, in the balance sheet set out above, is surplus to operating requirements and could be used to help to finance the planned expansion of activity. Your bank has been approached to finance any shortfall.

Required:

(a)   A summarised profit and loss account for 1983 and a summarised balance sheet at 31 December 1983, under alternative I, assuming sales of widgets increase to 150,000 units.   *9 marks*

(b)   A summarised profit and loss account for 1983 and a summarised balance sheet at 31 December 1983, under alternative II, assuming sales of widgets increase to 150,000 units.   *9 marks*

(c)   A full discussion of the two alternatives, including an assessment of the effect of the company failing to achieve additional sales of 50,000 units. You should support your discussion with calculations of the break-even point on the *additional* sales (i.e., the amount of additional sales required to ensure that profits earned in 1983 are equal to those earned in 1982).   *12 marks*

Notes:

1. Assume that the calculations are being made on 1 January 1983.

2. The balance on the bank account or the bank overdraft may be treated as the balancing item in the balance sheets you prepare.

3. The forecast accounts should be presented in columnar format.

4. Ignore interest payable, if any.

Total 30 marks

15 ROWAN

Rowan recently won a premium bond prize of £50,000. At present he is employed as a travelling salesman with an annual income of £4,000 and a company car which is worth £1,000 a year to him. His wife works as a receptionist and her salary is £2,000 p.a. He has been exploring two investment possibilities.

(i) To invest his money in a local company. The proposal is that, with the £50,000 available, he should acquire 20,000 shares, which the firm intends to issue in order to finance a plan for expansion. The firm's managing director informs him: 'Our annual profits are at present in the region of £30,000, of which two thirds are paid out in dividends. As a result of the expansion profits should increase by 25% all of which will be added to the current annual dividend.' At present the company's share capital consists of 80,000 shares with a nominal value of £1 each. Under this option Rowan would play no part in the management of the company.

(ii) To acquire a shop which has recently come on to the market. The cost would be £60,000 and this includes stocks to which a value of £15,000 is attached. Finance would be provided out of his winnings and by realising some investments currently yielding a 'safe' return of 10% p.a. (gross). These investments can be added to or reduced without affecting the rate of return. The following estimates are provided concerning this business:

Average annual rate of stock turnover	10
Gross profit as a percentage of sales	25%
Overhead expenses	£33,000

If this option is pursued, Rowan can either run the business with the help of his wife, both working full-time, or engage a manager at an annual salary of £8,000. Management salaries are not included in the overhead expenses shown above.

Required:

(a) A numerical analysis of the options open to Rowan, presented in a manner which will help him to make comparisons. Confine your calculations to the information given.

(b) An indication of the alternative you would recommend on the basis of the information given.

Note: Ignore taxation.

20 marks

16 OMEGA LTD

Omega Ltd is a retail trading concern, currently planning its operations for the year ending 31 May 1985. The company's summarised final accounts for the year ended 31 May 1984 are as follows:

Trading, and profit and loss account, year ended 31 May 1984

	£	£
Sales		80,000
Less: Cost of sales		60,000
Gross profit		20,000
Less: Overheads:		
Establishment expenses	7,000	
Administrative expenses	2,000	
Selling expenses	5,000	
		14,000
Net profit		6,000

Balance sheet as at 31 May 1984

	£	£
Fixed assets at cost		45,000
Less: Depreciation		20,250
		24,750
Current assets		
Stock in trade	10,000	
Debtors	8,000	
Bank	7,850	
	25,850	
Less: Current liabilities		
Creditors	5,600	
Net current assets		20,250
		45,000
Ordinary share capital		30,000
Retained earnings		15,000
		45,000

The company's plans for the year ending 31.5.85 are as follows:

(i) Sales volume to increase by 50% compared with previous year, but with no change in selling prices.

(ii) Overhead expenditure:

Establishment: reduced by £2,000 compared with previous year.
Administrative: 50% increase over previous year.
Selling: 100% increase over previous year.

(iii) Significant relationships:

Debtors are expected to be $16\tfrac{2}{3}\%$ of sales.
Net profit margin is to be 5%.
Creditors are to be the same percentage of purchases as in previous years.
Rate of stock turnover will be 12 times p.a. (one month).
Last year it was 5 times p.a.

(iv) Other information:

All purchases and sales are on credit.
In April 1985 a piece of land will be bought for £20,000.
In May 1985 a further £5,000 will be spent on additional fixtures.
There will be no creditors for fixed assets at 31 May 1985.
All fixed assets are depreciated at 5% p.a. straight-line, and the sum is already charged to the above figure for establishment expenses.

Required:

(a) The budgeted trading and profit and loss account of Omega Ltd for the year to 31.5.85 and the balance sheet at that date.

(b) A total bank account to prove the correctness of the bank balance in (a) above.

30 marks

ANSWERS

1 DEF LTD

Total bank account

Receipts	£000	Payments	£000
Opening balance in credit	55	Payments to suppliers	
Debtors from last year		this year (W3)	1,108
settled in full	212	Operating costs (W2)	144
Cash from sales this year (W1)	1,215	Dividend paid	50
Ordinary shares issued	150	Plant bought	130
		Corporation tax paid	115
		Debentures repaid	20
		Closing balance in credit	65
	1,632		1,632

Workings

1   Cash receipts from this year's sales are:

	£000	£000
Total sales		1,450
Less: Year-end debtors, good	232	
bad	3	235
Cash receipts		1,215

2

	£000
Operating costs	168
Less: Depreciation, a non-cash expense	16
	152
Increase in creditors	(4)
Decrease in prepayments	(4)
Cash payments	144

3   Payments to trade suppliers will be purchases for the year plus £17,000 (the decrease in creditors).

	£000
Therefore, cost of sales	1,026
Add: Stock increase	65
Purchases	1,091
Add: Creditors decreased	17
Cash payments	1,108

Tutorial notes

(a) Those with greater ability in double-entry accounting may have arrived at the cash paid for operating costs as follows:

Operating costs

	£000		£000
Prepayment b/d	4	Accrual b/d	Nil
Cash (the balancing figure)	144	Profit and loss account	168
Depreciation	16	Prepayment c/d	Nil
Accrual c/d	4		
	168		168

(b) Since cost of sales (£1,026,000) is purchases adjusted by stock changes (i.e., opening and closing) and £65,000 extra stocks were held at the year end, then £1,091,000 must have been bought.

2 DISCOUNT LTD

(a) In order to break even, the sales must produce sufficient gross profit to cover the overheads.

In the year ended 31.3.83, the overheads will be:

	£
Rent	7,000
Wages	14,000
Administration etc.	8,000
Depreciation (i.e., 12½% × 8,000)	1,000
	30,000

Gross profit required = 20% × Sales

Therefore sales = $\dfrac{30,000}{0.2}$ = £150,000

(b) **Budgeted balance sheet as at 31.3.83**

	Cost £	Depreciation £	Net £
Fixed assets			
Freeholds	19,200	Nil	19,200
Fixtures and fittings	8,000	1,200	6,800
	27,200	1,200	26,000

		£
Current assets:		
Stock (W1)	12,000	
Debtors (W2)	4,500	
	16,500	

Less: Current liabilities	£	
Creditors (W3)	14,763	
Overdraft (balancing item)	4,037	
		18,800

Net current assets		(2,300)
Net assets employed		23,700

Financed by:		
Capital: shares		25,000
Less: Profit and loss account (loss)		(1,300)
Shareholders' funds		23,700

(c) **Budgeted source and application of funds statement for year ended 31.3.83**

Sources:	£
Net profit for year	Nil
Add: Depreciation for year	1,000
Funds from trading	1,000
Other sources	Nil
Less: Applications:	Nil
Net inflow of funds	1,000

Represented by increases in working capital:	
Stock decrease	(1,900)
Debtors decrease	(700)
Creditors decrease	2,037
Overdraft decrease	1,563
Net increase	1,000

Workings

1   Stock at 31.3.83

Cost of sales = 80% × £150,000 =	£120,000
Stock = 10% × £120,000 =	£12,000

2   Debtors at 31.3.83

    Credit sales = 36% × £150,000 =   £54,000
    Debtors = (1/12) × £54,000 =   £4,500

3   Creditors at 31.3.83

	£
Cost of sales	120,000
Stock at 31.3.83	12,000
	132,000
Stock at 31.3.82	13,900
Purchases for year	118,100

    Creditors = (1½/12) × £118,100 =   £14,763

Tutorial note

The bank overdraft is the balancing item in the balance sheet. It can be checked by producing a total bank account as follows:

Total bank account

Receipts	£	Payments	£
Debtor cash from last year	5,200	Opening overdraft	5,600
Sales, cash terms	96,000	Rent	7,000
Sales, credit terms		Wages	14,000
(i.e., £54,000 less £4,500)	49,500	Administration, etc.	8,000
		Creditors paid from last year	16,800
		Purchases this year	
Closing overdraft	4,037	(i.e., 118,100 less 14,763)	103,337
	154,737		154,737

3 HENRY

(a) Gross profit = Sales × 40%, and
    Cost of sales = 60% × Sales

To provide Henry's estimated profit, gross profit must be sufficient to cover:

		£
Overheads:	Wages	5,000
	Rent	4,000
	Sundries	4,000
	Depreciation	600
		13,600
and Profit		2,400
		16,000

(b) **Budgeted balance sheet as at 31.12.85**

	£	£
Fixed assets		
Equipment		6,000
Less: Depreciation		600
		5,400
Current assets		
Stock	3,100	
Debtors (W1)	6,400	
	9,500	
Less: Current liabilities		
Creditors (W2)	2,400	
Overdraft (balancing item)	1,500	
	3,900	
		5,600
		11,000
Financed by:		
Capital		10,000
Net profit		2,400
Less: Drawings		(1,400)
Net worth		11,000

(c) **Budgeted source and application of funds statement for the year ended 31.12.85**

	£	£
Sources:		
Net profit for year		2,400
Add: Depreciation for year		600
Funds from trading		3,000
Other sources:		
Capital injected		10,000
		13,000
Applications:		
Equipment bought	6,000	
Drawings	1,400	
		(7,400)
Net inflow of funds		5,600
Represented by increase in working capital:		
Stocks increase		3,100
Debtors increase		6,400
Creditors increase		(2,400)
Bank overdraft increase		(1,500)
Net increase		5,600

(d) Extra sales to clear £1,500 overdraft:

Cash flow from £1 sales:

		£
Sales		1.00
Purchases 60% × 1.00 =	0.60	
Less: Credit by Henry (5/50 weeks) × 0.60 =	0.06	
	0.54	
Credit taken by customers (8/50 weeks) × 1.00 =	0.16	
		0.70
Cash flow per £1 sales		0.30

Extra sales required = 1,500/0.3 =	5,000
Budgeted sales	40,000
	45,000

Workings

1 Debtors

   8/50 weeks, i.e., 16% × Sales = 0.16 × £40,000 = £6,400

2 Creditors

   5/50 weeks, i.e., 10% × Purchases

   Purchases = 60% × Sales, since there is no stock increase. Therefore creditors at 31.12.85 = 10% × (£40,000 × 0.6) = £2,400

Tutorial notes

(a) No allowance has been made for any stock increases to help generate extra sales.

(b) An alternative calculation for part (d), could be:

Cash required for a nil bank balance at 31.12.85:

	£
Equipment	6,000
Stock	3,100
Overheads (13,600 − 600)	13,000
Drawings	1,400
	23,500
Less: Capital introduced	10,000
	13,500

Sales required: 13,500/0.3 = £45,000

(c) The overdraft £1,500 can be proved as follows:

Bank account

		£			£
Capital		10,000	Equipment		6,000
Sales	£40,000		Stock		3,100
Less: Debtors	£6,400	33,600	Wages		5,000
			Rent		4,000
Balance, overdraft		1,500	Sundry expenses		4,000
			Drawings		1,400
			Purchases: 0.6 × £40,000 = £24,000		
			Less: Creditors	£2,400	21,600
		45,100			45,100

4 BAIN LTD

(a) To provide a profit of £5,000 the contribution required from sales must be as follows:

	£
Fixed overheads:	
Rent	7,000
Depreciation	4,000
Directors' remuneration	5,000
	16,000
Profit required	5,000
	21,000

Analysis of the profit statement shows:

		£000	%
Sales		120	100
Cost of sales	72		60
Wages	18		15
Sundry expenses	12	102	10
			85
Contribution towards fixed expenses and profit		18	15
			100

Since the contribution is 15% × Sales:

Sales (producing £5,000 profit) = £21,000/0.15 = £140,000

(b) **Estimated balance sheet as at 30.6.84**

	£	£
Equipment at cost		48,000
Less: Depreciation (W1)		16,000
		32,000
Current assets		
Stock	9,000	
Debtors (W2)	24,500	
	33,500	
Less: Current liabilities		
Creditors (W3) £7,000		
Overdraft, balancing item £1,500		
	8,500	
		25,000
		57,000
Financed by:		
Capital		30,000
Revenue reserves		27,000
Shareholders' funds		57,000

(c) Extra sales required to convert £1,500 overdraft to £1,000 credit, i.e., to produce £2,500 cash at 30.6.84:

	£
Cash flow from sales of £1:	
Sales	1.000
Variable costs	0.850
	0.150
Add: Increase in creditors for purchases	
Purchases = 60% × Sales (0.6)	
Period of credit (£6,000/£72,000) × 0.6	0.050
Less: Increase in debtors	
Period of credit (£21,000/£120,000) × 1.00	(0.175)
Cash flow per £1 sales	0.025

	£
Therefore extra sales required = £2,500/0.025 =	100,000
Add: Budgeted sales	140,000
Sales required for year ended 30.6.84	240,000

Workings

1   Depreciation (accumulated by 30.6.84):

	£
Balance at 30.6.83	12,000
Add: Depreciation for year	4,000
	16,000

2   Debtors at 30.6.84:

(£21,000/£120,000) × £140,000 =   £24,500

3   Creditors at 30.6.84:

(£6,000/£72,000) × 60% × £140,000 =   £7,000

Tutorial notes

The contribution, towards fixed overheads and profit, is sales less the variable costs. From the summary in part (a) it can be seen that:

	% of sales
Cost of sales	60
Wages	15
Sundries	10
Variable costs	85
Contribution	15
	100

This relationship of contribution to sales is known as the profit volume ratio (P/V ratio).

5 GRIFFIN LTD

(a) Budgeted balance sheet as at 31.12.85

		£	£
Fixed assets at cost			40,000
Less: Depreciation			4,000
			36,000
Current assets			
Stock (W2)		25,000	
Debtors (W3)		30,000	
		55,000	
Less: Current liabilities			
Creditors (W4)	16,250		
Overdraft, balancing figure	16,250		
		32,500	
Net current assets			22,500
			58,500
Capital at 31.12.84 (W5)			47,500
Net profit for year (W1)			11,000
Shareholders' funds			58,500

(b) Calculation of revised stock figure

$$\text{Liquid ratio} = \frac{\text{Debtors}}{\text{Current liabilities}} = \frac{30,000}{\text{CL}} = 1.2$$

Therefore $CL = \dfrac{30,000}{1.2} = £25,000$

		£
Since net current assets per (a)	=	22,500
Current liabilities (see above)	=	25,000
Current assets (stock and debtors)	=	47,500
Less: Debtors		30,000
Stock at 31.12.85		17,500

Workings

1 Profit for year

	£
Sales	150,000
Cost of sales	120,000
Gross profit (20%)	30,000

Overheads:	£	
General	15,000	
Depreciation (10% × 40,000)	4,000	19,000
		11,000

2 Stock

Since the stock turn = 6 times, average stock = $\dfrac{120,000}{6}$ = £20,000

Average stock = (Opening and closing stock)/2 = £20,000

Therefore closing stock = £25,000

3 Debtors

Debtors = Sales (£150,000) × (72/360 days) = £30,000

4 Creditors

Creditors = Purchases × (45/360) days (i.e., 1/8)

Purchases:	£
Cost of sales	120,000
Add: Stock increase, £25,000 − £15,000 =	10,000
	130,000

Therefore creditors = £130,000 × $\dfrac{1}{8}$ = £16,250

5 Capital at 31.12.84

From opening balance sheet

	£		£
Capital	47,500	Fixed assets	40,000
Overdraft (½ × £15,000)	7,500	Stock	15,000
	55,000		55,000

6 CROWTON LTD

Budgeted balance sheet as at 31.12.77

	£	£
Fixed assets		20,000
Current assets		
Stock	5,000	
Debtors (W1)	10,000	
Bank (W3)	3,000	
	18,000	
Less: Current liabilities		
Creditors (W2)	6,000	12,000
		32,000
Share capital (W7)		20,800
Net profit for year (W4)		3,200
Shareholders' funds		24,000
Medium-term liabilities		
Debenture loan 10% (W5)		8,000
		32,000

Workings

1. Debtors = Sales (£60,000) × (2/12 months) = £10,000

2. Creditors = Purchases (£36,000) × (2/12) = £6,000

3. Bank balance = Current assets less (Stock and debtors)

   Current assets = 3 × Current liabilities
                    = 3 × £6,000 = £18,000

   Therefore bank balance = £18,000 − (£5,000 + £10,000) = £3,000

4. Profit for year

	£
Sales	60,000
Cost of sales	36,000
	24,000
Less: Wages and expenses	20,000
Profit before interest	4,000
Interest (1/5 × 4,000)	800
Profit	3,200

5   Debentures

Since interest is £800 (per W4), £8,000 × 10%

Debentures will be issued, i.e., 800/0.1 = £8,000

6   Shareholders' funds

	£
Assets total, per balance sheet	32,000
Assets financed by debentures	8,000
Assets financed by shareholders	24,000

7   Share capital (to be issued) = £24,000 less £3,200 = £20,800

7 MARTIN

(a) **Budgeted balance sheet as at 30.6.78**

	£	£	£
Fixed assets			36,000
Current assets			
Stock		12,000	
Debtors (W1)		30,000	
		42,000	
Less: Current liabilities			
Creditors (W2)	7,500		
Overdraft (W3)	6,500		
		14,000	
Net current assets			28,000
			64,000
Financed by:			
Capital			31,000
Net profit for year (W4)			15,000
Less: Drawings			(2,000)
Net worth			44,000
Medium-term liabilities			
15% loan (W5)			20,000
			64,000

(b) Calculation of lowest current ratios

	July £	August £	September £	
Stock	12,000	12,000	12,000	
Debtors	15,000	30,000	30,000	
	27,000	42,000	42,000	steady
Creditors	7,500	7,500	7,500	steady
Interest outstanding	250	500	750	increasing by £250 per month
Overdraft*	3,000	16,500	15,000	reducing by £1,500 per month
	10,750	24,500	23,250	reducing

Current ratio at 31.8.77 = $\dfrac{42,000}{24,500}$ = 1.71:1

*Cash flow

	£			
Capital	31,000			
Loan	20,000			
	51,000			
Fixed assets	36,000			
Stock	12,000			
Expenses	6,000	54,000	(6,000)	(6,000)
		(3,000)		
Creditors			(7,500)	(7,500)
		(3,000)	(13,500)	(13,500)
Debtors				15,000
Excess of receipts over payments		(3,000)	(13,500)	1,500	continues at £1,500 per month

The lowest current ratio, i.e., $\dfrac{\text{current assets}}{\text{current liabilities}}$ occurs at the end of August, since from then onwards the current liabilities are steadily reduced, while the current assets remain at £42,000.

Workings

1. Debtors = Sales (£180,000) × (2/12) = £30,000

2. Creditors = Purchases (£90,000) × (1/12) = £7,500
   (Note: Purchases = cost of sales, since stock does not change.)

3   Overdraft

   Current liabilities = 1/3 current assets = 1/3 × 42,000
   = £14,000
   Creditors (W2)   £ 7,500

   Overdraft   £ 6,500

4   Profit   £   £
    Sales   180,000
    Less: Purchases   90,000
          Expenses   72,000   162,000

    Profit before interest   18,000
    Less: Interest (1/6 × 18,000)   3,000

                                                              15,000

5   Debentures = $\dfrac{\text{Interest per W4}}{\text{Rate of interest}} = \dfrac{£3,000}{0.15} = £20,000$

6   Capital to be introduced

    Total assets per balance sheet at 30.6.78   £64,000

                                                                £
    Profit for year retained (£15,000 − £2,000)   13,000
    Loan capital per W5   20,000
    Balance financed by original capital   31,000

                                                             64,000

8   **SPANNER LTD**

(a) **Budgeted balance sheet as at 31 March 1978**
                                                     £   £
    Fixed assets   88,000
    Less: Accumulated depreciation   31,000

    (W1)   57,000

    Current assets
      Closing stocks (W2)   10,000
      Debtors (W2)   25,000

                                                 35,000

		£	£	£
	Less: Current liabilities			
	Creditors	£11,000		
	Overdraft, balancing item	£1,000		
			12,000	
				23,000
				80,000
	Financed by:			
	Capital			50,000
	Reserves (£22,000 + £8,000)			30,000
				80,000

(b) Cash made available by:

	£
Stock reduction (£13,000 − £10,000)	3,000
Debtors reduction (£29,000 − £25,000)	4,000
	7,000

(c) Effect on bank balance of taking 15 days credit

	£
Purchases = Cost of sales =	120,000
Less: Stock reduction (i.e., £13,000 − £10,000)	3,000
	117,000

Therefore creditors = £117,000 × (15/360) = £4,875

	£
Creditors per balance sheet, see (a)	11,000
Creditors calculated above	4,875
Reduction in creditors = increase in overdraft	6,125
Overdraft per balance sheet, see (a)	1,000
Amended overdraft	7,125

Workings

1 Fixed assets at cost

	£
Balance at 31.3.77	75,000
Purchases	13,000
	88,000
Accumulated depreciation	
Balance at 31.3.77	25,000
Depreciation for year	6,000
	31,000

2   Stock at 31.3.78 = £120,000 × (30/360) = £10,000

Debtors at 31.3.78 = £200,000 × (45/360) = £25,000

9 KENDAL LTD

(a) **Forecast balance sheet at 31 March 1985**

			£000
Fixed assets at cost (920 + 270)			1,190
Less: Accumulated depreciation (170 + 130)			300
			890

Current assets

	£		
Stocks: 350 × (150/100)	525		
Trade debtors: 320 × (150/100) × (125/100)	600		
	1,125		

Less: Current liabilities

	£		
Trade creditors: 200 × (150/100)	300		
Corporation tax due: 180 + 16	196		
Overdraft, balancing item	90	586	539
			1,429

Share capital	1,000
Profit and loss account (205 + 224)	429
	1,429

(b)

Bank finance required by 1.6.84:		Working capital at 1.6.84:	
	£000 £000	£000	£000
To purchase of fixed assets	270		
Increase stocks by	175		525
Increase debtors	280		600
	725		1,125
Less: Sale of Investments			
(70 + 24 + 16)	110		
Increase in creditors	100	300	
Profit before depreciation	60		
	270		
	455		
Less: Bank balance at 31.3.84	35		
	420	420	
			720
			120 Tax*
			840

(i) Current ratio

	31.3.84 £000	1.6.84 £000	31.3.85 £000
CA	775	1,125	1,125
CL	320	840	586
	2.4:1	1.34:1	1.92:1

(ii) Liquid ratio $\left(\dfrac{\text{Cash and debtors}}{\text{CL}}\right)$

	31.3.84 £000	1.6.84 £000	31.3.85 £000
	425	600	600
	320	840	586
	1.3:1	0.71:1	1.02:1

*Corporation tax has been included as a current liability in all three calculations.

It can be seen that both of these solvency ratios are comparatively weak at 1.6.84, but will have strengthened to a respectable current ratio of 1.92:1 and a liquidity ratio of 1.02:1 by 31.3.85.

Of more significance than these solvency ratios, is the estimation of cash flow, and the major capital items that have to be paid out of that cash flow. From June onwards this appears to be £45,000 per month, which over a full year will be £540,000 out of which £120,000 tax will have to be paid on 1.1.85. Within a year, therefore, the bank borrowing will have been repaid out of profits. Admiration for this excellent performance must, however, be tempered by consideration of the interest (to be ignored in the calculations) and the ability of the firm to increase output and profitability by 50%, almost instantaneously, and to generate this increase with capital that has increased from £1,205,000 at 31.3.84 to £1,429,000 at 31.3.85. These figures taken from the respective balance sheets show capital will increase by only 18.6%.

Provided an analysis of the firm's cost structure and method of the projected expansion supports the budgeted figures an assessment of the financial implication would probably be favourable, particularly if past data has been reliable.

Management's intention to fund the project within a year out of retained profits (since no dividends appear in the profit and loss account) may be reassuring to the bank, though the minority shareholders' attitudes should be considered.

Tutorial note

This question clearly illustrates the limitations of cash budgets for periods as long as a year. One can see from part (a) that Kendal Ltd requires bank funding of £90,000 at 31.3.85 but agreement, when the budgets are being produced, of an overdraft limit of about that figure would prove calamitous, since the bank funding required in June 1984 is more than £400,000.

The bank may well agree not to lend this large amount, but the managing director, being aware of the problem, could seek alternative funding. Note that the bank overdraft is the best form of finance in this case, since it is only required for a relatively short time and is self-liquidating.

When there are great fluctuations in the finance required, it is necessary to produce cash budgets for each quarter or even each month. Such monthly cash budgets simply summarise receipts and payments for the period and add monthly net cash flows to the opening balance — see chapter 5.

10 BASKETWEAVERS LTD

(a) **Trading and profit and loss accounts for years ended:**

		31.12.81			31.12.82	
	units	£	£	units	£	£
Sales	(20,000)		60,000	(18,000)		54,000
Less: Materials		18,000			22,500	
Direct wages		20,000			25,000	
Rent		6,000			6,000	
Manufacturing expenses		11,500			11,500	
Cost of production	(20,000)	55,500		(25,000)	65,000	
Less: Stock	Nil	Nil	55,500	(7,000)	18,200	46,800
Profit	(20,000)		4,500	(18,000)		7,200

(b) The higher profit in 1982 is due entirely to the higher output reducing the average fixed cost of goods produced, as shown below:

		1981 £		1981 £
Variable cost per unit:	$\dfrac{38{,}000}{20{,}000}$	1.900	$\dfrac{47{,}500}{25{,}000}$	1.90
Fixed cost per unit:	$\dfrac{17{,}500}{20{,}000}$	0.875	$\dfrac{17{,}500}{25{,}000}$	0.70
Total cost per unit		2.775		2.60
Selling price		£3.000		£3.000
Profit per unit		£0.225		£0.40
Sales (Units)		20,000		18,000
Profit for year		£4,500		£7,200

The apparent paradox that the firm's profit can be 60% higher on a 10% lower turnover at a constant selling price, is explained by the accounting policy of valuing stock at full cost price (known as total absorption cost), i.e., including fixed overheads. This procedure is endorsed by SSAP 9 on stock and work in progress, provided costs are absorbed on a normal basis. At 31.12.82, Basket-weavers Ltd is carrying forward into 1983 £4,900 of fixed expenses, i.e., (7,000/25,000 units) × £17,500, to be set against future income rather than being written off in the year, 1982, in which it was incurred.

Since the expenses listed can be categorised as variable costs or fixed costs, the following contribution statement would be an appropriate alternative to that shown in part (a):

		1981 £		1982 £
Selling price	3.00			
Variable cost	1.90			
Contribution per unit	1.10			
Contribution	(20,000 units)	22,000	(18,000 units)	19,800
Less: Fixed overheads		17,500		17,500
			Less: (7/25) 4,900	12,600
Profit		4,500		7,200

When the stock is ultimately sold, the profits are likely to be £4,900 lower than they would have been if fixed overheads had not been carried forward in the stock valuation.

11 RADIOS LTD

(a)

		1983 £			1984 £	
Sales	(9,000 × £10)	90,000		(11,000 × £10)	110,000	
Cost of sales:	£			£	£	
Opening stock	–				18,400	
Raw materials	14,300			13,000		
Variable costs	18,700			17,000		
Fixed costs	68,200			68,200		
Cost of manufacture	(11,000) 101,200		(10,000)	98,200		
Closing stock	(2,000) 18,400		(1,000)	9,820		
	(9,000) 82,800	82,800	(9,000)	88,380	88,380	106,780
Profit		7,200				3,220

Note: Stocks have been valued at full cost, using the FIFO, i.e., 'First in, first out', basis.

(b) Although sales in quantity and value were more than 20% higher in 1984, the profit was more than halved. This was due entirely to the method of stock valuation adopted; stock has been valued in line with accepted practice at cost including a proportion of fixed overheads. This means that Radios Ltd has carried forward in its stock valuation fixed expenses of £12,400 (i.e., (2,000 units stock/11,000 units made) × £68,200), from 1983, when the costs were incurred, to a later period when the stock was sold — assumed to be early 1984 using the FIFO basis. The relevant amount being carried forward from 1984 is only £6,820, i.e., (1,000 units/10,000 units) × £68,200.

The profits of the two years may be compared as follows:

1983			£	£
Sales	9,000 @	£10.0	90,000	
Costs		9.2	82,800	
Profit		0.8	7,200	

1984				£
Sales	2,000 @	10.00	20,000	
Cost		9.20	18,400	
Profit		0.80	1,600	1,600
Sales	9,000 @	10.00	90,000	
Cost		9.82	88,380	
Profit		0.18	1,620	1,620
			11,000	3,220

In 1983, unit cost was £9.20 based on 11,000 units.
In 1984, unit cost was £9.82 based on 10,000 units.

Average cost increased considerably because of the high fixed expenses, £68,200, and the relatively low output, 10,000 units, to share (absorb) the cost.

Tutorial note

An alternative contribution statement would be:

	1983			1984		
	£				£	
Contribution*	(9,000 × £7)	63,000		(11,000 × £7)	77,000	
Less: Fixed overheads	68,200		Less: Fixed over-			
Less: carried forward	12,400	55,800	heads		68,200	
			brought forward	12,400		
			carried forward	(6,820)	73,780	
Profit		7,200			3,220	

*Selling price £10.00 less variable cost = £7.

12 SEESAW LTD

Option B is typical of the more capital intensive method of operation, in that lower variable cost (materials and labour) per unit can be achieved only at the cost of higher fixed overheads, which can only be recovered from a higher output. From the diagram, showing profitability related to sales, it can be seen that option A is better than B up to a level of 7,500 units.

There is no indication of potential sales at the price of £50, and, therefore, comparisons have been made, in the attached table, between the profit at 8,000 units (since 80% utilisation of maximum capacity is a reasonable level) as well as 10,000 units.

It should be noted that, although B will provide £55,000 compared with A's £48,000 at a sales level of 8,000 units, the margin of safety is only 22.9% compared with A's 37.5%. The margin of safety is the amount by which sales can fall without making a loss. For A this fraction is $(8,000 - 5,000)/8,000 = 37.5\%$ and for B it is $(8,000 - 6,167)/8,000 = 22.9\%$.

There is insufficient data to make a fair financial comparison; the financial cost of fixed expenses, payable in advance, is less than that of variable expenses, which are payable in arrears as they are consumed.

Supporting calculations

	A			B
	£			£
Selling price	50			50
Variable cost	34			20
Contribution per unit	(32%) 16		(60%)	30
Fixed expenses	£80,000			£185,000
Break-even point	$\dfrac{80,000}{16}$	5,000 units	$\dfrac{185,000}{30}$	6,167 units
Maximum profit for 10,000 units	160,000 − 80,000	£80,000	300,000 −185,000	£115,000
Profit on sales of 8,000 units	128,000 − 80,000	£48,000	240,000 −185,000	£55,000
Margin of safety*, on budgeted sales of 8,000 units	$\dfrac{3,000}{8,000}$	37.5%	$\dfrac{1,833}{8,000}$	22.9%

*The proportion by which budgeted sales can fall before break-even point is reached.

Comparison of both options at budgeted sales of 8,000 units and 10,000 units:

Profit statement:	A		B	
Units	8,000	10,000	8,000	10,000
	£	£	£	£
Sales @ £50 each	400,000	500,000	400,000	500,000
Less: Variable costs	272,000	340,000	160,000	200,000
Contribution	128,000	160,000	240,000	300,000
Less: Fixed expenses	80,000	80,000	185,000	185,000
Profit	48,000	80,000	55,000	115,000

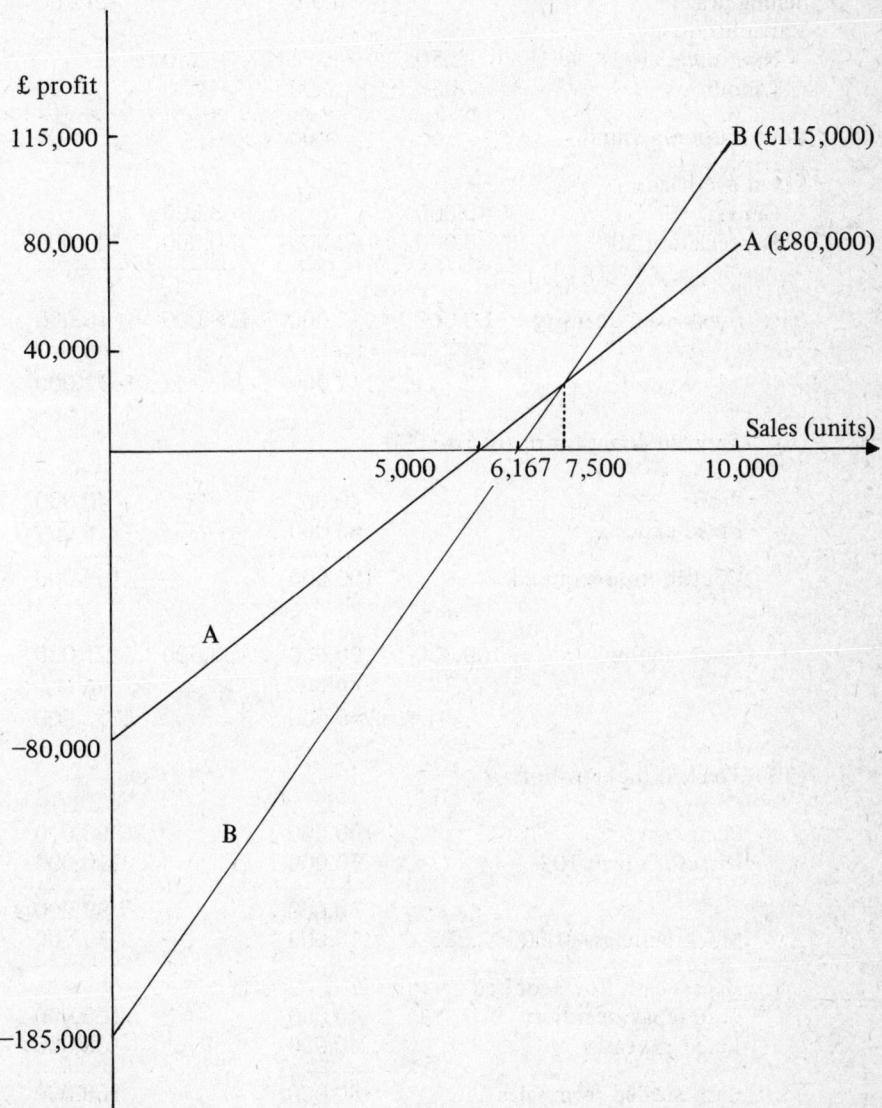

This diagram illustrates the relative profitability of the two options at various levels of activity. Note that at a sales figure of 7,500 units* they are equally profitable; at that level of sales the profit is £40,000, i.e., (7,500 × 16) − £80,000.

$$\text{*}\frac{\text{Difference in fixed costs}}{\text{Difference in contribution}} = \frac{185{,}000 - 80{,}000}{30 - 16} = 7{,}500 \text{ units}$$

13 CAVALINO LTD

(a)

		I		II	
		£	£	£	£
Selling price			12.00		12.00
Variable costs					
Raw materials		2.50		2.50	
Labour		4.50	7.00	1.50	4.00
Contribution per unit			5.00		8.00
Fixed overheads					
General		40,000		68,000	
Depreciation 20%		20,000	60,000	60,000	128,000

(i) Break-even quantity $\dfrac{60{,}000}{5}$ = 12,000 units i.e., £144,000 $\dfrac{128{,}000}{8}$ = 16,000 units i.e., £192,000

(ii) To yield target profits of £40,000

	£	£
Profit	40,000	40,000
Fixed expenses	60,000	128,000
Contribution required	100,000	168,000

Sales required $\dfrac{100{,}000}{5}$ = 20,000 units i.e., £240,000 $\dfrac{168{,}000}{8}$ = 21,000 units i.e., £252,000

(iii) To clear the overdraft

	£	£
Plant cost	100,000	300,000
Director's loan 70%	70,000	210,000
	30,000	90,000
Stock purchase, 4,000 × £2.5	10,000	10,000
Excess cash flow required to repay overdraft	40,000	100,000
Fixed expenses	40,000	68,000
Cash needed from sales	80,000	168,000

	I		II	
Cash flow contribution per unit				
Contribution per (a)	5.00		8.00	
Less: Debtors (2/12) × £12	2.00		2.00	
	3.00		6.00	
Sales required	80,000/3	26,667 units	168,000/6	28,000 units
Sales value required to clear overdraft		£320,000		£336,000

(b)

	I	II
Potential profit based on 30,000 units sold:		
Contribution	(30,000 × £5) 150,000	(30,000 × £8) 240,000
Less: Fixed expenses	60,000	128,000
	90,000	112,000

Although method II is more directly profitable with a P/V ratio of 67% (i.e., £8 contribution/£12 sales) compared with method I's P/V ratio of 42% (i.e., 5/12), the fixed expenses to be recovered, before the firm can earn a profit, are £128,000 contrasted to £60,000 for method I. The two methods may be compared, in the first place, by considering the budgeted sales to meet target, the break-even point, and the margin of safety.

	I (units)		II (units)	
Budgeted sales to meet target as in (a) (ii)		20,000		21,000
Break-even sales		12,000		16,000
Margin of safety	(40%)	8,000	(24%)	5,000
Sales to clear overdraft as in (a) (iii)		26,667		28,000
Margin of safety	(55%)	14,667	(43%)	12,000

As is usual with more capital intensive methods, higher turnover is required and there is a lower margin of safety (or margin of error in making estimates). Since annual sales of 30,000 are possible, there seems little doubt that the estimates and budgets will be attained.

Additional information that may be relevant would include data about when the overheads have to be paid. Interest on the overdraft has been ignored in the calculation; if substantial fixed overheads have to be paid in advance, as is often the case, much of the financial benefit of method II could be lost.

Variable costs are usually paid in arrears, slightly in the case of wages, rather more for materials.

Information is also required about the wages cost. If equally 'beneficial' uses cannot be found for the work force, the real cost of method II could be much higher.

Tutorial note

The P/V ratio (profit/volume) is the contribution expressed as a percentage of the sales. It is, therefore, a product's direct profitability.

14 ALUMINEX LTD

(a) Alternative I

Profit and loss account for 1983

		£000
Sales 150,000 × £5		750
Less: Variable costs:		
Day	300	
Night	225	
	525	
Depreciation	20	
Other fixed costs 120		
+ 2	122	667
Profit		83

Balance sheet at 31.12.83

	£000
Fixed assets	200
Less: Depreciation (80 + 20)	100
	100
Working capital, 200 × $\frac{150}{100}$	300
Bank, balancing item	28
	428
Share capital	200
Retained profits (145 + 83)	228
	428

(b) Alternative II

Profit and loss account for 1983

			£000
Sales			750
Less: Variable costs		450	
Depreciation (10%)	20		
	12	32	
Other fixed costs 120			
+40	160	642	
Profit			108

Balance sheet at 31.12.83

		£000
Fixed assets (200 + 120)		320
Less: Depreciation		
(80 + 20 = 100)		
(10% × 120 = 12)		112
		208
Working capital		300
Bank overdraft, balancing item		(55)
		453
Share capital		200
Retained profit	145	
	108	253
		453

(c) Immediate finance required:

		£
I	Working capital	100,000
	Less: Deposit account	25,000
		75,000
II	Working capital	100,000
	Fixed assets	120,000
		220,000
	Less: Deposit account	25,000
		195,000

In terms of immediate finance I is quite modest, particularly as the cash flow generated will more than clear the borrowing within a year; also the additional sales figure to break even is only 4,000 units, i.e.

$$\frac{2,000}{5.0 - (3.0 \times 1.5)}.$$

If only 130,000 units are sold the profit will be £73,000.

Alternative II requires immediate finance of £195,000, of which £55,000 will still be outstanding at 31.12.83. Additional sales needed to break even will be 26,000 units i.e.,

$$\frac{40,000 + 12,000}{5.00 - 3.00}$$

If sales are 130,000 units the profit will be £68,000, i.e., £5,000 less than in alternative I, at the same output.

130,000 units:		I		II	
	£000	£000		£000	£000
Sales 130,000 × £5		650			650
Variable cost:					
Day	300		130,000 × 3 = 390		
Night 3 × 1.5 × 30,000	135				
	435				
Depreciation	20		(20 + 12) =	32	
Fixed expenses (120 + 2)	122	577	(120 + 40) =	160	582
Profit		73			68
Break-even*: 100,000 + 4,000 =		104 units	100,000 + 26,000 =	126 units	

* Break-even is being used in the special sense of making the same profit as before, i.e., it relates to the additional sales.

From these figures it can be seen that I is less risky, although temporarily, at least, overtime and similar payments are inefficient (higher cost of wages for people who are tired).

15 ROWAN

(a) OPTION A: Stay in present employed position, and invest money

	£
Rowan's salary	4,000
Value of company car	1,000
Wife's salary	2,000
£50,000 invested @ 10% 'safe' present return	5,000
	12,000

OPTION B: Stay in present employed situation, but invest in local firm

	£
Rowan's salary, plus value of car, plus wife's salary	7,000
Present dividend: £20,000 on 80,000 shares = 25%	
Expected new dividend: £20,000 plus ¼ of £30,000 = £27,500, on 100,000 shares = 27½%	
Rowan's share £27,500 × $\frac{20,000}{100,000}$ =	5,000
	12,500

OPTION C: Purchase a shop, managed by Rowan and his wife

Budgeted trading and profit and loss account

	£	
Sales	200,000	(100%)
Cost of sales (10 × £15,000)	150,000	(75%)
Gross profit	50,000	(25%)
Less: Overheads	33,000	
Net profit	17,000	

	£
Net profit from shop	17,000
Less: Loss of interest from investments, £10,000 @ 10%	(1,000)
	16,000

OPTION D: Purchase shop, remain in present employment and employ a manager

		£
Rowan's salary		4,000
Value of car		1,000
Wife's salary		2,000
Income from shop	16,000	
Less: Manager's salary	(8,000)	
		8,000
		15,000

(b) The placement of Rowan's premium bond prize into 'safe' investments in option A may be contrasted with option B where certain risks are possible. There is, of course, the chance that the capital value of the shares may appreciate. However, if risk is to be avoided option A seems more favourable.

As to the shop, if Rowan and his wife manage the enterprise themselves they would seem to maximise their return, rather than employ a manager where problems could also develop (theft or loss of customers through lack of attention). But how skilled are they in shop management and are they suited to it — also what are their job prospects in their present employment?

Subject to the above, they may settle on option C.

16 OMEGA LTD

(a) Budgeted trading and profit and loss account for year ending 31.5.85

	£	£
Sales (W1)		120,000
Less: Opening stock	10,000	
Purchases (W5)	92,000	
Closing stock (W5)	(6,000)	
Cost of sales		96,000
Gross profit (W4)		24,000
Less: Overheads (W3):		
Establishment expenses	5,000	
Administration expenses	3,000	
Selling expenses	10,000	18,000
Net profit (W2)		6,000

Budgeted balance sheet as at 31.5.85

		£	£
Fixed assets at cost			70,000
Less: Depreciation to date (W6)			23,750
			46,250
Current assets			
Stock in trade (W5)		6,000	
Trade debtors (W7)		20,000	
		26,000	
Less: Current liabilities			
Trade creditors (W8)	9,200		
Overdraft, balancing figure	12,050	21,250	4,750
			51,000
Financed by:			
Ordinary share capital			30,000
Retained profits (W9)			21,000
			51,000

(b) **Total bank account**

Receipts	£	Payments	£
Opening balance in credit	7,850	Fixed assets bought	25,000
Debtors last year settled in full	8,000	Establishment expenses (i.e., £5,000, less depreciation for year £3,500)	1,500
Cash from sales this year (i.e., £120,000 less £20,000)	100,000	Administration expenses	3,000
		Selling expenses	10,000
		Creditors from last year paid in full	5,600
Closing overdraft	12,050	Cash purchases this year (i.e., £92,000 less £9,200)	82,800
	127,900		127,900

Workings

1. Sales: £80,000 × (150/100) = £120,000

2. Profit: 5% × £120,000 (sales) = £6,000

3   Overheads: Establishment, £7,000 − £2,000 = £5,000
    Administration, £2,000 × (150/100) = £3,000
    Selling, £5,000 × (200/100) = £10,000

4   Gross profit = Profit + Overheads = £6,000 + £18,000 = £24,000
    Cost of sales = Sales − Gross profit = £120,000 − £24,000 = £96,000
    Purchases = Cost of sales + closing stock − opening stock

5   Stock: Average stock = $\dfrac{\text{Cost of sales}}{\text{Stock turn}} = \dfrac{£96,000}{12} = £8,000$
    Since the opening stock = £10,000.
    Closing stock = (2 × £8,000) − £10,000 = £6,000.
    Purchases = Cost of sales − stock reduction = £96,000 − £4,000 = £92,000.

		£
6	Fixed assets: £45,000 + £5,000 + £20,000 =	70,000
	Depreciation: £20,250 + (5% × 70,000) =	23,750
		46,250

7   Debtors = $16\tfrac{2}{3}\%$ × £120,000 (sales) = £20,000

8   Creditors = Purchases × 1/10*

    *Calculations for previous year:

	£
Average stock = £60,000/5	12,000
Average stock × 2	24,000
Closing stock from balance sheet	10,000
Opening stock at 31.5.83	14,000

    Purchases = Cost of sales − stock reduction = £60,000 − £4,000 = £56,000

    Credit period = $\dfrac{\text{Creditors}}{\text{Purchases}} = \dfrac{5,600}{56,000} = \dfrac{1}{10}$ (of a year)

    Creditors at 31.5.85 = £92,000 × 1/10 = £9,200

9   Retained profits: £15,000 + £6,000 = £21,000

Tutorial notes

(a) Since the net profit % was given as 5%, the net profit must be calculated immediately after the sales, and the gross profit, cost of sales, and stock found by working up the trading account.

(b) The gross profit % for the year ending 31.5.85 is only 20% (£24,000/£120,000) compared with 25% (£20,000/£80,000) in the previous year. Presumably this fall in gross profit % is due to Omega Ltd's inability (or intention as part of a marketing strategy), to pass on increased costs of purchases to its customers.

(c) Some of the workings for items appearing in the profit and loss account and balance sheet are quite complex and thus require to be shown in separate workings. Others are quite simple, merely requiring the addition or multiplication of two figures, and can thus be shown conveniently in brackets on the face of the answer.

For example, the budgeted trading and profit and loss account could be:

	£	£
Sales (£80,000 × $\frac{150}{100}$)		120,000
Less: Opening stock	10,000	
Purchases (W)	92,000	
Closing stock	(6,000)	96,000
		24,000
Less: Overheads:		
Establishment expenses (£7,000 − £2,000)	5,000	
Administration expenses 2,000 × (150/100)	3,000	
Selling expenses 5,000 × (200/100)	10,000	18,000
Net profit (5% × £120,000)		6,000

5   Cash budgets

INTRODUCTION

There is no need to stress the importance of this chapter since every bank has amongst its stationery a form to take this information. Its purpose is to determine points in time when overdrafts are likely to peak.

Students must be aware that budgeting cash or bank balances at the end of a financial year (e.g., inserting cash or overdraft as the balancing item in a balance sheet), does not provide details of the variation that can take place during the year. Bank balances can often be much lower than normal, shortly before the peak selling times when larger stocks have to be bought and paid for. Similarly in January when many companies pay their corporation tax, cash balances may be abnormally low.

You must be able to assess the real level of borrowing required and to monitor progress by producing quarterly or even monthly statements, called variously cash flow statements, cash budgets or cash forecasts.

THE PROCEDURE

1   Head columns appropriately.

2   **Enter receipts**, mainly from debtors, i.e., normally the sales of some earlier period, after allowing for the time-lag between sale and receipt of money.

3   Enter other items of income — usually quite few in number.

4   Total the receipts.

5   **Enter the payments:**

    (a)   purchases, after allowing the appropriate time-lag;
    (b)   expenses — most of which will be paid in the month to which they relate;
    (c)   occasional payments: capital expenditure; taxation; dividends.

6   Total payments.

7   Deduct (6) from (4) to show excess.

8   Enter balance brought forward.

9   Add (7) to (8) and enter in column, i.e., month-end balance.

The receipts from debtors, and the payments to creditors are both related to the same sales figure. It is convenient, therefore, to enter the monthly sales either in a box in the appropriate monthly column, or immediately above the column. The debtors will be sales adjusted for time-lag; while the purchases will be the cost of sales (sales × the appropriate figure to remove gross profit) adjusted for stock changes and time period adjusted for credit allowed by suppliers (see pro forma opposite).

SUGGESTED METHOD FOR ANSWERING THE QUESTION

Questions in this chapter are best answered by using the now familiar 'layout technique'. In this instance rule up your monthly grid layout, leaving a good gap on the right-hand side for outstanding cash items, e.g., debtors, creditors, accruals, prepayments. Consider also the 'box' approach within the monthly columns which makes the timing of sales and purchases a separate and prior operation to the receiving and paying of cash, which in itself can be complicated. The boxes also facilitate balancing expected sales, with purchases necessary to continually top-up stocks.

Additions and subtractions should be worked with care, and then all items transposed into a set of budgeted final accounts where, as in Chapter 4, the layout should be prepared first.

'Monthly' cash flow forecast

	Jan	Feb	Mar	Apr	May	Jun	Jul	Aug	Sep	Oct	Nov	Dec	Outstanding items for balance sheet at 31 December 19....
Receipts													
Sales: Actual	☐	☐	☐	☐	☐	☐	☐	☐	☐	☐	☐	☐	→ £ Debtors
Cash													
Payments													
Purchases: Actual	☐	☐	☐	☐	☐	☐	☐	☐	☐	☐	☐	☐	→ £ Accruals (£ Prepayments)
Cash													→ £ Creditors
Opening stocks** Actual	☐												
Cash													
Stock increase* Actual						☐							
Cash													
Opening bank balance													
Net receipts													
Closing bank balance													

*If stock does not vary from month to month, 'purchases' will be the same as 'cost of sales' and the purchases 'actual' box will be directly proportionate to the sales 'actual' box. When stock does change it will then appear as a separate item; an increase or occasionally a decrease.

**Only use this entry if the cash flow is for a 'new' business. Otherwise the closing stock in the existing balance sheet automatically becomes the opening stock in the year under review.

QUESTIONS

1 PHILIP'S VEGETABLE STALL

Philip, aged 17, is in his first year at a sixth form college. He particularly wants to go on the college ski-ing holiday arranged for November 1984.

He has decided to start a Saturday mornng roadside vegetable stall outside his father's market garden, and is trying to decide whether he can do enough trade to raise the £400 needed for the holiday, over the next six months.

He estimates that his sales each Saturday will be:

1984	May	Jun	Jul	Aug	Sep	Oct
£	60	68	76	96	76	76

There are five Saturdays in May and August.

He can be quite certain as to one quarter of the above, as a family friend is matron of the Old Peoples' Home in their local village, and he makes an agreed weekly delivery to her. Unlike his roadside cash sales, he will allow the Home one month's credit before requiring payment.

Philip will take all his vegetables from his father on a weekly basis, and mark them up by $33\frac{1}{3}\%$.

In an attempt to encourage him in his venture, his father has agreed to waive payment for purchases for one month, except for October; he will also take back from him each Saturday anything he has not sold.

Required:

(a) A monthly cash forecast for the six months to 31 October 1984 showing the accumulated cash surplus or cash deficit, so as to indicate whether Philip will have sufficient funds after six months for his holiday.

(b) A budgeted trading and profit and loss account for the six months, and a budgeted balance sheet as at 31 October 1984, *thus proving the correctness of the cash flow forecast.*

20 marks

2 ISIS ROWING EQUIPMENT

Isis Rowing Equipment is to start trading on 1 January 1985 with capital of £12,000 in cash.

The following management policy is agreed beforehand:

(a) Fittings and equipment costing £7,000 and goods for resale costing £5,600 will be acquired during December 1984 but both items will be paid for during January 1985.

(b) Selling prices are arranged to give 25% gross profit on the selling price, that is, a 'mark-up' of 33⅓% on cost.

(c) All sales are to be on credit terms and customers are expected to pay their accounts one month following the month of sale. Estimated sales for the first quarter (January-March 1985) are expected to run at £4,000 each month and in the second quarter (April-June) to reach £6,000 each month.

(d) The purchasing and stocking policy is:

   (i) All goods sold during a month are to be replaced as soon as practicable and definitely within that month (*i.e., goods sold in January are replaced in January*).

   (ii) As with the initial purchase of goods for resale which is paid for in January ((a) above), suppliers will allow one month's credit (that is, payment is to be made for the 'goods for resale' bought during any month, in the next month).

(e) Wages and expenses of £920 per month will be paid in cash during each month.

(f) Rates of £200 for the half-year ending June will be paid in January 1985.

(g) Depreciation on fittings and equipment for the period January-June 1985 is estimated at £600.

Prepare:

(a) A monthly cash forecast for the six months ending 30 June 1985.

(b) A forecast trading and profit and loss statement for the six months and a balance sheet at 30 June 1985.

20 marks

3 MAIL ORDER LTD

John is planning the incorporation of a company, Mail Order Ltd, in December 1978.

The company will have a capital of 30,000 £1 ordinary shares which will be issued for cash in December 1978. In the same month Mail Order Ltd will purchase equipment for £8,000 and stocks of goods for £6,500. The equipment will be paid for immediately, but Mail Order Ltd will take one month's credit on all purchases of goods. The company will keep its stocks of goods replenished at £6,500 throughout the year to 31 December 1979.

It is estimated that in January and February 1979. Mail Order Ltd will make cash sales of £3,000 per month. The cash sales will increase to £4,500 in March and continue at that monthly level throughout the remainder of the year.

The company will also make instalment credit sales at the estimated level of £6,000 per month throughout the year. Payment for the sales will be receivable in 12 monthly instalments, the first instalment being received in the month in which the sale is made. The company will recognise profit on all sales made during the year, and for the purposes of this question bad debts can be ignored.

Mail Order Ltd will earn a constant gross profit margin of $33\frac{1}{3}\%$ on all sales, calculated on sales value.

From 1 January 1979 the company will incur wages and expenses of £2,100 per month, which will be paid in the month in which they are incurred.

Premises will be rented at a cost of £5,000 per year, payable quarterly in advance. The first payment will be made in December 1978.

Equipment is to be depreciated in the company's accounts at the rate of 10% per year on cost.

Required:

(a) Calculations revealing clearly the amount and month of the company's estimated maximum overdraft or minimum bank balance in 1979.

(b) The company's estimated profit and loss account for 1979 and the estimated balance sheet at 31 December 1979.

Note: Make all calculations on the basis of calendar months. Ignore taxation.

30 marks

4 P. BLAIR

Peter Blair has worked for some years as a sales representative, but has recently been made redundant. He intends to start up in business on his own account, using £15,000 which he currently has invested with a building society. He has a number of good business contacts, and is confident that his firm will do well, but thinks that additional finance will be required in the short term. Peter also maintains a bank account showing a small credit balance, and he plans to approach his bank for the necessary finance. Peter, whom you have known for some time, asks you for advice. He provides the following additional information:

(i) Arrangements have been made to purchase fixed assets costing £8,000. These will be paid for at the end of September and are expected to have a five-year life, at the end of which they will possess a nil residual value.

(ii) Stocks costing £5,000 will be acquired on 28 September, and subsequent monthly purchases will be at a level sufficient to replace forecast sales for the month.

(iii) Forecast monthly sales are £3,000 for October, £6,000 for November and December, and £10,500 from January 1984 onwards.

(iv) Selling price is fixed at the cost of stock plus 50%.

(v) Two months' credit will be allowed to customers but only one month's credit will be received from suppliers of stock.

(vi) Running expenses, including rent but excluding depreciation of fixed assets, are estimated at £1,600 per month.

(vii) Blair intends to make monthly cash drawings of £1,000.

Required:

(a) A cash forecast for the six months to 31 March 1984, showing the accumulated cash surplus or deficit at the end of each month. *9 marks*

(b) A forecast trading and profit and loss account for the six months to 31 March 1984, and a forecast balance sheet at 31 March 1984, showing the accumulated cash surplus or deficit as a separate item. *11 marks*

(c) A full assessment of Blair's forecasts and financial requirements from a lender's viewpoint. *10 marks*

Note: Ignore interest payable, if any.

Total 30 marks

5 CANTON LTD

Canton Ltd was recently incorporated and plans to commence trading on 1 June 1979. During May the company will issue 200,000 ordinary shares of £1 each at par and the cash will be subscribed at once. During the same month £130,000 will be spent on plant and £50,000 will be invested in stock, resulting in a cash balance on 1 June of £20,000.

Plans for the twelve months commencing 1 June 1979 are as follows:

(i) Stock costing £40,000 will be sold each month at a mark-up of 25%. Customers are expected to pay in the second month following the sale.

(ii) Month-end stock levels will be maintained at £50,000 and purchases will be paid for in the month following delivery.

(iii) Wages and other expenses will amount to £6,000 per month, payable in the month during which the costs are incurred.

(iv) Bad debts are expected to be incurred at the rate of 2% of sales.

(v) Plant will have a 10-year life and no scrap value. Depreciation is to be charged on the straight-line basis.

(vi) No provision is to be made for corporation tax in view of the capital allowances which are to be claimed in respect of the new plant.

Required:

(a) A cash budget for Canton Ltd which will be sufficient to reveal the maximum overdraft requirement on the basis of the information available. Do not continue the cash budget for more months than necessary.

(b) The company's estimated trading and profit and loss account for the year ending 31 May 1980 and estimated balance sheet at 31 May 1980.

(c) A calculation of the *additional* sales which would be needed in order to produce *additional* profits sufficient to cover a dividend of 6% on the issued share capital. For this purpose you may regard depreciation and 75% of wages and other expenses as fixed costs and the remainder as directly variable with output.

Note: The company's bank has agreed to provide the necessary overdraft facilities.

30 marks

6 N. BERMAN

Norman Berman is a trader whose draft balance sheet as at 30 June 1982 is as follows:

Balance sheet at 30 June 1982

Capital	£000		£000	£000
Balance at 1 July 1981	120	Fixed assets at cost		89
Add: Net profit	24	Less: Depreciation		31
Less: Drawings	(18)			—
	—			58
Balance at 30 June 1982	126	Current assets		
		Stock in trade	64	
Current liabilities		Trade debtors	35	
Trade creditors	32	Bank	1	100
	—		—	—
	158			158
	==			==

There is a buoyant demand for Berman's products, and sales have increased steadily over the years. The following forecasts and estimates are made for the year ending 30 June 1983.

(i) Forecast monthly sales are as follows:

   1982:   July-December £40,000 per month
   1983:   January-June £45,000 per month
           July-December £50,000 per month.

(ii) The gross profit margin will be 20% on sales.

(iii) It is Berman's policy to maintain stocks, at the end of each month, sufficient to cover the expected sales for the following *two* months.

(iv) The period of credit allowed to customers and obtained from suppliers is expected to remain the same as for the year ended 30 June 1982, i.e., one month.

(v) Berman has sufficient accommodation for the planned increase in sales, but vehicles and equipment costing £20,000 will need to be purchased and paid for in December 1982.

(vi) Wages and general expenses (including an allowance for bank interest) are paid for in the month that they are incurred and will amount to £5,000 per month.

(vii) The depreciation charge for the year is to be £12,000.

(viii) Berman will withdraw £2,000 each month for personal use.

(ix) Berman's bank has agreed to provide any overdraft facilities required during the year ended 30 June 1983 and will charge interest at a rate of 18% p.a.

Required:

(a) A forecast cash statement, showing the bank balance or overdraft at the end of each month, for the year ending 30 June 1983. *10 marks*

(b) Berman's forecast profit and loss account for the year ending 30 June 1983. *6 marks*

(c) Berman's forecast balance sheet at 30 June 1983. *8 marks*

(d) A discussion of the respective merits of bank overdraft finance as compared with loan finance, in the light of Berman's requirements, assuming that he could alternatively finance the purchase of vehicles and equipment by raising a five-year loan at a fixed interest rate of 15% p.a. *6 marks*

Notes:

Ignore taxation.

Assume for the purpose of the question that your calculations are being made on 1 July 1982 and that the year to 30 June 1983 consists of twelve months of equal length.

Total 30 marks

7 REGENT

Regent, a trader, has been in business for a number of years. The summarised trading and profit and loss account for 1981 was as follows:

Summarised trading and profit and loss account, 1981

	£	£
Sales (all on credit)		240,000
Less: Variable costs: purchases	180,000	
Fixed costs: general expenses*, etc.	42,000	222,000
Net profit		18,000

*General expenses include depreciation of £12,000 on fixed assets.

Regent believes that profits can be improved by increasing the sales of his product for which there exists a strong demand. The following plans and estimates are made:

(i) In January 1982 Regent will issue a circular informing customers that the period of credit allowed will be increased from one to two months on all sales from 1 February.

(ii) The more favourable credit terms will produce an increase in monthly sales, over 1981 levels, of 10% for February to June 1982, and 20% thereafter.

(iii) The period of credit received from suppliers will remain unchanged at one month.

(iv) It is Regent's policy to maintain stocks at a level equivalent to expected sales over the forthcoming two months. Stocks at 31 December 1981 were £30,000.

(v) General expenses accrue evenly during the year and, depreciation apart, are paid for on a monthly basis.

At 31 December 1981 Regent's bank balance stands at £3,000. Regent's bank has agreed to provide overdraft facilities up to a limit of £13,000 for the forthcoming twelve months.

Required:

(a) A cash budget showing the forecast bank balance or overdraft at the end of each month during 1982. *16 marks*

(b) Comments, in the light of your calculations under (a), on the bank's requirement that the overdraft should not exceed £13,000. *4 marks*

Notes:

(i) Assume that 1982 consists of twelve months of equal length.
(ii) Trading transactions occurred at an even rate during 1981.

Total 20 marks

8 WRENBURY

Wrenbury, who has maintained an account with your bank for a number of years, plans to undertake a business venture for which finance is required.

At present, your client is a sales representative and he receives an annual salary of £8,000. He has recently been approached by an official of a company based overseas who offers to supply Wrenbury with a range of goods similar to those he sells on behalf of his present employer. The official claims that the goods he offers are of a higher quality than those currently being marketed in the United Kingdom and, after examining samples, Wrenbury fully agrees with this assessment.

During the course of discussions Wrenbury makes the following comments:

> I will need to maintain stocks of goods costing approximately £4,000. These will have to be delivered during December 1980 if I am to start business in the new year.
>
> I have spoken to a number of contacts who have promised me orders amounting to £9,000 and £12,000 respectively for the quarterly periods January-March 1981 and April-June 1981. From July 1981 onwards I expect sales to be steady at a rate of £60,000 p.a.
>
> The goods which I will be selling produce, on average, a gross profit of 20% on selling price.
>
> I intend to conduct most of my business from home, but I will need additional premises in which to keep the stocks of goods. I have found a small warehouse which I have been told I can use for the period 1 December 1980-31 May 1982 for £540, payable in January 1981. There should be no problem in finding alternative premises if the owner is unwilling to renew these arrangements in 1982. My telephone bill which is at present £50 per quarter, and which amount I will continue to pay privately, will probably rise to £200 per quarter as the result of running the business from my home. I estimate other incidental business expenses at £200 per quarter payable in cash.
>
> I will arrange for monthly supplies of goods sufficient to replace items sold. The overseas company is willing to allow two months' credit for all supplies, including the initial stocks to be delivered in December, and I will have to offer similar terms to my customers.
>
> I will need a van to transport the goods. I can get one delivered in December 1980 for £7,000 provided I pay cash at once. I expect it will last five years and be worth about £2,500 at the end of that time.

You discover that Wrenbury owns some investments which he purchased recently for £3,200; their present market value is only £2,600. Wrenbury will require the bank to meet all his other cash needs if the project is to be undertaken.

Required:

(a) A cash budget for each of the four quarters of 1981, showing the cash surplus or deficit at the end of each quarter.

(b) An estimated profit statement for 1981.

(c) A reconciliation of the forecast change in the cash position over the next 12 months with the estimated profit figure.

(d) Your reasoned assessment of Wrenbury's proposals.

Notes:

1. Ignore taxation.
2. Sales and purchases will occur at an even rate during each quarter of 1981.
3. Ignore interest on any forecast cash deficit.

30 marks

9 SUBSIDIARY ENGINEERING LTD

A holding company has established a new subsidiary company, called Subsidiary Engineering Ltd, on 1 November specifically for the manufacture and selling of a new product. The holding company will inject for working capital purposes, £30,000 cash on 1 December. Plant and machinery is being transferred from another company in the group, value £144,000.

The variable production cost per unit is expected to be:

	£
Direct materials	4.0
Direct wages	4.0
Variable production overhead	1.0
Variable production cost	9.0

Fixed overheads estimated at £48,000 p.a. are expected to be incurred in equal amounts each month from 1 December.

Production will commence in December and sales on 1 January. The estimated sales for the first four months are:

	Units	Sales value £
January	6,200	66,650
February	6,800	73,100
March	5,400	58,050
April	6,000	64,500

The following information is to be taken into consideration:

(i) Stocks, finished goods: 75% of each month's invoiced sales units to be produced in the month of sale and 25% of each month's invoiced sales units to be produced in the previous month.

(ii) Stocks, direct materials: 50% of direct materials required for each month's production to be purchased in the previous month. Direct materials to be paid for in the month following purchase.

(iii) Direct wages to be paid 75% in the month used and 25% in the following month.

(iv) Variable production overhead: 40% to be paid in the month of usage and the balance in the following month.

(v) Fixed overhead: 20% to be paid in the month in which it is incurred and 50% in the following month. The balance represents depreciation of fixed assets.

(vi) Payments to be received from customers as follows:

	£
January	13,258
February	42,409
March	61,722

Required:

(a) A cash flow forecast for the months of November to March.

(b) A set of budgeted final accounts (manufacturing, trading, profit and loss, and balance sheet) to the end of January, to show the position after the first month. *Note*: stock is to be valued at variable cost.

30 marks

ANSWERS

1 PHILIP'S VEGETABLE STALL

(a)   **Cash flow forecast**

1984			May	Jun	Jul	Aug	Sep	Oct	
Receipts									
Sales:	Actual	£	300	272	304	480	304	304	
	Cash: ¾ now		225	204	228	360	228	228	
	¼ in one month			75	68	76	120	76	£76 debtors
			225	279	296	436	348	304	
Payments									
Purchases:	Actual		225	204	228	360	228	228	
	Cash			225	204	228	360	228	
								228	
			Nil	225	204	228	360	456	
Opening balance			Nil	225	279	371	579	567	
Net receipts			225	54	92	208	(12)	(152)	
Closing balance			225	279	371	579	567	415	

(b) **Budgeted trading and profit and loss account for half year to 31.10.84**

	£
Sales	1,964
Less: Purchases	1,473
Gross profit/Net profit	491

Budgeted balance sheet as at 31.10.84

	£
Current assets	
Debtors	76
Cash/Bank	415
	491
Financed by:	
Capital at the beginning	Nil
Net profit	491
Less: Drawings	(Nil)
Net worth	491

Notes on part (a)

(i) Insert monthly sales into the appropriate boxes.

(ii) Apportion these figures:

¾ into present month;

¼ into the following month (in respect of October's sales, this amount will appear on the balance sheet as debtors).

(iii) Use a similar procedure for the purchases, but in this case the whole amount is payable in the following month, except for October's purchases.

Note: Since Philip marks up the cost price of his purchases by $33\tfrac{1}{3}\%$ (i.e. $\tfrac{1}{3}$) to arrive at the selling price, the cost is 75% (i.e. ¾) of the selling price and the gross profit % is 25% (i.e. ¼).

(iv) Complete the cash plan by doing the additions.

Notes on part (b)

(i) Philip's profit for the period is simply sales less purchases, since there are no stocks and no overheads.

(ii) The projected balance sheet at 31.10.84 contains two assets:

	£
Cash	415 (per cash budget)
Debtors	76
	491

and since there are no creditors or other liabilities the capital will be:

£
491

Philip started with no capital and thus the £491 increase in capital is explained completely by the projected profit.

2 ISIS ROWING EQUIPMENT

(a) Cash flow forecast 1985

	Dec	Jan	Feb	Mar	Apr	May	Jun	
Receipts								
Sales: 100% Actual	✕	4,000	4,000	4,000	6,000	6,000	6,000	
Cash			4,000	4,000	4,000	6,000	6,000	£6,000 debtors
Capital		12,000						
	Nil	12,000	4,000	4,000	4,000	6,000	6,000	
Payments								
Fittings and equipment		7,000						
Opening stock Actual	5,600							
Cash		5,600						
Purchases: 75% Actual	✕	3,000	3,000	3,000	4,500	4,500	4,500	
Cash			3,000	3,000	3,000	4,500	4,500	£4,500 creditors
Wages and expenses		920	920	920	920	920	920	
Rates, half-year		200						
	Nil	13,720	3,920	3,920	3,920	5,420	5,420	
Opening balance		Nil	(1,720)	(1,640)	(1,560)	(1,480)	(900)	
Net receipts		(1,720)	80	80	80	580	580	
Closing balance		(1,720)	(1,640)	(1,560)	(1,480)	(900)	(320)	

(b) **Budgeted trading and profit and loss account for period to 30.6.85**

	£	£
Sales		30,000
Less: Opening stock	5,600	
Purchases	22,500	
Closing stock	(5,600)	
		22,500
Gross profit		7,500
Less: Depreciation	600	
Other overheads:		
Wages and expenses	5,520	
Rates	200	
		6,320
Net profit		1,180

Budgeted balance sheet as at 30.6.85

		£	£
Fixed assets at cost			7,000
Less: Depreciation			600
			6,400
Current assets			
Stock		5,600	
Debtors		6,000	
		11,600	
Less: Current liabilities			
Creditors	4,500		
Overdraft	320		
		4,820	
			6,780
			13,180
Financed by:			
Capital			12,000
Net profit			1,180
Net worth			13,180

Tutorial notes

1. In the cash flow note that:

   (i) opening stocks are only bought *once*;
   (ii) with gross profit 25%, cost of sales is 75%.

   Then, as opening and closing stocks are identical, purchases must be equal in amount to cost of sales, so that the monthly purchases needed to replace sales will be ¾ of the sales figure.

   Thus the stock level of £5,600 is automatically maintained.

2. Depreciation appears in the profit and loss account but not in the cash flow forecast, since it is a *non-cash expense*.

3. Since monthly purchases replace goods sold, the original stock value of £5,600 will still be there at the end of the period.

3 MAIL ORDER LTD

(a)

Cash flow forecast

	1978 Dec	Jan	Feb	Mar	Apr	May	Jun	Jul	Aug	Sep	Oct	Nov	1979 Dec	
Receipts														
Capital, ordinary shares	30,000													
Sales: Actual	☒	9,000	9,000	10,500	10,500	10,500	10,500	10,500	10,500	10,500	10,500	10,500	10,500	£33,000 debtors
Cash		3,000	3,000	4,500	4,500	4,500	4,500	4,500	4,500	4,500	4,500	4,500	4,500	
Credit		500	1,000	1,500	2,000	2,500	3,000	3,500	4,000	4,500	5,000	5,500	6,000	
	30,000	3,500	4,000	6,000	6,500	7,000	7,500	8,000	8,500	9,000	9,500	10,000	10,500	
Payments														
Opening stock: Actual	6,500													
Cash	8,000	6,500												
Equipment	☒													
Purchases: Actual		6,000	6,000	7,000	7,000	7,000	7,000	7,000	7,000	7,000	7,000	7,000	7,000	£7,000 creditors
Cash			6,000	6,000	7,000	7,000	7,000	7,000	7,000	7,000	7,000	7,000	7,000	
Wages and expenses	1,250	2,100	2,100	2,100	2,100	2,100	2,100	2,100	2,100	2,100	2,100	2,100	2,100	(£834) prepaid
Rent				1,250			1,250			1,250			1,250	
	9,250	8,600	8,100	9,350	9,100	9,100	10,350	9,100	9,100	10,350	9,100	9,100	10,350	

	Dec	Jan	Feb	Mar	Apr	May	Jun	Jul	Aug	Sept	Oct	Nov	Dec
Net receipts	20,750	(5,100)	(4,100)	(3,350)	(2,600)	(2,100)	(2,850)	(1,100)	(600)	(1,350)	400	900	150
Closing bank balance	20,750	15,650	11,550	8,200	5,600	3,500	650	(450)	(1,050)	(2,400) Max o/d	(2,000)	(1,100)	(950)
Credit sales calculation £6,000 monthly over 1 year													
J		500	500	500	500	500	500	500	500	500	500	500	500
F			500	500	500	500	500	500	500	500	500	500	500
M				500	500	500	500	500	500	500	500	500	500
A					500	500	500	500	500	500	500	500	500
M						500	500	500	500	500	500	500	500
J							500	500	500	500	500	500	500
J								500	500	500	500	500	500
A									500	500	500	500	500
S										500	500	500	500
O											500	500	500
N												500	500
D													500

Debtors
1 × £500
2   £500
3   £500
4   £500
5   £500
6   £500
7   £500
8   £500
9   £500
10 £500
11 £500
———
66 at £500 = £33,000

(b) **Trading and profit and loss account for period ended 31.12.79**

	£	£
Sales		123,000
Less: Opening stock	6,500	
Purchases	82,000	
Closing stock	(6,500)	
Cost of sales		82,000
Gross profit		41,000
Less: Wages and expenses	25,200	
Rent (13 months)	5,416	
Depreciation of equipment	800	
		31,416
Net profit		9,584

Balance sheet as at 31.12.79

		£	£
Fixed assets			
Equipment			8,000
Less: Depreciation			800
			7,200
Current assets			
Stocks		6,500	
Debtors		33,000	
Rent prepaid (2 months)		834	
		40,334	
Less: Current liabilities			
Creditors	7,000		
Overdraft	950		
		7,950	
			32,384
			39,584
Capital introduced			30,000
Retained profit			9,584
			39,584

4 P. BLAIR

(a)

Cash flow forecast 1984

	Sep	Oct	Nov	Dec	Jan	Feb	Mar	
Receipts								
Sales: Actual	✗	3,000	6,000	6,000	10,500	10,500	10,500	£10,500 + £10,500 debtors
Cash				3,000	6,000	6,000	10,500	
Capital	15,000							
	15,000	Nil	Nil	3,000	6,000	6,000	10,500	
Payments								
Fixed assets	8,000							
Opening stock: Actual	5,000							
Cash		5,000						
Purchases: Actual	✗	2,000	4,000	4,000	7,000	7,000	7,000	£7,000 creditors
Cash			2,000	4,000	4,000	7,000	7,000	
Expenses		1,600	1,600	1,600	1,600	1,600	1,600	
Drawings		1,000	1,000	1,000	1,000	1,000	1,000	
	8,000	7,600	4,600	6,600	6,600	9,600	9,600	
Opening balance	Nil	7,000	(600)	(5,200)	(8,800)	(9,400)	(13,000)	
Net receipts	7,000	(7,600)	(4,600)	(3,600)	(600)	(3,600)	900	
Closing balance	7,000	(600)	(5,200)	(8,800)	(9,400)	(13,000)	(12,100)	

(b) **Budgeted trading and profit and loss account for half-year to 31.3.84**

	£	£
Sales		46,500
Less: Opening stock	5,000	
Purchases	31,000	
Closing stock	(5,000)	
		31,000
Gross profit		15,500
Less: Depreciation for half-year	800	
Other overheads	9,600	
		10,400
Net profit		5,100

Budgeted balance sheet as at 31.3.84

	£	£
Fixed assets at cost		8,000
Less: Depreciation		800
		7,200
Current assets		
Stock	5,000	
Debtors	21,000	
	26,000	
Less: Current liabilities		
Creditors	7,000	
Overdrafts	12,100	
	19,100	
		6,900
Net current assets		14,100
Financed by:		
Capital		15,000
Net profit		5,100
Less: Drawings		(6,000)
Net worth		14,100

(c) The maximum overdraft appears in the month of February at £13,000; are bankers happy with this sum? As regards gearing, it is probably acceptable to bankers since £15,000 of Mr Blair's money corresponds with £13,000 of the banks.

Each month should now show a reduction of £900 in the overdraft; thus by the end of September next year the facility should be £12,100 less (6 × £900) = £6,700 overdrawn, if all goes to plan and the cash flow is considered accurate.

Budgeted trading and profit and loss account to 30.9.84

	£
Sales* (100%)	109,500
Less: Cost of sales (66⅔%)	73,000
Gross profit	36,500
Less: Running expenses	19,200
Depreciation	1,600
Net profit	15,700

*(extra 6 months (from 31 March to 30 September) × £10,500) + £46,500

The cash flow from trading for the year, taken into the balance sheet would be £17,300 (i.e., net profit £15,700 plus the book entry of depreciation £1,600 added back). This should easily cater for drawings of £12,000, bank interest (which has not been taken into consideration) and also correct the working capital position shown at the half-way stage of about 1.4 to 1, which is a little weak.

5 CANTON LTD

(a)

Cash flow forecast

	1979 May	Jun	July	Aug	Sep	Oct	Nov	Dec	1980 May	Cash outstanding
Receipts										
Sales 100% Actual	☒	50,000	50,000	50,000	50,000	50,000				£100,000 debtors
Cash					(1,000)	(1,000)				(£2,000) bad debts
Less: Bad debts				(1,000)						
Ordinary £1 shares	200,000									
	200,000	Nil	Nil	49,000						
Payments										
Plant and equipment	130,000									
Purchases 80% Actual	☒	40,000	40,000	40,000	40,000					£40,000 creditors
Cash			40,000	40,000	40,000					
Opening stock: Actual	50,000									
Cash	50,000	6,000	6,000	6,000						
Wages and expenses		6,000	6,000	6,000						
	180,000	46,000	46,000	46,000						
Opening balance	Nil	20,000	14,000	(32,000)						September to May inclusive @ £3,000 positive per month =
Net receipts	20,000	(6,000)	(46,000)	3,000						
Closing balance	20,000	14,000	(32,000) (Max)	(29,000)						(2,000)

136

(b) **Budgeted trading and profit and loss account for 31.5.80**

	£000	£000
Sales		600
Less: Opening stock	50	
Purchases	480	
Closing stock	(50)	
		480
Gross profit		120
Less: Depreciation	13	
Other overheads		
Bad debts	12	
Wages, etc.	72	
		97
Net profit		23

Budgeted balance sheet as at 31.5.80

		£000	£000
Fixed assets at cost			130
Less: Depreciation			13
			117
Current assets			
Stock		50	
Debtors		98	
		148	
Less: Current liabilities			
Creditors	40		
Overdraft	2		
		42	
			106
			223
Financed by:			
Capital			200
Net profit retained			23
Shareholders' funds			223

(c) For a 6% dividend, extra profit needed = £12,000.

	At present		**For 6% Div.**
Sales	600,000 (100%)		80,000 (100%)
Less: Variable overheads			
Cost of sales	(480,000)		↑
Bad debts	(12,000)		
¼ Wages and expenses	(18,000)		
Contribution	90,000 (15%)	Contribution	12,000 = (15%)
Less: Fixed overheads			↑
¾ Wages and expenses	(54,000)		Nil
Depreciation	(13,000)		Nil
Net profit	23,000	Extra	12,000

Thus, by working backwards from the extra £12,000 profit needed, £80,000 more sales will be needed.

Tutorial notes

The Cash Flow Forecast:

(i) Shows maximum overdraft in July of £32,000, reducing then by £3,000 each month, i.e., £2,000 overdrawn by May 1980.

(ii) Bad debts are shown as deductions from cash sales, in the same way as discounts allowed.

6 N. BERMAN

(a)   Cash flow forecast (£000)

	1982 Jul	Aug	Sep	Oct	Nov	Dec	1983 Jan	Feb	Mar	Apr	May	Jun		
Receipts														
Sales: 100% Actual	[40]	[40]	[40]	[40]	[40]	[40]	[45]	[45]	[45]	[45]	[45]	[45]	[50]	[50] debtors
Cash		40	40	40	40	40	40	45	45	45	45	45	45	
Debtors from last year	35													
	35	40	40	40	40	40	40	45	45	45	45	45		
Payments														
Vehicle and equipment						20								
Wages and expenses	5	5	5	5	5	5	5	5	5	5	5	5		
Drawings	2	2	2	2	2	2	2	2	2	2	2	2		
Purchases: 80% Actual	[32]	[32]	[32]	[32]	[32]	[32]	[36]	[36]	[36]	[36]	[36]	[36]	[40]	[40] creditors
Cash	(64)	32	32	32	32	32	32	36	36	36	36	36	36	
(2-month stockholding)	(64)	(64)	(64)	(64)	(68)	(72)	(72)	(72)	(72)	(72)	(76)	(80)		
Necessary Stockpiling					[4]	[4]					[4]	[4]		
Necessary stock, Cash						4	4					4	4	creditors
Creditors from last year	32													
	39	39	39	39	39	63	43	43	43	43	43	47		
Opening balance	1	(3)	(2)	(1)	Nil	1	(22)	(25)	(23)	(21)	(19)	(17)		
Net receipts	(4)	1	1	1	1	(23)	(3)	2	2	2	2	(2)		
Closing balance	(3)	(2)	(1)	Nil	1	(22)	(25)	(23)	(21)	(19)	(17)	(19)		

(b) **Forecast trading and profit and loss account for year to 30.6.83**

	£000	£000
Sales		510
Less: Opening stock	64	
Purchases	424	
Closing stock	(80)	
		408
Gross profit		102
Less: Depreciation	12	
Other overheads:		
Wages and expenses	60	
		72
Net profit		30

(c) **Forecast balance sheet as at 30.6.83**

		£000	£000
Fixed assets at cost			109
Less: Depreciation			43
			66
Current assets			
Stock		80	
Debtors		45	
		125	
Less: Current liabilities			
Creditors	40		
Overdrafts	19		
		59	
			66
			132
Financed by:			
Capital			126
Net profit			30
Less: Drawings			(24)
Net worth			132

(d) To purchase the vehicle and equipment, £20,000 via overdraft facilities assumes that Berman can generate sufficient funds to maintain adequate and safe working capital. The budgeted balance sheet appears to have a strong working capital base, at 125 to 59 (2 to 1). Also, the cash flow from trading operations is £42,000 (net profit £30,000 + depreciation £12,000) and with Berman withdrawing £24,000, some £18,000 is re-invested (subject to tax). Only if expansion is rapid, may loan finance be necessary, so as to protect the working capital structure. The overdraft should prove the most inexpensive method, and preferable, but only if expansion slows down.

7 REGENT

(a)

Cash flow forecast (£000)   1982

	Jan	Feb	Mar	Apr	May	Jun	Jul	Aug	Sep	Oct	Nov	Dec	
Receipts													
Sales: Actual	[20]	[22]	[22]	[22]	[22]	[22]	[24]	[24]	[24]	[24]	[24]	[24]	
Cash		20		22	22	22	22	22	24	24	24	24	24 + 24 debtors
Debtors, last year	20	20	Nil	22	22	22	22	22	24	24	24	24	
Payments													
General expenses (W5)	2.5	2.5	2.5	2.5	2.5	2.5	2.5	2.5	2.5	2.5	2.5	2.5	
Creditors, last year (W4)	15												
Purchases: Actual (W1)	[15]	[16.5]	[16.5]	[16.5]	[16.5]	[16.5]	[18]	[18]	[18]	[18]	[18]	[18]	18 creditors
Cash		15	16.5	16.5	16.5	16.5	16.5	18	18	18	18	18	
(2-months stock level)	(30)	(33)	(33)	(33)	(34.5)	(36)	(36)	(36)	(36)	(36)	(36)	(36)	
Stock pile: Actual (W2)	[1.5]				[1.5]	[1.5]							
Cash	1.5	3				1.5	1.5						
	17.5	20.5	19	19	19	20.5	20.5	20.5	20.5	20.5	20.5	20.5	
Opening balance	3	5.5	5	(14)	(11)	(8)	(6.5)	(5)	(3.5)	Nil	3.5	7	
Net receipts	2.5	(0.5)	(19)	3	3	1.5	1.5	1.5	3.5	3.5	3.5	3.5	
Closing balance	5.5	5	(14)	(11)	(8)	(6.5)	(5)	(3.5)	Nil	3.5	7	10.5	

(b) The cash flow shows £14,000 as the maximum overdraft and this exceeds the limit by £1,000.

While it is doubtful whether a banker would insist on this (since there will be credit balances in a few months time), the only way to achieve it if need be, would be by stock reductions of £1,000 for one month only.

Again, a very strong cash flow position exists of £38,500 over the year from trading operations (net profit £26,500 + depreciation for year £12,000).

Workings

1. Purchases = 75% × sales, i.e., 180,000/240,000 (from trading account).

2. Stock, to support sales from February onwards:

	£
2 × £16,500 =	33,000
Less: Stock in January	30,000
Stock increase	3,000

Similarly, stock to support sales from August onwards:

	£
2 × £18,000 =	36,000
Less: Stock in July	33,000
Stock increase	3,000

3. Receipts in January from debtors at 31.12.81:

   1/12 × £240,000 = £20,000

4. Receipts in January to creditors at 31.12.81:

   1/12 × £180,000 = £15,000

5. Monthly general expenses:

	£
Annual expenses	42,000
Less: Depreciation	12,000
	30,000

   Monthly payment = 1/2 × £30,000 = £2,500

8 WRENBURY

(a)

Quarterly cash forecast for 1981

	1	2	3	4	Balance sheet:
Receipts					
Sales	9,000	12,000	15,000	15,000	10,000
	(6,000)	6,000	8,000	10,000	
		(8,000)	(10,000)	(10,000)	
	3,000	10,000	13,000	15,000	
	3,000	10,000	13,000	15,000	
Payments					
Stock	4,000				
Purchases (W1)	7,200	9,600	12,000	12,000	8,000
	(4,800)	4,800	6,400	8,000	
	2,400	(6,400)	(8,000)	(8,000)	
Rent	540				
Telephone	150	150	150	150	
Other expenses	200	200	200	200	
	7,290	8,350	10,750	12,350	
Excess of receipts over payments	(4,290)	1,650	2,250	2,650	
Balance b/f (W2)	(4,400)	(8,690)	(7,040)	(4,790)	
Balance c/f	(8,690)	(7,040)	(4,790)	(2,140)	2,140

(b) **Estimated profit statement for 1981**

	£	£
Sales		51,000
Less: Cost of sales (80% × £51,000)		40,800
Gross profit (20%)		10,200
Less: Overheads		
Rent: £540 − (5/18 × £540)	390	
Telephone	600	
Expenses	800	
Depreciation: (£7,000 − £2,500)/5	900	2,690
Profit for year		7,510

(c)

	£	£
Bank overdraft at 1.1.80 (cost of van)	7,000	
Less: Investments sold	2,600	4,400
Bank overdraft at 31.12.80 per budget (a)		2,140
Improvement in cash position		2,260

This improvement has been financed by:

	£	£
Profit	7,510	
Add: Depreciation, a non-cash expense	900	
	8,410	
Expenses not yet paid – purchases	8,000	
	16,410	16,410
Less: Income not yet received – debtors	10,000	
Profit tied up in stock	4,000	
Expenses paid in advance – 5 months' rent	150	14,150
Profit converted into cash flow		2,260

(d) The cash flow forecast shows neither Wrenbury's drawings nor bank interest charges, both of which will worsen the position. Enquiries must be made as to his likely drawings especially as his previous salary of £8,000 may be unachievable in his first year of self-employment. Next year, however, with sales of £60,000 and a prevailing gross profit margin of 20%, i.e., £12,000, and running expenses held at the year one level of £2,690, net profit could be £9,310 and give him a better living.

Workings

1. Purchases = 80% × sales, i.e., 100% − 20% gross profit.

2. Overdraft at 1.1.80:

	£
Payment for van in December	7,000
Less: Sale of investments	2,600
	4,400

9 SUBSIDIARY ENGINEERING LTD

(a)

Cash flow forecast

		Nov	Dec	Jan	Feb	Mar	Apr
Receipts							
Sales:	Units			6,200	6,800	5,400	6,000
	£ Actual			66,650	73,100	58,050	64,500
Working capital injected	Cash		30,000	13,258	42,409	61,772	
			30,000	13,258	42,409	61,772	
Payments							
Units produced	25%		1,550	1,700	1,350	1,500	?
	75%		–	4,650	5,100	4,050	4,500
Direct materials, £4 per unit:	£ Actual 50%	3,100	12,700	12,900	11,100	?	
	50%		3,100	12,700	12,900	11,100	
Direct wages, £4 per unit	Cash		3,100	15,800	25,600	24,000	
	75%		4,650	19,050	19,350	16,650	5,550
	25%			1,550	6,350	6,450	
Variable overheads, £1 per unit	40%		620	2,540	2,580	2,220	
	60%			930	3,810	3,870	3,330
Fixed overheads	20%		800	800	800	800	
£4,000 monthly	50%			2,000	2,000	2,000	2,000
			9,170	42,670	60,490	55,990	
Net receipts		–	20,830	(29,412)	(18,081)	5,782	
Closing bank balance		–	20,830	(8,582)	(26,663)	(20,881)	

(b) **Budgeted manufacturing, trading and profit and loss account for the month ending 31 January 19. .**

	£	£
Sales		66,650
Less: Purchases of raw materials (W1)	44,500	
Closing stock of raw materials (W2)	(12,900)	
Raw materials consumed	31,600	
Direct wages (W3)	31,600	
Prime cost	63,200	
Factory overheads		
Variable (W4)	7,900	
Fixed (W5)	5,600	
Depreciation of plant and machinery (W6)	2,400	
Cost of production	79,100	
Deduct: Closing stocks of finished goods (W7)	(15,300)	
	63,800	63,800
Net profit		2,850

Budgeted balance sheet as at 31 January 19 . .

	£	£
Fixed assets: plant and machinery		144,000
Less: Depreciation		2,400
		141,600
Current assets		
Stocks of raw materials (W2)	12,900	
Stocks of finished goods (W7)	15,300	
	28,200	
Debtors (W9)	53,392	
	81,592	
Less: Current liabilities		
Creditors for raw materials (W1) 25,600		
Accruals for variable overheads (W8) 3,810		
Accruals for fixed overheads 2,000		
Accruals for wages 6,350		
Overdraft from cash forecast 8,582		
	46,342	
Net current assets		35,250
Net assets employed		176,850
Financed by:		
Share capital (W10)		174,000
Retained profit		2,850
Shareholders' funds		176,850

Workings

1. Purchases:
   November-January = £3,100 + £15,800 + £25,600 = £44,500, of which £25,600 is outstanding at 31 January.

2. Stock of raw materials:
   January purchases not consumed till February: £12,900

3. Direct wages:
   £4.0 × 7,900* = £31,600

4. Variable overhead:
   £1.0 × 7,900* = £7,900

   *7,900 units were produced in December and January i.e.:

   1,550
   1,700
   4,650

   7,900

5. Fixed overheads:
   70% × £48,000 = £33,600 × (2/12 months) = £5,600

6. Depreciation:
   30% × £48,000 = £14,400 × (2/12) = £2,400

7. Stock:
   7,900 units made – 6,200 units sold = 1,700 units
   1,700 units valued at variable cost = 1,700 × £9 = £15,300

8. Accruals for variable overheads, fixed overheads and wages appear as payments in the February column of the cash flow forecast.

9. Debtors:

	£
Sales	66,650
Less: Cash received	13,258
Debtors	53,392

10. Share capital:

	£
Plant and machinery	144,000
Working capital	30,000
	174,000

Tutorial note

Much of the detailed working appears in the cash flow forecast, since all three statements are related to the sales and production plans.

6 Profit/cash/working capital

INTRODUCTION

This chapter is important since working capital is the most important element of a firm's capital structure. The ability to pay one's creditors in the short term is more important than the ability to produce profit.

The questions are concerned with the effect on budgeted working capital of alternative management actions and policy. The chapter can be seen as a natural development of the previous two chapters on budgeting.

The budgeting of working capital is the most important element of short-term planning since a major component is the bank balance out of which all creditors have to be met. If the working capital appearing on the forecast balance sheet is not acceptable, in terms of size, components or the relationship of components, the impact of alternative policies and transactions must be considered.

Students must remember that there are two aspects to all transactions; thus alternative policies will affect two components of the balance sheet. Only those which affect:

(a) stock;
(b) debtors;
(c) cash; and
(d) current liabilities,

come within the definition of working capital.

Since alternative policies may also affect profit, students must consider the impact on profit at the same time as the effect on working capital, as illustrated in the table overleaf.

SUGGESTED METHOD FOR ANSWERING THE QUESTION

Following the completion of the budgets management will consider the effect of each decision separately in the initial stages. Alter the budgeted balance sheet, taking each decision separately as required by the question.

Policy or action	Total working capital	Cash	Profit	Other balance sheet items
1 Allowing longer credit period to debtors	No change	Decrease		
2 Allowing higher discount to debtors	Decrease	Decrease	Decrease	
3 Receiving longer credit from creditors	No change	Increase		
4 Receiving higher discount from creditors	Increase	Increase	Increase	
5 Increasing stockholding, i.e. reducing stock turn	No change	Decrease		
6 Sale of fixed assets	Increase	Increase		Decrease fixed assets
7 Issue shares or debentures	Increase	Increase		Increase capital
8 Issue bonus shares	No change			Increase capital and decrease reserves
9 Revalue property	No change			Increase fixed assets and increase reserves
10 Provision for depreciation	No change		Decrease	Decrease fixed assets
11 Provision for bad debts	Decrease		Decrease	
12 Provision for stock loss	Decrease		Decrease	

Note that in 1, 3 and 5 the alternative policy has no effect on working capital, because more than one component will change and the net effect is nil.

QUESTIONS

1 DUMBLE LTD

The directors of Dumble Ltd are considering the company's estimated financial situation in 1985. The following estimates relate to the company's expected activities in 1985:

	£
Sales	240,000
Purchases	150,000
Depreciation	7,000
Net profit	13,000

It is estimated that 60% of the company's sales will be on credit and 40% for cash.

Consistent with the above information, the estimated balance sheet for the year ending 31 December 1985 is shown below:

	£			£
Issued share capital	75,000	Freehold property at cost		54,000
Profit and loss account	55,000	Plant at cost	£62,000	
Trade creditors	16,000	Less: Depreciation	£18,000	
				44,000
		Stocks		28,000
		Trade debtors		18,000
		Bank		2,000
	146,000			146,000

It can be assumed that all transactions will take place at an even rate throughout the year.

The directors are interested in the effects which would occur if the following changes were made to the estimates:

(a) 80% of sales to be made on credit and 20% for cash.

(b) Depreciation for 1985 to be amended to £11,000.

(c) The average period of credit to be taken from suppliers to be amended to two months.

(d) A provision of £2,000 to be made for doubtful debts at 31 December 1985.

(e) Freehold property to be revalued at £60,000.

Required:

A statement showing the net profit, bank balance or overdraft, and the current ratio (working capital ratio) for 1985 which would result from making each individual amendment. For any items which are unaffected by an amendment, show the appropriate figures derived from the original estimates.

Consider each amendment *independently* and present your answer in a table, as shown below:

Amendment	Net profit 1985	Bank balance or (overdraft) 31.12.85	Current ratio 31.12.85
(a)			
(b)			
(c)			
(d)			
(e)			

Notes:

(1) Ignore taxation.

(2) Assume that the amendment will not alter the amount of bank interest payable.

20 marks

2   ELLIS LTD

According to financial projections for 1985, currently being examined by the management of Ellis Ltd, the company's balance sheet at 31 December 1985 is expected to be as follows:

	£		£	£
Share capital	100,000	Property		61,000
General reserve	50,000	Equipment	82,000	
Profit and loss account	63,000	Less: Accumulated depreciation	30,000	
	213,000			52,000
Trade creditors	40,000	Stocks		80,000
Bank overdraft	10,000	Debtors		70,000
	263,000			263,000

Certain figures relating to the company's projected activities for 1985 are shown below:

	£
Sales	640,000
Purchases	300,000
Depreciation	6,000
Profit	20,000

Amendments to the estimates are under discussion, and the company's management is interested in the effects of the following possible changes:

(a) Depreciation for the year 1985 to be amended to £9,000.

(b) New equipment to be purchased for £5,000 on 31 December 1985.

(c) Collections from debtors to be altered, so that in the balance sheet at the end of the year debtors would be equal to one and a half months' sales.

(d) Advantage to be taken of cash discounts for prompt payment. This would result in average discounts of 3% being obtained on two-thirds of the company's purchases during 1985. No benefit from cash discounts had been assumed in the original estimates. As a result of the changed payment procedures, the trade creditors in the balance sheet at 31 December 1985 would be equivalent to one month's purchases.

(e) £10,000 to be transferred to general reserve from the balance on profit and loss account.

Required:

A statement showing the profit, bank balance or overdraft, and the current ratio (working capital ratio) for 1985 which would result from making each individual amendment. For any items which are unaffected by an amendment, show the appropriate figures derived from the original estimates.

Consider each amendment *independently* and present your answer in a table shown below:

Amendment	Profit 1985	Bank balance or (overdraft)	Current ratio
(a)			
(b)			
(c)			
(d)			
(e)			

Notes:

(1) Ignore taxation.

(2) Assume that the amendment will not alter the amount of bank interest payable.

20 marks

3 TILE LTD

The estimated balance sheet of Tile Ltd at 31 December 1985 is shown below:

	£		£	£
Issued share capital (£1 ordinary shares)	50,000	Property		37,000
Profit and loss account	68,000	Equipment at cost	80,000	
Trade creditors	36,000	Less: Depreciation	29,000	
Bank overdraft	14,000			51,000
		Stocks and work in progress at cost		50,000
		Trade debtors		30,000
	168,000			168,000

The following information also relates to the estimates made for the year ending 31 December 1985.

	£
Credit sales	240,000
Purchases	150,000
Depreciation	8,000
Net profit	9,000

The directors of Tile Ltd are reviewing the above estimates and are considering making the following amendments:

(a) Depreciation for the year to be amended to £10,000.

(b) The average period of credit allowed to customers to be amended to one calendar month. (Assume transactions take place at an even rate throughout the year.)

(c) The purchase of goods for £12,500, which the original estimates assumed would be acquired on credit in December 1985, to be deferred until January 1986.

(d) A bonus (scrip) issue of ordinary shares, comprising one new £1 share for every two shares held at 30 June 1985, to be made to shareholders by capitalisation from the balance of the profit and loss account.

Required:

A statement showing the bank balance or overdraft, the current (or working capital) ratio, and the net profit for 1985 which would result from making each individual amendment. For any items which may be unaffected by an amendment show the figures from the original estimates.

Consider each amendment *independently* and present your answer in a table, as shown below:

Amendment	Net profit for 1985	Bank balance or overdraft	Current ratio 31.12.85
(a)			
(b)			
(c)			
(d)			

Notes:

(1) Ignore taxation.

(2) Assume that the amendments will not alter the amount of bank interest payable.

20 marks

4 MONTEAGLE LTD

The directors of Monteagle Ltd are considering the company's estimated financial situation for 1981. The following forecasts relate to the company's expected activities in 1981.

Forecast profit and loss account 1981

	£	£
Sales		600,000
Less: Purchases	480,000	
Stock increase during 1981	(30,000)	
Cost of goods sold		450,000
Gross profit		150,000
Less: Depreciation	20,000	
Other overhead expenses	100,000	
		120,000
Net profit		30,000

Forecast balance sheet as at 31 December 1981

	£		£	£
Ordinary share capital (£1 shares)	100,000	Freehold property at cost		40,000
Profit and loss account	65,000	Plant at cost	80,000	
Trade creditors	40,000	Less: Depreciation	35,000	
				45,000
		Stocks		50,000
		Trade debtors		60,000
		Bank		10,000
	205,000			205,000

It is to be assumed that 1981 consists of 12 months, each of 30 days, and transactions take place at an even rate throughout the year.

The directors intend to undertake an expansion of business activity at the beginning of 1982 and are considering ways of improving the forecast financial position as at 31 December 1981. The following suggested courses of action have been put forward:

(a) Make a bonus (capitalisation) issue of shares to existing shareholders on the basis of one additional £1 share for every two shares held at present.

(b) The average period of credit taken from suppliers to be amended to 45 days.

(c) Revalue the freehold property to £60,000.

(d) Increase the depreciation charge for 1981 to £32,000.

(e) Arrange for a long-term loan of £15,000 to be made to the company on 31 December 1981.

(f) The average period for which stocks are held to be amended to 60 days.

Required:

A statement showing the net profit for 1981 and the bank balance (or overdraft) and the current (working capital) ratio at 31 December 1981 which would result from taking each course of action *separately*. For any items which are unaffected by a course of action, show the original figure derived from the above accounts.

Consider each course of action *separately* and present your answer in a table, as shown below.

Course of action	Net profit 1981 £	Bank balance or (overdraft) 31 December 1981 £	Current ratio 31 December 1981
(a) (b) (c) (d) (e) (f)			

Notes:

(1) Ignore taxation.

(2) Assume that no course of action will alter the amount of bank interest payable, if any.

20 marks

ANSWERS

1 DUMBLE LTD

	Net profit 1985 £	Bank balance (overdraft) £		Current ratio
Budgeted	13,000	2,000	(48/16)	3.0 to 1

Amendments

(a)	(W1)	13,000	(4,000)	2.6 to 1
(b)	(W2)	9,000	2,000	3.0 to 1
(c)	(W3)	13,000	11,000	2.28 to 1
(d)	(W4)	11,000	2,000	2.88 to 1
(e)	(W5)	13,000	2,000	3.0 to 1

Workings and tutorial notes

1   Profit is made at the moment of sale, irrespective of cash or credit terms, i.e., no change.

Bank balance will fall if more credit is given:

60% on credit = £144,000

20% more = £48,000, i.e. $\frac{1}{3}$ more.

Debtors may be expected to rise by $\frac{1}{3}$ (= £6,000), cash withheld.

Working capital will now become:

Stocks: £28,000   Overdraft: £4,000
Debtors: £24,000   Creditors: £16,000

i.e., 2.6 to 1 current ratio.

2   Depreciation increased by £4,000 so reducing net profit. Cash and working capital are unaffected by this book expense.

3   Profit is unaltered; there is merely a change in credit terms. Bank balance will improve if credit terms from suppliers are extended, or fall if credit terms are shortened:

	£
2 months' terms = (1/6) × £150,000 =	25,000
Less: Creditors at present	16,000
Improvement in bank	9,000

Working capital:

	£		
Stocks:	28,000	Creditors:	£25,000
Debtors:	18,000		
Bank:	11,000		
	57,000		

i.e., 2.28 to 1 current ratio

4   Debtors reduced by £2,000, together with net profit; bank, no change.

Working capital:

	£		
Stocks:	28,000	Creditors:	£16,000
Debtors:	16,000		
Bank:	2,000		
	46,000		

i.e., 2.875 to 1 current ratio

5   No change, to profit (from trading), bank balance or working capital, merely a book entry by which a £6,000 revaluation reserve is created.

2   ELLIS LTD

		Net profit 1985 £	Bank balance (overdraft) £		Current ratio
Budgeted		20,000	(10,000)	(150/50)	3.0 to 1

Amendments

(a)	(W1)	17,000	(10,000)	3.0 to 1
(b)	(W2)	20,000	(15,000)	2.73 to 1
(c)	(W3)	20,000	(20,000)	2.67 to 1
(d)	(W4)	26,000	(19,000)	3.41 to 1
(e)	(W5)	20,000	(10,000)	3.0 to 1

Workings

1   Net profit only affected by £3,000 extra depreciation charge.

2   Capital expenditure does not affect the profit and loss account, but alters the bank account, and therefore the working capital.

3   1½ months' credit allowed to customers is £640,000/8 = £80,000. Thus the cash position will worsen by £10,000 and the current ratio change to (160/60) = 2.67.

	£000		£000
Stocks	80	Creditors	40
Debtors	80	Overdraft	20
	160		60

4 Discounts received are £6,000, i.e., £300,000 × $\frac{2}{3}$ @ 3%. They reduce cash paid out and improve profits. Creditors, however, are reduced to £25,000 which means an outflow of cash from the bank of £15,000, i.e., £40,000 − £25,000.

Working capital change:

	£		£
Stocks	80	Creditors	25
Debtors	70	Bank overdraft (10 − 6 + 15)	19
	150		44

5 No changes, as this is a transfer only within the reserves of the company.

3 TILE LTD

	Net profit 1985 £	Bank balance (overdraft) £		Current ratio
Budgeted	9,000	(14,000)	(80/50)	1.6 to 1

Amendments

(a)	(W1)	7,000	(14,000)	1.6 to 1
(b)	(W2)	9,000	(4,000)	1.75 to 1
(c)	(W3)	9,000	(14,000)	1.8 to 1
(d)	(W4)	9,000	(14,000)	1.6 to 1

Workings

1 The increase of depreciation by £2,000 only affects net profit.

2 Debtors are reduced to £20,000, i.e., (240,000/12), thus releasing £10,000 cash to reduce the overdraft to £4,000.

$$\frac{CA}{CL} = \frac{50 + 20}{36 + 4} = \frac{70}{40} = 1.75$$

3 Stocks fall to £37,500 and creditors to £23,500, so that the current ratio alters, but not profit or the overdraft.

$$\frac{CA}{CL} = \frac{80 - 12.5}{50 - 12.5} = 1.8$$

4 The capitalisation does not alter any of the three figures. It is merely an issue of shares out of reserves already accumulated.

4 MONTEAGLE LTD

		Net profit 1981 £	Bank balance (overdraft) £		Current ratio
Budgeted		30,000	10,000	(120/40)	3.0 to 1
Course of action					
(a)	(W1)	30,000	10,000		3.0 to 1
(b)	(W2)	30,000	30,000		2.33 to 1
(c)	(W3)	30,000	10,000		3.0 to 1
(d)	(W4)	18,000	10,000		3.0 to 1
(e)	(W5)	30,000	25,000		3.37 to 1
(f)	(W6)	30,000	(15,000)		2.45 to 1

Workings and tutorial notes

1 No change; a bonus issue affects share capital and reserves.

2 £480,000 × (1½/12) = £60,000 creditors. Bank balance rises by £20,000.

$$\frac{CA}{CL} = \frac{140}{60} = 2.33$$

3 No changes — revaluation reserve created.

4 A further £12,000 book expense against profits.

5 A capital injection unaffecting profit, but altering bank balances and hence working capital.

Bank = 10,000 + 15,000 = 25,000; CA = 120,000 + 15,000 = 135,000

$$\frac{CA}{CL} = \frac{135}{40} = 3.37$$

6 £450,000/6 (two months) = £75,000. The stock increase, £25,000, reduces cash and creates an overdraft.

$$\frac{CA}{CL} = \frac{120 - 10 + 25}{40 + 15} = \frac{135}{55} = 2.45$$

7 Share and business valuations

INTRODUCTION

This chapter is important from the lending banker's point of view since shares and similar investments are frequently offered as collateral. The adequacy of this collateral depends upon the value of the shares which in their turn depend upon the value of the company. Since most shares are not quoted, the ability to place realistic valuations on such investments is of great importance, particularly as there are three or four ways of approaching the problem. Even Inland Revenue experts will disagree fundamentally on valuations.

A share represents an interest in a company and is, therefore, valued either as an entitlement to a share of future profits, or as an interest in the net assets that comprise the company. The majority of shareholders are interested in dividends. On the other hand a majority shareholder who may be able to liquidate a company, is probably more interested in the realisable value of the company's assets. Shares are valued on the bases represented by these two interests, and students must be fully conversant with the following:

(a) **Yield basis**

    (i) Earnings yield

        If a company distributed all of its profit it could not grow and would, therefore, never be in a position to increase its dividend. Since the shareholder has an interest in the retained as well as the distributed profit, shares are normally valued on the basis of the profits or earnings expected, using an average of recent years as the best indicator of what the future earnings will be. The earnings are then capitalised by applying an appropriate profit/earnings ratio (that of similar companies), or dividing by the required yield, e.g., if shareholders require a 12½% yield from a company generating 15p per share profit, they are valuing the shares at £1.20, i.e., 15p × 8 or 15p/0.125.

    (ii) Dividend yield

        In circumstances where the shareholder has little or no influence over dividend policy, it may be more appropriate to capitalise dividends by dividing the dividend by the appropriate yield required on shares in that type of business. Usually a growth factor is built into the calculations. If there is no indication of growth, this method may not be appropriate.

(b) **Net assets basis**

On this basis, the share's value is simply the net assets, or equity, divided by the number of shares.

There are three bases upon which the assets may be valued:

(i) Book value

This is the balance sheet value for the equity (net assets), which includes share capital and reserves. This valuation is the result of the accounting conventions and policies adopted in the past and generally is not realistic in terms of realisable value.

(ii) Liquidation or break-up value

In theory this gives figures closer to the current sale value of the assets. However, the valuations can be highly subjective and artificial since there is generally no intent to separate the assets.

(iii) Replacement cost

Modern accounting theory and practice as postulated in current cost accounting requires balance sheets to show assets at their 'value to the business' as a going concern. This is generally replacement cost, or deprival value, and may be considered by some as more relevant to share valuation than the break-up value.

SUGGESTED METHOD FOR ANSWERING THE QUESTIONS

As with ratios, successful answers to these questions depend initially on memorising the various yield equations and being able to comment upon them.

QUESTIONS

1 BISCUITS LTD

Biscuits Ltd is a private company controlled by X, who has deposited his shares in the company with his bank to secure an overdraft for his other business activities.

In order to estimate the value of the company's shares the bank obtained the information given below:

Summarised balance sheet of Biscuits Ltd 31 December 1983

	£		£
Issued share capital:		Fixed assets	11,000
£1 ordinary shares	10,000		
Reserves	4,000	Current assets	13,500
Profit and loss account	5,000		
Current liabilities	5,500		
	24,500		24,500

The company's profit for the year ended 31 December 1983 was appropriated as follows:

	£
Net profit for the year	3,000
Ordinary dividends for the year	500
Retained profit	2,500

At 31 December 1983 a professional valuer considered that, in the event of a forced sale, the company's assets would realise on liquidation:

Fixed assets	£17,500
Current assets	£10,000

Similar private companies have recently been sold at values giving an earnings yield of 10%.

On the London Stock Exchange ordinary shares of public companies in the same industry as Biscuits Ltd currently have a dividend yield of 4%.

Required:

(a) A table, to be completed in the following form:

	Valuation of a £1 ordinary share in Biscuits Ltd
(i) Balance sheet basis (i.e., net asset book value per share)	
(ii) Break-up (i.e., liquidation) basis	
(iii) Dividend yield basis	
(iv) Earnings yield basis	

(N.B. Confine your calculations to the information provided above.)

(b) Comment briefly on the limitations of the valuations you have calculated.

Ignore taxation.

20 marks

2 FLOYD LTD

Mardyke Ltd has made an offer to acquire the ordinary shares of Floyd Ltd. John, who owns 1,000 £1 ordinary shares in Floyd Ltd, would receive for his entire holding £2,000 in cash plus £1,000 9% debenture stock in Mardyke Ltd.

The debenture stock in Mardyke Ltd will be quoted on the Stock Exchange when it is issued; debenture stocks in companies which involve similar risks to Mardyke Ltd are currently valued on a basis which gives a yield of 10% p.a. (For simplicity, redemption dates can be ignored; i.e., assume perpetual debenture stock.)

John is trying to reach a decision on whether he should accept the offer, and he hopes that the following information will provide the answer:

Summarised balance sheet of Floyd Ltd at 31 December 1983:

	£		£
£1 ordinary shares	500,000	Fixed assets at cost	
Reserves	340,000	less depreciation	680,000
Current liabilities	460,000	Current assets	620,000
	1,300,000		1,300,000

Excerpt from the profit statement of Floyd Ltd for the year ended 31 December 1983:

	£
Trading profit	138,000
Less: Interst paid on short-term loans	6,000
Net profit	132,000
Less: Dividends for 1974	60,000
Retained profit	72,000

According to a recent stockbroker's report 'the property assets of Floyd Ltd are reliably estimated to have a saleable value of £1 million'. It can be assumed that saleable values of the other fixed assets would be negligible and that current assets would realise their balance sheet figures.

The shares of Floyd Ltd are quoted on the Stock Exchange, and shares in quoted companies in the same industry currently have an average price-earnings ratio of 10 and an average dividend yield of 5% p.a.

Required:

(a) Calculations showing the value of Mardyke's offer for John's shares in Floyd Ltd, and valuations for those shares on *four further* valuation bases. Adopt widely known valuation bases and state which you have used, in a table as follows:

Valuation basis	Valuation of 1,000 ordinary shares in Floyd Ltd
(i) Offer from Mardyke Ltd	
(ii)	
(iii)	
(iv)	
(v)	

(b) Comment very briefly on your results and the limitations of the valuation bases you have used.

Note: Ignore taxation.

20 marks

3 BROCK'S DOCK LTD

Brock's Dock Ltd builds and repairs small coastal craft. About 40% of the company's shares are held by its directors; the remainder are held by members of the Brock family, who are not involved in the company's day-to-day activities.

The company's summarised balance sheets and profit information for the past three years are shown below:

Balance sheets at 31 December

	1981 £000	1982 £000	1983 £000
Issued share capital, shares of £1 each	100	100	100
Reserves	59	54	70
Creditors	64	70	81
Bank borrowing	77	96	109
	300	320	360
Freehold property	130	130	130
Equipment less depreciation	50	60	58
Stocks and work-in-progress	51	58	71
Debtors	69	72	101
	300	320	360

Profit information for years ended 31 December

	1981 £000	1982 £000	1983 £000
Cost of goods and expenses	338	404	425
Depreciation of equipment	15	16	17
Directors' remuneration	20	25	30
Dividends	10	10	12
Retained profit (transfer from reserves)	17	(5)	16
	400	450	500

Brock's Dock has received an offer of £210,000 for its property from a marina development group. The directors of Brock's Dock Ltd are considering the proposal, and have discussed the position with their bankers. The bank borrowing is secured by a charge over the property, and the directors were negotiating with the bank over borrowing facilities when the purchase offer was received.

The directors have taken professional advice on the value of the property, and have been informed that in normal circumstances the property could be sold for about

£150,000. If the existing property were sold, it would cost the company some £170,000 to acquire similar property for the continuance of its business operations.

You are given the following estimates for net realisable values and replacement costs of the equipment and stock of Brock's Dock Ltd at 31 December 1983:

	Net realisable value £000	Replacement cost (in similar condition) £000
Equipment	25	78
Stocks and work-in-progress	30	90

Debtors are all considered good. If the company were to be wound up, there would be liquidation costs, redundancy payments, etc., of some £20,000.

Henry, a director, who is particularly anxious that the company should continue in operation, has discovered that similar companies have recently been sold for amounts equal to six times 'maintainable earnings'. He is prepared to purchase shares of any shareholders in Brock's Dock Ltd for the same valuation. For this purpose 'maintainable earnings' would be defined as average profit over the past three years. Profit would be calculated in the usual accounting manner, after the deduction of depreciation and directors' remuneration.

A shareholder, who is not a director, on hearing of the proposals under consideration, commented that he was more interested in the dividend income from the shares than in their saleable value. (Dividend yields on listed shares in companies in the same industry as Brock's Dock Ltd are currently about 8% per year.)

Required:

(a) A table, completed in the following form, showing valuations for *one* ordinary share in Brock's Dock Ltd, adopting the bases shown.

		Valuation of an ordinary share in Brock's Dock Ltd at 31 December 1983
(i)	Nominal value	
(ii)	Book value	
(iii)	Break-up value (i.e., liquidation after property sale to marina group)	
(iv)	Replacement cost basis	
(v)	'Maintainable earnings' basis (i.e., Henry's offer)	
(vi)	Dividend yield basis	

(b) Comment on the relevance of your valuations to the shareholders of Brock's Dock Ltd.

Note: Assume that you are making all valuations at 31 December 1983, and confine your calculations to information provided in the question. Ignore taxation.

30 marks

4 CONNECTICUT PLC

The directors of Connecticut plc, who own 50% of the company's ordinary shares, have approached the bank requesting a renewal of the overdraft facility of £50,000 for a further 12 months. Connecticut's share quotation was suspended last month because of irregularities concerning the purchase and sale of the company's shares by one of its directors. The director has since resigned and it is expected that the Stock Exchange will resume dealing in the company's shares in the near future.

The following historical cost information has been extracted from previously published accounts:

Balance sheet at 31 December 1982

	£000	£000
Fixed assets		
Equipment at cost less depreciation		800
Current assets		
Stocks	810	
Debtors	580	
	1,390	
Current liabilities		
Trade creditors	316	
Proposed dividends	100	
Bank overdraft	24	
	440	
Net current assets		950
		1,750
Capital and reserves		
Ordinary shares (£1 each)		1,000
Reserves		550
		1,550
10% preference shares		200
		1,750

Profit and loss accounts

	1980 £000	1981 £000	1982 £000
Net profit for the year	126	210	240
Less: Dividends: ordinary shares	(80)	(80)	(80)
preference shares	(20)	(20)	(20)
Retained profit for the year	26	110	140

The following additional information is provided:

(i) Depreciation of £60,000 per year has been charged on the equipment during each of the last three years. The equipment is old and in need of replacement; annual depreciation based on current replacement cost would be in the region of £76,000.

(ii) On investigation, the stock in the balance sheet shown above was found to be overvalued by £14,000.

(iii) The profit for 1980 was arrived at after deducting an exceptional loss of £56,000 arising from the liquidation of a major customer.

(iv) It is estimated that the equipment and stocks possess respective liquidation values of £240,000 and £600,000. The debtors would be collected in full and liquidation costs would amount to £52,000.

(v) A recent article in the financial press estimated a dividend yield of 12% and an earnings yield of 20% for other companies in Connecticut's industry.

Required:

(a) A table, completed in the following form, showing valuations for the entire ordinary share capital of Connecticut plc.

		Valuation
(i)	Earnings yield basis (based on average earnings for the last three years, after making appropriate adjustments).	
(ii)	Liquidation (break-up basis).	
(iii)	Dividend yield basis.	

18 marks

(b) Comments on the significance of the above-mentioned valuations, paying particular attention to the request for a renewal of the overdraft facility.

12 marks

Notes:

(1) Assume that you are making the valuations at 31 December 1982.

(2) Ignore taxation.

Total 30 marks

5 TONGUE LTD

The entire share capital of Tongue Ltd, an unlisted company, is held by the directors. They have decided to sell their shares and wish to discover their likely value prior to approaching a number of prospective purchasers. Should they fail to agree a price with a buyer the company will be liquidated and the assets sold off piecemeal. The following facts and information are provided:

(i) **Balance sheet of Tongue Ltd at 31 December 1980**

	£000	£000
Fixed assets		
Freehold properties at cost		260
Equipment at cost less depreciation		624
Current assets		
Stock	279	
Debtors	193	
Bank	26	
	498	
Less: Current liabilities	164	
Working capital		334
		1,218
Financed by		
Ordinary shares (£1 each)		600
Reserves		618
		1,218

(ii) **Extracts from the published profit and loss accounts for the last three years:**

	1978 £000	1979 £000	1980 £000
Depreciation	90	90	90
Directors' remuneration	100	116	120
Net profit before deducting dividend	130	144	167
Dividend	90	90	90

It was discovered that stock was over-valued at the end of 1977 by £24,000.

The directors have increased directors' remuneration in order to minimise the aggregate tax liability; a realistic charge for services rendered would be £75,000 p.a. The equipment is old and in need of replacement; annual depreciation based on current replacement cost would be in the region of £120,000.

(iii) One of the directors, Alfred, expresses the view that it is most appropriate to value shares on the basis of the price/earnings ratio. For this purpose he argues that earnings should be defined as the average reported profits for the last three years, after making 'proper' charges for depreciation and directors' remuneration and correcting the stock error made in 1977.

(iv) Relevant data relating to two listed companies engaged in the same line of business as Tongue Ltd:

	Dividend yield	Price/earnings ratio
Company 1	9%	5.4
Company 2	11%	6.6

(v) Figures obtained from experts for items appearing in the balance sheet of Tongue Ltd at 31 December 1980:

	Replacement values £000	Liquidation values £000
Freehold properties	600	600
Equipment	946	216
Stock	290	320

Required:

(a) A table completed in the following form, showing valuations for the entire share capital of Tongue Ltd:

		Valuation
(i)	Price/earnings basis (with earnings computed on the basis proposed by Alfred)	
(ii)	Book value basis	
(iii)	Liquidation (break-up) basis	
(iv)	Replacement cost basis	
(v)	Dividend yield basis	

(b) Comment on the significance of the above valuations in the light of the following comment made by Tongue Ltd's bank manager, when asked for his advice: 'None of these valuations is of much interest since the price depends on negotiation and expectations regarding likely future cash flows.'

Notes:

(1) Assume you are making the valuations at 31 December 1980.

(2) Ignore taxation and liquidation costs.

30 marks

ANSWERS

1 BISCUITS LTD

(a)   Valuation of £1 ordinary share

(i)   Balance sheet basis

$$\text{Value} = \frac{\text{Net assets}}{\text{No. of shares}} = \frac{19{,}000}{10{,}000} = £1.90$$

(ii)   Break-up basis

	£
Assets	27,500
Liabilities	5,500
	22,000

Share value = £22,000/10,000 =   £2.20

(iii) Dividend yield basis

$$\text{Value} = \frac{\text{Dividend}}{\text{Yield}} = \frac{£500/10{,}000}{0.04} = £1.25$$

(iv) Earnings yield basis

$$\text{Value} = \frac{\text{Earnings}}{\text{Earnings yield}} = \frac{£30{,}000/10{,}000}{0.10} = £3.00$$

(b)   Limitations

(i)   Asset valuations are subject to accounting conventions, which do not necessarily provide 'real value' figures.

(ii)   Such a valuation is only appropriate when the business needs to be liquidated. X's business is a going concern.

(iii) Whereas the value may be appropriate for a minority shareholder with no influence over dividend policy, the dividend yield basis is not suitable for X's controlling shareholding. Also the 4% yield of listed companies must be adjusted for private companies.

(iv) Though earnings yield is the most appropriate basis, the information in this case is limited to one year, which is not adequate for assessing maintainable profits.

2 FLOYD LTD

(a)
				Value of 1,000 shares
				£
	(i)	Offer from Mardyke	1,000 × £2.90 (W1)	2,900
	(ii)	Book value	1,000 × £1.68 (W2)	1,680
	(iii)	Liquidation value	1,000 × £2.32 (W3)	2,320
	(iv)	Earnings yield basis	1,000 × £2.64 (W4)	2,640
	(v)	Dividend yield basis	1,000 × £2.40 (W5)	2,400

(b) The five valuation bases have provided results varying from a low of £1,680 to high of £2,900, which from John's point of view would, therefore, appear reasonable.

Comments on the five valuations:

(i) Since this is the value of an external offer, it can be taken as Mardyke's minimum assessment of the value to them; presumably, because they see Floyd Ltd as a subsidiary capable of making a significant contribution to group profits.

(ii) Although this may be an accurate statement of net assets as valued by agreed accounting conventions, it is unlikely to represent saleable value, e.g., stock is valued at cost rather than saleable value.

(iii) This is highly subjective; the value of a business as a going concern would probably be greater and the value on a 'forced' sale considerably lower.

(iv) Only one year's figures are available; these may be untypical of the business activities and, therefore, unsuitable as the basis for predicting future earnings.

(v) As a minority shareholder, the owner's interest is in regular dividends, and possibly capital appreciation. Dividend payments and dividend growth depend upon the directors' policy. The dividend was well covered this year (2.2 times) suggesting reasonable dividend security.

Workings

		Value	per share
		£	£
1	Mardyke's offer		
	Cash	2,000	
	9% debenture stock: 1,000 × (9/10) (note a)	900	
		2,900	2.90
2	Book value of net assets		
	Share capital (500,000)	500,000	
	Reserves	340,000	
		840,000	1.68

		Value £	per share £
3	Break-up value		
	Value as in (W2)	840,000	
	Add: Extra value of fixed assets (1,000,000 − 680,000)	320,000	
		1,160,000	2.32

4   Earnings yield basis

Value of company = Annual profit × P/E ratio (note b)

£132,000 × 10 = £1,320,000   2.64

5   Dividend yield basis

$$\text{Value} = \frac{\text{Dividend}}{\text{Yield}} = \frac{£60,000}{0.05} = £1,200,000 \qquad 2.40$$

Tutorial notes

(a) An irredeemable (undated) debenture paying £90 p.a. has a value of £900 if an acceptable yield, or return, is 10%, i.e., 90/0.10 = £900.

(b) Since the earnings yield = Earnings/Price (E/P), it is the reciprocal or inverse of the Price/Earnings ratio (P/E).

3 BROCK'S DOCK LTD

(a) Basis of valuation

		Value of one ordinary share £
(i)	Nominal value	1.00
(ii)	Book value (£170,000/100,000)	1.70
(iii)	Break-up value (W1)	1.56
(iv)	Replacement cost (W1)	2.49
(v)	Maintainable earnings (W2)	1.20
(vi)	Dividend yield (3)	1.50

(b) The minimum value is £1.56, but as a going concern, in which assets are stated at value to the business (i.e., replacement cost) the shares are worth £2.49. Rarely are shares valued on this basis, since the value of a company, which is not being sold, is the present value of the cash flows it will generate. One would expect, therefore, that the earnings basis would give the most appropriate value.

The calculation of maintainable profits has been reduced to £20,000 by 1982's low profit. If earnings had been maintained average profits would be about

40% higher, taking £1.20 (as in (v) above) to about £1.70. However, the P/E ratio of 6 already takes into account the variability of earnings in this type of business.

The non-director shareholders, although holding minority shareholdings, have significant influence, proved by their ability to maintain the dividend in times of reduced profit; however, they cannot force a sale so that the dividend yield may be more appropriate. The shares are more risky than marketable shares and a more appropriate yield could be 10%, giving a value of 10/8 = £1.25.

Workings

1 Net assets basis

		Break-up value £000		Replacement cost £000
Assets				
Property		210		170
Equipment		25		78
Stock		30		90
Debtors		101		101
		366		439
Less: Creditors	81		81	
Bank	109	190	109	190
		176		249
Less: Costs		20		
		156		249
Per share		£1.56		£2.49

2 Maintainable earnings

	1981	1982	1983
Profit retained	17	(5)	16
Dividends	10	10	12
	27	5	28

Average = 60/3 = £20,000

Valuation = £20,000 × 6 = £120,000, i.e., £1.20 per share

3 Dividend yield

Current dividend (1983): 12%, i.e., 12,000/100,000

Yield on similar (but quoted shares) = 8%

Share value = £1.00 × (12/8) = £1.50

4 CONNECTICUT PLC

(a)   Valuation
                                                                                             £

    (i)   Earnings yield basis (W1)   850,000
    (ii)   Liquidation basis (W2)   728,000
    (iii) Dividend yield basis (W3)   667,000

Note: These are ex div. valuations. The cum div. value is £80,000 higher.

(b) (i)   This is generally considered the most appropriate way to value the equity shares of companies, since it 'capitalises' the profits attributable to the ordinary shareholders, whether they are distributed or not.

     (ii) This method is not appropriate since there appears to be no real danger of having to liquidate, particularly if the overdraft facility is renewed. Without renewal of the facilities the company does not have the cash to pay even the preference dividend which requires £20,000. However, the company is generating a positive net cash flow of about £25,000 per month, i.e.

$$\frac{\text{Profit} + \text{Depreciation}}{12} = \frac{£240,000 + £60,000}{12}$$

Against this must be set the need to replace fixed assets for which a more permanent loan will be negotiated. Gearing would increase the return to shareholders. Profits do not appear to vary and thus risk does not appear high.

     (iii) This valuation is on the low side since the dividends have been consistently low. Earnings for the ordinary shareholders have more than doubled, while the dividend has remained the same. Those who look to dividends as their sole income from the company (50% of the shareholders) may agitate to have the dividend increased.

General observation

The bank may insist on a deposit of, say, 20% of the directors' shares as collateral for the overdraft (value of company about £800,000, i.e., between (i) and (ii)).

Since the directors own half the shares the value of the deposit would be about £80,000.

Workings

1	Earnings basis	1980	1981	1982
		£000	£000	£000
	Profit	126	210	240
	Adjustments: Depreciation	(16)	(16)	(16)
	Stock valuation			(14)
	Extraordinary item	56		
		166	194	210

		£000
Average profits = 570/3 =		190
Less: Preference dividends		20
Earnings for ordinary shareholders		170
Valuation of company = £170,000/0.2 =		£850,000

2   Liquidation basis

		£000
Net assets per balance sheet		1,550
Less: Equipment (800 − 240)	560	
Stock (810 − 600)	210	
Costs	52	822
		728

3   Dividend yield basis

$$\text{Value} = \frac{\text{Dividends}}{\text{Yield}} = \frac{£80,000}{0.12} = £666,666$$

5   TONGUE LTD

(a)

		Valuation £
(i)	P/E basis (W1)	972,000
(ii)	Book value basis (W2)	1,218,000
(iii)	Liquidation basis (W3)	1,191,000
(iv)	Replacement cost basis (W4)	1,891,000
(v)	Dividend yield basis (W5)	900,000

(b)   The bank manager's comments are fair in that the price does depend on negotiation and expected cash flows, but unreasonable in dismissing the valuations as being 'of not much interest', since they form the basis of negotiation and are based on expectations of profits and returns which are related to cash flow. In the absence of specific knowledge of changing circumstances, the past and the present provide the best guide to the future.

Consideration of the five valuations:

(i)   Using a P/E ratio is the most usual way of valuing quoted shares, provided the earnings have been calculated on an understandable and standard basis. Tongue Ltd is not a quoted company and its shares are owned by the managers. The P/E ratio used in the calculation (the average for two listed companies) is thus not appropriate. Possibly, a lower P/E ratio should be used, giving an even lower valuation.

(ii)   Since the individual assets comprising the valuation are not valued at present sale price, or even value to the business as a going concern, the figures need adjusting.

(iii) This is the minimum value of the net assets and normally the lowest figure the vendors would accept.

(iv) The current (or replacement) cost represents a reasonable valuation of the net tangible assets of the business as a going concern.

If £216,000 is a realistic assessment of the equipment's value, replacement requires a further £730,000 finance, suggesting that this valuation is far in excess of the firm's real worth.

(v) Past dividends and potential dividends provide a realistic basis for the valuation of shares in large listed companies, managed rather than controlled by their directors. This basis is clearly inappropriate to Tongue Ltd.

The bank manager is right in suggesting that more consideration be given to future expectations and possibly explaining the low 'earnings' valuation relative to the 'break-up' value, suggesting the existence of negative goodwill.

Workings

1. Earnings (average) basis

	1978	1979	1980
	£000	£000	£000
Profit per accounts	130	144	167
Stock error (GP increase)	24		
Depreciation adjustment	(30)	(30)	(30)
Directors' remuneration	25	41	45
	149	155	182

Average profit for 3 years = 486/3 = £162,000

Appropriate P/E ratio (average for companies 1 and 2)* is 6.

Share valuation: 6 × £162,000 = £972,000

*See part (b) of answer.

2. Book value basis

Value of equity per balance sheet: £1,218,000

3. Liquidation basis

		£000
Value as above		1,218
Freehold property	(600 – 260)	340
Equipment	(216 – 624)	(408)
Stock	(320 – 279)	41
		1,191

4	Replacement cost basis		£000
	Value as in W2 above		1,218
	Freehold property	(600 – 260)	340
	Equipment	(946 – 624)	322
	Stock	(290 – 279)	11
			1,891

5   Dividend yield basis

     Regular dividends paid: £90,000
     Yield required (average of companies 1 and 2):   10%

     Valuation: £90,000/0.1 = £900,000

     *See part (b) of answer.

8 Liquidation

INTRODUCTION

This topic is directly related to a banker's legal and practical studies both of which are examined. It is of great importance since the lending banker has more than one interest in a company's solvency. The banker is a creditor (often unsecured in respect of overdrafts and loans) and is therefore immediately concerned with the order of preference as defined by law. His second interest is in the residual value of the company's shares if they have been taken as collateral (see previous chapter).

Liquidation (or winding up) of a company usually occurs when the company is unable to pay its debts. However, there are other instances when liquidation may occur and all creditors and shareholders are paid in full.

Questions centre around the former series of liquidations, i.e., insufficient assets to clear debts, so that some creditors will only receive part of their claim — this is called a dividend in the liquidation.

Be sure that you are familiar with the order of priority of repayment:

(a) Debtors who hold a fixed charge, e.g., mortgage over land or the 'fixed' element of a debenture.

(b) Costs of the liquidation, i.e., mainly liquidators' expenses.

(c) Preferential debts: these include rates and VAT for the preceeding 12 months; one year's assessment for income and corporation tax (the Revenue can select a year); employees' wages and salaries for the last four months, up to a maximum figure; compensation for holiday pay accrued; and redundancy.

(d) Holders of a floating charge: since these are fourth, many banks avoid floating charges, in favour of a so-called 'fixed charge', even on debtors. Further, the charge may be invalid in a liquidation, unless it has existed for 12 months, or it can be proved that the company was solvent when it was taken.

(e) Unsecured creditors: these are usually trade and expense creditors. The category will also receive any of the fixed and floating charge creditors who, although holders of security, remain unsatisfied (in part) as to their debt.

(f) Preference shareholders: these are non-voting shareholders, whose shareholding bears a fixed rate of interest.

(g) Ordinary shareholders: these are voting shareholders who thus own the enterprise. They have no guaranteed dividend and are the principal risk takers.

You will have to use the above priority list in all questions, and also consider reconstruction schemes (see chapter 9) and other alternatives which will not only benefit the bank, but creditors in general.

SUGGESTED METHOD OF ANSWERING THE QUESTIONS

Since the order of preference for the payment of debts is of paramount importance, the order must be learned and candidates must practise the interpretation thereof.

QUESTIONS

1 EASTGATE LTD

One of your bank's customers, Jeremiah, has deposited 6,000 shares in Eastgate Ltd as security for a personal bank overdraft on which £2,460 is at present outstanding. You have heard that, at a meeting between the directors and creditors of Eastgate Ltd held on 20 April 1981, it was decided to liquidate that company. Certain facts and estimates were examined by the meeting. These include:

(i) **Balance sheet of Eastgate Ltd at 19 April 1981**

	£	£		£	£
Share capital (£1 shares)		100,000	Goodwill at cost		22,000
Reserves at 31 December 1980	70,000		Freehold property at cost		45,000
Loss for 1981 to date	68,000		Plant and machinery at cost less depreciation		48,000
		2,000			115,000
		102,000	Quoted investments (market value £16,000)		12,000
12% debenture		50,000	Current assets:		
Current liabilities:			Stock	108,000	
Creditors	209,000		Debtors	194,000	
Bank overdraft	68,000				302,000
		277,000			
		429,000			429,000

(ii) The following asset values are considered to be relevant in a liquidation:

	£
Plant and machinery	10,000
Stock	47,000
Debtors	160,000

There was significant disagreement regarding the likely value of the freehold property. The majority accepted a valuation of £60,000 recently obtained from a firm of surveyors. A minority argued that, in view of development potential in the area where this property was located, a sale figure of £150,000 was likely to be much nearer the mark.

(iii) Eastgate Ltd's bank holds a fixed charge on the freehold property as security for the overdraft.

(iv) Of the £209,000 creditors, £57,000 were estimated as being preferential.

(v) The debenture is secured by a floating charge over the assets of Eastgate Ltd, other than the freehold property. There are no arrears of debenture interest.

(vi) Liquidation expenses are estimated at £6,000.

Required:

(a) Calculations of the amounts which would be received by each of the providers of finance, assuming that the majority view regarding the value of the freeholds is correct and that the other information proves accurate. You should show clearly the order of priority for repayment.

(b) An indication of the effect on the findings under (a) if the minority view regarding the value of the freeholds proves to be correct.

Note: Ignore taxation.

20 marks

2 ALLERTON LTD

The following is the summarised balance sheet of Allerton Ltd at 31 March 1984:

	£000		£000
Issued share capital, £1 shares	400	Freehold building at cost less	
Profit and loss account	80	depreciation	40
		Plant and equipment at cost	
	480	less depreciation	504
12% debentures repayable 1990	400		
Sundry creditors	205		544
Bank overdraft	195	Stocks	420
		Debtors	316
	1,280		1,280

The bank overdraft is secured by a fixed charge on the freehold building; the debentures, all held by Shipley plc, are secured by a floating charge over the remaining assets of Allerton.

Allerton has been trading unprofitably for over two years and is now finding it impossible to meet its financial obligations. A meeting of creditors has been called to examine its affairs, and the following proposals are put forward for consideration:

I Piecemeal liquidation of the company

It is estimated that the company's assets, sold individually, would realise the following amounts:

	£000
Freehold building	70
Plant and equipment	20
Stocks	290
Debtors	250

Liquidation costs are estimated at £10,000 and sundry creditors, in the above balance sheet, include preferential creditors of £30,000.

II Sale of company as a going concern

Shipley would purchase the shares for a token sum and pay immediately the preferential creditors, in full, and the other sundry creditors and the bank 20p in the £ on account of the amounts shown as due to them in the above balance sheet. Seventy-five per cent of the balances then remaining outstanding would be repaid after one year but would not attract interest during the interim period.

Assume that:

(i)   The current rate of interest on all forms of borrowing is 12%.

(ii) The £195,000 overdraft in the balance sheet included interest to date.

(iii) The calculations are being made on 1 April 1984.

(iv) Piecemeal liquidation, if selected, would occur immediately; alternatively the company could be sold to Shipley at once.

Required:

(a) Calculations showing the amount which would be received by the bank under each proposal. *14 marks*

(b) A brief explanation of the relative merits of the two proposals from the bank's point of view. *6 marks*

Total 20 marks

3 SHAFTSBURY LTD

The East Bank today (23 April) received the following balance sheet prepared for its customer Shaftsbury Ltd:

Balance sheet at 20 April 1982

	£		£
Issued share capital (£1 ordinary shares)	50,000	Fixed assets Freehold property at cost	20,000
Reserves	23,000	Plant at cost less depreciation	172,000
10% debenture (secured on freehold property)	50,000		192,000
Current liabilities:		Current assets	
Bank overdraft	45,000	Stocks	67,000
Sundry creditors	117,000	Debtors	26,000
	285,000		285,000

Shaftsbury Ltd is a long established company which traded profitably until a few years ago. Following the expiration of exclusive patent rights on a particularly profitable product line, results declined dramatically. Over the last 12 months the company's cash flow problems have steadily increased. The overdraft facility at present stands at £45,000 and carries a second charge on the company's freehold property.

A meeting has been arranged for next Friday to consider the company's future. The above balance sheet will be presented to the meeting and the following proposals discussed:

(1) Immediate liquidation of the company: in these circumstances it is estimated that the freehold property would realise £65,000, the plant £21,000, the stock £40,000 and the debtors would pay up in full. Preferential creditors, included in the balance sheet figure for creditors, amount to £27,000.

(2) Cline Ltd has made an offer to take over the entire business activities of Shaftsbury Ltd. Under the terms of the offer the East Bank would receive 80% of the balance due, but repayment would not be made until exactly one year from the date of the creditors' meeting. No further interest would be considered to accrue on the balance due to East Bank during the 12-month period.

(3) Reorganisation and capital reconstruction: the management of Shaftsbury Ltd are planning a reorganisation of the company's activities which will restore profitability to reasonable levels almost immediately. The reorganisation will be linked with a capital reconstruction scheme. Under this scheme the existing shareholders will be asked to accept two £1 shares in exchange for every five shares currently held. The bank will be asked to accept 10,000 £1 shares as consideration for one half of the present overdraft. If this proposal is acceptable to creditors, the shareholders have indicated their willingness to take up a further 30,000 £1 shares for cash and the balance remaining outstanding to the bank would be repaid from the proceeds of this issue. The directors are confident that, if this proposal is put into effect, profits of £40,500 p.a. will be earned for the foreseeable future, of which two-thirds will be paid out as dividends and the remainder reinvested.

Notes:

(i) Assume that the East Bank earns 15% p.a. on all its lending and that the amounts in the balance sheet include interest accrued to date.

(ii) Assume, for convenience, that any adopted proposal would be implemented immediately with payments received immediately unless otherwise stated.

(iii) Ignore expenses of realisation and liquidation and assume that no changes have occurred between 20 April and 23 April 1982.

(iv) Ignore taxation.

Required:

(a) Calculations showing clearly the amounts the East Bank would receive under each of the three proposals. 20 marks

(b) An examination of the relative financial merits of the proposals from the viewpoint of the East Bank. 10 marks

Total 30 marks

4 LOWDOWN LTD

The following is the summarised balance sheet of Lowdown Ltd at 15 September 1978:

	£		£
Issued share capital	50,000	Leasehold property, less	
Revenue reserves	64,000	depreciation	40,000
Debentures	32,000	Equipment, less depreciation	38,000
Bank loan	30,000	Stocks	70,000
Creditors	49,000	Debtors	72,000
		Cash	5,000
	225,000		225,000

The debentures, which are held by one of the company's directors, are secured by a floating charge over the company's assets and are payable between 1992 and 1995.

The bank loan is secured by a charge over the leasehold property.

Lowdown Ltd is a publishing company and has recently lost a court case for publishing a libel in a book produced by the company. The company now owes damages and legal costs totalling £53,000, which do not appear in the balance sheet shown above. Consequently, a meeting of creditors has been called to consider the company's affairs. Two proposals are to be considered at the meeting:

I   Immediate liquidation of the company

In these circumstances the company's assets would realise the following amounts:

	£
Leasehold property	20,000
Equipment	12,000
Stocks	18,000
Debtors	65,000
Cash	5,000

Estimated liquidation costs would be £16,000.

Preferential creditors for £12,000 are included among creditors in the balance sheet.

The damages and legal costs of the libel action can be assumed to rank as unsecured creditors.

II   Takeover by Jackal Press

Jackal Press would be prepared to acquire the shares of Lowdown Ltd for a token sum. Jackal Press would provide funds for continuing the operations of Lowdown Ltd, and preferential creditors would be immediately paid in full. But all other liabilities (including those to the debenture-holder and the bank) would be subject to a moratorium of one year. At the end of the year, 85 pence in the £ would be paid on those liabilities irrespective of their nature, and in exchange the holders of those liabilities would be required to waive all claims (including security) and interest.

Jackal Press offers undoubted financial guarantees to back its proposals.

Assume that:

(i)   The current rate of interst on all forms of borrowing is 12%.
(ii) The debentures and bank loan in the balance sheet include interest to date.
(iii) The proposal adopted would be put into effect immediately.
(iv) No changes have occurred since the balance sheet date.

Required:

(a)   Calculations showing the amounts which would be received by the bank and unsecured creditors under both proposals.

(b)   Brief comments on the relative merits of the proposals from the bank's viewpoint.

20 marks

5   FASTFOODS LTD

Fastfoods Ltd is in financial difficulties.

The company's estimated balance sheet at 28 April is shown below:

	£		£
Issued capital (£1 ordinary shares)	25,000	Freehold property at cost	17,000
Profit and loss account	7,000	Equipment at cost less	
10% debenture stock	12,000	depreciation	122,000
Sundry creditors	103,000	Stocks at cost	25,000
Bank overdraft with Eastern Bank	17,000		
	164,000		164,000

Fastfoods Ltd operates a number of retail outlets for 'take-away' cooked food; most of these outlets are rented. Its largest supplier is Catercorp Ltd, which holds all the debenture stock and is also a trade creditor for £60,000; the latter amount is included with sundry creditors in the balance sheet.

The sundry creditors in the balance sheet also include preferential creditors for £11,000.

The bank overdraft is secured by a charge over the freehold property of Fastfoods Ltd, and the debenture stock is secured by a floating charge over the company's assets.

A meeting of the creditors of Fastfoods Ltd has been called for tomorrow, to consider the following alternatives:

(1) Immediate liquidation of the company, which would result in the following estimated amounts for realised assets:

	£
Freehold property	14,000
Equipment	51,000
Stocks	10,000

(2) An offer of support from Catercorp Ltd which would permit the reconstruction of Fastfoods Ltd.

Under the reconstruction, the debentures held by Catercorp Ltd would be converted into £1 ordinary shares at par, and for every £100 of the £60,000 trade debt owed to Catercorp Ltd there would be issued 55 £1 ordinary shares in the reconstructed company. The balance of the trade debt owed to Catercorp would be written off against the assets of Fastfoods Ltd.

The existing shareholders of Fastfoods Ltd would receive one £1 ordinary share in the reconstructed company for every five presently held.

A further 30,000 £1 ordinary shares in Fastfoods Ltd would be issued to Catercorp Ltd in exchange for the introduction of £30,000 cash; these new funds would be sufficient to enable the reconstructed company to meet the remainder of its liabilities as they fall due.

It has been estimated by the management of Catercorp Ltd that after reconstruction, Fastfoods Ltd should earn regular net profits of £12,000 per year.

Assume that Catercorp Ltd can currently earn 15% p.a. on new investments involving similar risks to those which would be incurred by investing in Fastfoods Ltd.

Assume that the adopted proposal would be implemented immediately.

Use the figures provided, without deducting expenses for liquidation or reconstruction, and without adding safety margins to your calculations.

Required:

(a) Calculations showing the total amount Catercorp Ltd would receive if Fastfoods Ltd were liquidated.

(b) Numerical comparisons showing which of the two proposals is more advantageous to Catercorp Ltd.

(c) Calculation of the annual net profit the reconstructed Fastfoods Ltd would need to earn in order to provide Catercorp Ltd with the same financial results as it would obtain from liquidation.

(d) Comment briefly on which of the two proposals you consider the Eastern Bank might be inclined to support.

Note: Ignore taxation.

30 marks

6 HOME BUILDERS LTD

Western Bank today received the following balance sheet relating to its customer Home Builders Ltd:

Balance sheet at 10 April 1984

	£			£
Issued share capital	40,000	Equipment, at cost less		
Profit and loss account	16,200	depreciation		16,000
Taxation due	8,000	Work in progress at cost:		
Loan from Propinvest Ltd		Site A	£93,000	
(secured on site A)	71,000	Site B	£49,000	
Loan from Western Bank				142,000
(secured on site B)	40,000	Stocks and other work in		
Trade creditors	35,000	progress		41,000
Overdraft (Western Bank)	6,000	Debtors		17,200
	216,200			216,200

The balance sheet was accompanied by a statement from the company's auditors stating that the balance sheet has been based on the company's accounting records, but there has been insufficient time to assess the validity of certain items in the balance sheet, particularly with regard to the net realisable value of current assets.

Home Builders Ltd has had cash flow problems for some time, and the balance sheet has been prepared for presentation to a meeting of creditors to be held tomorrow for the consideration of the company's financial situation.

From discussions with Home Builders Ltd and its accountants, Western Bank has ascertained that the only preferential creditors are for taxation and £2,000 of the bank's overdraft, which was advanced for wages. The secured creditors are as stated in the balance sheet; sites A and B are small developments containing houses at different stages of construction.

Three proposals are to be discussed at the creditors' meeting, as follows:

(1) Immediate liquidation of the company. The estimated net proceeds of realisation would be:

	£
Equipment	5,000
Work in progress:	
Site A	60,000
Site B	30,000
Stocks and other work in progress	20,000
Debtors	15,000

(2) An offer from the local government authority to take over site A for £64,000, and site B for £36,000. These amounts would be paid to the secured lenders on completion of all work on the sites, which can be assumed to be exactly one year from the date of the creditors' meeting. The remaining assets would be sold immediately for the amounts shown for liquidation above, and lenders on sites A and B would be treated as unsecured creditors for the balance of their loans.

(3) An offer from Octopus Ltd to acquire the share capital of Home Builders. Preferential creditors would be paid immediately in full. In one year's time all other creditors (secured and unsecured) would be paid 90 pence in the £ on their current claims against Home Builders Ltd. The financial reliability of Octopus Ltd is undoubted.

The existing shareholders of Home Builders Ltd would be prepared to cooperate with proposal (3).

Assume that Western Bank earns 15% p.a. on all its lending, and that the amounts shown in the balance sheet include accrued interest to date.

Assume for convenience that any adopted proposal would be implemented immediately on 24 April 1984, with payments being received immediately, unless otherwise stated.

Ignore expenses of realisation and liquidation, and any interest charges or changes in the situation between 10 April and 24 April 1984.

Use the figures given throughout; do *not* add extra safety margins in your calculations.

Required:

(a) Calculations showing clearly the amounts Western Bank would receive under each of the three proposals.

(b) An examination of the relative financial merits of the proposals from the viewpoint of Western Bank.

30 marks

7 THORNTON LTD

The balance sheet of Thornton Ltd, as at 31 August 1979, is as follows:

Balance sheet

	£		£
Share capital (£1 shares)	40,000	Goodwill	12,000
Reserves	(550)	Freehold property	8,000
10% debenture, 1990	10,000	Equipment at cost less	
Bank overdraft	25,000	depreciation	24,000
Rates and taxes	9,000	Stock	46,100
Other creditors	31,350	Debtors	24,700
	114,800		114,800

The bank overdraft carries a fixed charge over the freehold property and the debenture is secured by a floating charge over the remaining assets of Thornton Ltd.

The company was formed some years ago. After a period of profitable activity, business has steadily declined and a loss was reported for each of the last three years. The present position of the company has been further aggravated by the fact that the market for certain product lines has completely collapsed. As a result the company is now in severe financial difficulty and a meeting of the creditors is called for 2 September 1979 to consider its affairs.

The following proposals are put forward for consideration:

(I) Immediate liquidation of the company

In these circumstances it is estimated that the assets would realise the following amounts:

	£
Freehold property	15,000
Equipment	9,000
Stock	19,200
Debtors	24,700

It is discovered that 'other creditors' includes £9,350 that would rank as preferential in a liquidation, as well as the amounts due for rates and taxes. The liquidation expenses are estimated at £8,550.

(II) Reorganisation and capital reconstruction

The management of Thornton Ltd have informed the creditors that a complete reorganisation is presently taking place and that the removal of unprofitable lines will reverse the present trend within a couple of months. Accordingly, the directors have prepared a scheme of capital reconstruction for consideration. The plan is to revalue tangible assets at their liquidation values, and to write off goodwill and the debit balance on reserves. The shareholders would be asked to accept shares with a nominal value of 1p each in a 'one for one' exchange for shares presently held. After the exchange has taken place the shares will be consolidated into £1 shares. The bank and the non-preferential other creditors would be asked to reduce their claims to 95% and 70% of their present balances respectively. The non-preferential other creditors would obtain repayment of this revised amount in three months' time, and the bank would receive its repayment in 12 months' time. The shareholders have indicated their willingness to take up a further 20,000 £1 shares at par, to finance working capital requirements, if this proposal is adopted.

Required:

(a) A calculation of the amounts which would be received by each of the providers of finance under proposal (I), assuming the information proves accurate. You should show clearly the order of priority for repayment.

(b) The revised balance sheet of Thornton Ltd at 2 September 1979 under proposal (II).

(c) A consideration of the relative merits of the two proposals from the respective viewpoints of the bank, of the non-preferential other creditors, and of the shareholders.

Note:

The current interest rate on all forms of borrowing is 10%. The £25,000 overdraft includes interest to date.

You may assume that no changes have occurred since the balance sheet date and the selected proposal will be implemented immediately.

30 marks

ANSWERS

1 EASTGATE LTD

(a) Cash to be received by providers of finance (majority view re value of freeholds):

		£	
Sale of assets:			
Freehold property		60,000	
Plant and machinery		10,000	
Stocks		47,000	
Debtors		160,000	
Quoted investments		16,000	
Available		293,000	

Less: Priority repayments:			Outstanding £
(i) Secured creditors, with fixed charge – the bank	60,000		8,000
		233,000	
(ii) Liquidation expenses	6,000		
		227,000	
(iii) Preferential creditors	57,000		
		170,000	
(iv) Secured creditors, floating charge:			
12% debenture	50,000		
Available for unsecured creditors		120,000	

(v) Unsecured creditors: bank £8,000; others £152,000

Dividend:

Bank: (8/160) × £120,000 = £6,000

Others: (152/160) × £120,000 = £114,000

Debenture holders paid in full, £50,000.

Bank receives £66,000.

Unsecured creditors receive £114,000.

Shareholders do not receive any payment.

(b) Freeholds valued in accordance with minority views:

		£
Sale of assets (£293,000 + £90,000):		
Cash available		383,000
Less:		
(i) Fixed charge — bank	68,000	
(ii) Liquidation expenses	6,000	
(iii) Preferential creditors	57,000	
(iv) Floating charge:		
Debentures	50,000	
(v) Unsecured creditors	152,000	
		(333,000)
		50,000

(vi) Ordinary shares in issue: 100,000

Dividend: 50p in £1

Jeremiah's shares are now worth £3,000.

2 ALLERTON LTD

(a) Cash to be received by the bank under the following proposals:

(I) Piecemeal liquidation of the company

Sale of assets:	£000
Freehold building	70
Plant and equipment	20
Stocks	290
Debtors	250
Available	630

Priority repayments:			Outstanding £000
(i) Secured creditors, fixed charge — the bank	70		125
(ii) Liquidation costs	10		
(iii) Preferential creditors	30		
(iv) Secured creditors, floating charge: Shipley	400	510	
Available for unsecured creditors		120	

(v) Unsecured creditors: bank £125,000; others £175,000

Dividend:

Bank: (125/300) × £120,000 = £50,000

Others: (175/300) × £120,000 = £70,000

Thus the bank receives £120,000 of its overdraft of £195,000.

(II) Sale of the company as a going concern

Cash to the bank:
£195,000 × (20/100) = £39,000 now, and
£195,000 × (75/100) = £146,250 after 1 year.

(b) Relative merits of each proposal for the bank

	I Liquidation £	II Sale to Shipley £
Now	120,000	39,000
One year later:		
Interest at 12%	14,400	4,680
Balance on sale to Shipley		146,250
Total after one year	134,400	189,930

The sale to Shipley seems to be much the best proposition for the bank to accept. There is always an element of risk as to 'future prospect money', but Shipley is a public limited company, which has passed Stock Exchange scrutiny, and whose accounts are available in some detail.

3 SHAFTSBURY LTD

(a) Bank's cash receipts under each of the three proposals:

(1) Immediate liquidation

Sale of assets:	£
Freehold property	65,000
Plant	21,000
Stock	40,000
Debtors	26,000
Available	152,000

Priority repayments:
                                                              Outstanding £

(i) Secured creditors; fixed charge:
    1st debenture-holders   50,000   Nil
    2nd Bank   15,000   30,000
(ii) Preferential creditors   27,000
                              92,000

Available for unsecured creditors   60,000

(iii) Unsecured creditors: bank £30,000; others £90,000

Dividend:

Bank: (30/120) × £60,000 = £15,000

East Bank, under this proposal, obtains £30,000, i.e., £15,000 + £15,000

(2) The offer from Cline Ltd

80% of £45,000 = £36,000 but after one year's time.

(3) Reconstruction of company

	New ordinary shares
Existing shareholders, 2 for 5	20,000
Bank's shares (for ½ of the overdraft)	10,000
	30,000
Add: Existing shareholders taking new shares for cash	30,000
	60,000

	£
Bank is now repaid half its overdraft	22,500
Add: Dividends* to come	4,500
	27,000

*Dividends:
Annual profit = £40,500
Annual dividend (2/3) = £27,000
Bank holds 1/6 of the equity: (1/6) × £27,000 = £4,500

(b) Financial merits of each proposal for the bank

Proposal	(1) £	(2) £	(3) £
Now	30,000	—	22,500
After one year:			
Interest at 15%	4,500		3,375
80% of balance from Cline Ltd		36,000	
Dividend			4,500
Total after one year	34,500	36,000	30,375

The final proposal, however, provides dividends of £4,500 annually. At 15% cost of capital, this amounts in perpetuity to £4,500/15% = £30,000. Its comparative value, at the end of year one, now becomes £60,375, so that it is easily the most valuable.

Proposal three is, however, the most risky — will the reconstructed company make the profits it states?

Proposal one is the least risky, but has the lowest return value.

4 LOWDOWN LTD

(a) Cash to be received by the bank and unsecured creditors

   (I) **Immediate liquidation**

Sale of assets:	£
Leasehold property	20,000
Equipment	12,000
Stocks	18,000
Debtors	65,000
Cash	5,000
Available	120,000

Priority repayments:		Outstanding £
(i) Secured creditors, fixed charge – the bank	(20,000)	10,000
(ii) Liquidation expenses	(16,000)	
(iii) Preferential creditors	(12,000)	
(iv) Secured creditors, floating charge: Debenture	(32,000)	
Available for unsecured creditors	40,000	

   (v) Unsecured creditors: bank £10,000; others £90,000 (49 – 12 + 53)

   Dividend:

   Bank: (10/100) × £40,000 = £4,000

   Others: (90/100) × £40,000 = £36,000

   Unsecured creditors, who are non-preferential, receive £36,000. The bank receives £24,000 (i.e., £20,000 + £4,000).

   (II) **Takeover by Jackal Press**

   Bank receives 85% of £30,000 = £25,500 in one year.

   Unsecured creditors, non-preferential, receive 85% of (£37,000 + £53,000) = £76,500 in one year's time.

(b) Relative merits of each proposal

For the bank:	Now £	After one year £	Total after one year £
Proposal I	24,000 +	2,880 interest =	26,880
Proposal II	Nil	25,000	25,500

For unsecured
creditors:

	Now £	After one year £	Total after one year £
Proposal I	36,000 +	4,320 interest =	40,320
Proposal II	Nil	76,500	76,500

To put the company into liquidation seems best from the bank's point of view.

The proposal to allow Jackal Press to take over Lowdown would seem much the best for the unsecured creditors. Banks always avoid 'bad publicity' and would probably not force immediate liquidation, which would create very bad feelings in the locality.

5 FASTFOODS LTD

(a) Cash received by Catercorp Ltd if Fastfoods liquidated:

		£	
Sale of assets:			
Freehold property		14,000	
Equipment		51,000	
Stocks		10,000	
Available		75,000	
			Outstanding £
Less: Priority repayments:			
(i) Secured creditors with fixed charge — the bank		14,000	3,000
		61,000	
(ii) Preferential creditors		11,000	
		50,000	
(iii) Secured creditors with floating charge: Catercorp's debenture		12,000	
Available for general unsecured creditors		38,000	

(iv) Unsecured creditors: bank £3,000; Catercorp £60,000; others £32,000

Dividend:

Bank: (3/95) × £38,000 = £1,200

Catercorp: (60/95) × £38,000 = £24,000

Others: (32/95) × £38,000 = £12,800

Catercorp, originally owed £72,000, receives £36,000 only, and the bank, owed £17,000, receives £15,200, i.e., £14,000 + £1,200.

(b) Numerical comparison of the two options

	New shares
Reconstruction of Fastfoods	
£12,000 10% debenture stock	12,000
£60,000 trade debt to Catercorp × 55%	33,000
£30,000 cash injection by Catercorp	30,000
	75,000
25,000 original shares @ one for five	5,000
	80,000

Expected annual profits = £12,000.

Dividend to Catercorp: (75/80) × £12,000 = £11,250 p.a.

Under proposal one, Catercorp receives £36,000 and does not have to spend £30,000 on new shares mentioned above; this is effectively £66,000 to invest at 15%, i.e., £9,900 p.a. This is less than the benefits of proposal two.

(c) Calculation of the minimum annual net profit under the reconstruction for Catercorp to obtain the same results as under the liquidation: under the reconstruction, Catercorp owns 75/80 of Fastfoods shares. Therefore the £9,900 income under the liquidation must equal 75/80 of total profit. Therefore total minimum profit under the reconstruction must be £9,900 × (80/75) = £10,560.

(d) Under the liquidation the bank receives £15,200, forgoing £1,800. It must carefully consider the standing of Catercorp, together with its trading proposals, and, if all seemed well, it would probably support the reconstruction, in an attempt to recover its £17,000 together with interest and charges.

6 HOMEBUILDERS LTD

(a) Cash to be received by Western Bank:

(1) Immediate liquidation

Sale of assets:	£
Equipment	5,000
Work in progress, site A	60,000
Work in progress, site B	30,000
Other stocks	20,000
Debtors	15,000
Available	130,000

Less: Priority repayments: Outstanding
                                                                        £
(i) Secured creditors with fixed charges:
     Propinvest on site A   £60,000   11,000
     Western Bank on site B   £30,000   90,000   10,000
                                                 ──────
                                                 40,000
(ii) Preferential creditors:
     Tax due   8,000
     Bank's wage claim   2,000   10,000   4,000
                                                 ──────
Available for general unsecured creditors   30,000
                                                 ──────

(iii) Unsecured creditors: bank £14,000; Propinvest £11,000; others £35,000

Dividend:

Bank: (14/60) × £30,000 = £7,000

Bank, originally owed £46,000, receives £39,000, i.e., £30,000 + £2,000 + £7,000.

(2) Local government authority offer
                                                    £
Sale of assets as before   130,000
Add: Extra fund for: Site A   4,000
                     Site B   6,000
                                                 ──────
Available   140,000

Priority repayments: Outstanding
                                                                        £
(i) Secured creditors with fixed charges:
     Propinvest on site A   (64,000)   7,000
     Western Bank on site B   (36,000)   4,000
(ii) Preferential creditors as before   (10,000)
                                                 ──────
Available for unsecured creditors   30,000
                                                 ──────

(iii) Unsecured creditors: bank £8,000; Propinvest £7,000; others £35,000

Dividend:

Bank: (8/50) × £30,000 = £4,800

Thus the bank would receive £42,800 (£36,000 + £2,000 + £4,800) although the site money would not be received for one year.

(3) Takeover by Octopus

	£
Preferential creditor, paid in full	2,000
Secured and non-secured: 90% in one year's time:	
Loan £40,000	
Non-preferential overdraft £ 4,000 44,000 × 90% =	39,600
	41,600

(b) Relative merits of each proposal

Proposal	(1) £	(2) £	(3) £
Now	39,000	6,800	2,000
After one year:			
Interest at 15%	5,850	1,020	300
Payment from LGA		36,000	
Payments from Octopus			39,600
Total after one year	44,850	43,820	41,900

Undoubtedly from the bank's point of view immediate liquidation seems preferable. The unsecured creditors' position would also have to be calculated. If they benefited greatly by either of the other propositions, the bank might fall into line with them, so as to avoid bad publicity (often locally) of being 'the bank responsible for forcing the liquidation'.

7 THORNTON LTD

(a) Sums to be received by the providers of finance with immediate liquidation

Sale of assets:	£	
Freehold property	15,000	
Equipment	9,000	
Stock	19,200	
Debtors	24,700	
Available	67,900	

Priority repayments:		Outstanding £
(i) Secured creditors, fixed charge – bank	15,000	10,000
	52,900	
(ii) Liquidation expenses	8,550	
	44,350	
(iii) Preferential expenses: £9,350 + £9,000	18,350	
	26,000	
(iv) Secured creditors, floating charge: Debenture	10,000	
Available for general unsecured creditors	16,000	

(v) Unsecured creditors: bank £10,000; others £22,000

Dividend:

Bank: (10/32) × £16,000 = £5,000

Others: (22/32) × £16,000 = £11,000

While the debenture-holders and preferential creditors are repaid in full, the bank only receives £20,000 of its £25,000 debt. The other unsecured creditors receive £11,000 of their claim for £22,000. The ordinary shareholders receive nothing.

(b) Reconstructed balance sheet of Thornton Ltd as at 2.9.79

	£		£
Share capital (W3)	20,400	Freehold property	15,000
10% debentures	10,000	Equipment	9,000
Rates and taxes	9,000	Stock	19,200
Other creditors (W2)	24,750	Debtors	24,700
Overdraft (W1)	23,750	Cash from shares (W3)	20,000
	87,900		87,900

Workings

1   95% × £25,000 = £23,750

2   Other creditors (£31,350) less preferential (£9,350) =   £22,000

	£
Reduced to 70%	15,400
Add back preferential	9,350
	24,750

3   40,000 × 1p shares = £400 share capital, then consolidated into 400 × £1 shares. Extra £20,000 shares are issued for cash.

(c) Relative merits from the point of view of:

(i) The bank: immediate liquidation gives £20,000, plus interest at 10%, giving a total of £22,000 in one year's time, as opposed to £23,750 in one year under the reconstruction. The latter, although a larger payment, is more risky.

(ii) Non-preferential other creditors: they will receive £15,400 in three months' time under the reconstruction, which contrasts with £11,275 if immediate liquidation takes place, i.e., £11,000 + 10% interest for three months, which will, for them, probably outweigh the extra risk.

(iii) Shareholders: they receive nothing under the liquidation and may well be encouraged to inject the extra £20,000 if they feel that potential future profits will provide an adequate return.

9 Reorganisation of capital

INTRODUCTION

Specific questions on this topic are rare though the substance of the chapter is important because it is concerned with the rights of investors to income and capital repayment. The circumstances in which capital reorganisation is being considered are often similar to those of liquidations, for which it is often a better alternative.

Reduction of capital

Section 66 of the Companies Act 1948 allows a company to reduce its share capital in any manner it considers appropriate, including 'reduction of share capital which has been lost' (e.g., a debit balance on profit and loss account), or 'not represented by available assets', providing the reduction is authorised (by the articles of association), approved (by a special resolution), and sanctioned (confirmation by court). Remember that a scheme for the reduction of capital comprises two elements:

(a) The amount by which the various classes of capital are to be reduced;

(b) The amount by which the various assets including fictitious assets are to be reduced.

Redemption of capital

Students must be aware of the provisions of the 1981 Companies Act which extend to ordinary share capital what had previously only been available for preference share capital. Provided a company still has share capital which is not redeemable, it may issue redeemable ordinary share capital as well as redeemable preference share capital.

Remember that when share capital is redeemed out of profits, an amount equal to the nominal value of the shares so redeemed must be transferred from distributable profits to a capital redemption reserve. This means that the redeemed capital is replaced either by a new share issue for cash, or by the capitalisation of profits which would otherwise be distributable.

The capital redemption reserve is very much like issued share capital since it cannot be used for any other purpose than conversion into share capital (by a bonus issue) or as part provision of the amount required to effect a reduction of capital.

Reconstruction of capital

This is the general expression for the restructuring of a company's capital (often including loan capital as well as share capital), necessary to maintain the company as a going concern, rather than putting it into liquidation (see chapter 8). Any scheme, to be acceptable, must provide better terms for all interested parties than liquidation would.

The circumstances leading to liquidation and reconstruction are the same, i.e., the inability to pay liabilities as they become due because of past losses, or over-distributions. In order that the company may continue, further capital is required or at least some relief from debt payments, and therefore, reconstruction should not be considered until the worst of a company's troubles are over and profitable trading can be anticipated.

SUGGESTED METHOD FOR ANSWERING THE QUESTIONS

Since capital structure is concerned with the relative rights and expectations of investors to income and capital repayment, these questions must be tackled by comparing the present structure with the proposed structure, in terms of the above rights.

QUESTIONS

1 FORM LTD

Form Ltd made substantial losses in the early years of its existence, but has recently returned to profitability. The company's balance sheet at 31 August 1979 showed:

	£000		£000
Ordinary shares of £1	150	Net assets	215
7% preference shares of £1	50	Profit and loss account	25
6% debentures	40		
	240		240

The company is considering a scheme of reconstruction under the Companies Acts, along the following lines:

(a) The reconstructed company will be named Reform Ltd.

(b) It is expected that Reform Ltd will pay a total annual dividend of £10,000 on its ordinary shares, after meeting interest payments considered below.

(c) In exchange for every 100 7% preference shares in Form Ltd:

   (i) there will be issued £20 of 5% debenture stock in Reform Ltd *and* a number of £1 ordinary shares in Reform Ltd;

   (ii) the number of ordinary shares will be so determined that the expected annual income (debenture interest and ordinary share dividends) receivable by former preference shareholders will be the same as that due annually from their preference shares in Form Ltd.

(d) In exchange for every £100 6% debenture in Form Ltd:

   (i) there will be issued £80 of 5% debenture stock in Reform Ltd *and* a number of £1 ordinary shares in Reform Ltd;

   (ii) The number of ordinary shares will be so determined that the expected annual income (debenture interest and ordinary share dividends) receivable by former 6% debenture-holders will be equivalent to 7% p.a. on their former debenture holdings in Form Ltd.

(e) The issued ordinary share capital of Reform Ltd will consist of 125,000 £1 shares. After the issues of ordinary shares indicated above, the balance of the 125,000 shares will be issued on a *pro rata* basis in exchange for the ordinary shares of Form Ltd.

Ignore taxation, and any arrears or accruals of dividends or interest.

Required:

A table completed in the manner shown below, indicating the holdings of ordinary shares and debenture stock in Reform Ltd if the proposed reconstruction is adopted.

Holdings in Reform Ltd

	£1 ordinary shares	5% debenture stock
Form Ltd: Ordinary shareholders		
Preference shareholders		
Debenture holders		

20 marks

2 HAMMER LTD

Hammer Ltd has been in financial difficulties, and a scheme of reconstruction under the Companies Acts is being considered.

At present the company has the following share and loan capital:

	£
Ordinary shares of £1	250,000
8% preference shares of £1	60,000
12% debenture stock	200,000

Under the proposed scheme of reconstruction a new company, Hammer (1979) Ltd, would be formed. It is expected that Hammer (1979) Ltd would pay a total annual dividend of £15,000 after meeting interest on debenture stock considered below.

Hammer (1979) Ltd would take over all assets and liabilities of Hammer Ltd and would issue new 50 pence ordinary shares and new 15% debenture stock as follows:

(a) In exchange for every 10 preference shares in Hammer Ltd there will be issued £3 of 15% debenture stock *plus* a number of 50 pence ordinary shares in Hammer (1979) Ltd.

The number of 50 pence ordinary shares will be so determined that the expected annual income (debenture interest and ordinary share dividends) receivable by former preference shareholders will be the same as that due annually from the preference shares of Hammer Ltd.

(b) In exchange for every £100 12% debenture stock in Hammer Ltd there will be issued £40 of 15% debenture stock plus a number of 50 pence ordinary shares in Hammer (1979) Ltd.

The number of 50 pence ordinary shares will be so determined that the expected annual income (debenture interest and ordinary share dividends) receivable by former 12% debenture shareholders will be the same as that due annually from the debenture stock of Hammer Ltd.

(c) The issued share capital of Hammer (1979) Ltd will consist of 300,000 ordinary shares of 50 pence each. After the issues of ordinary shares mentioned above, the balance of the 300,000 shares will be issued on a *pro rata* basis in exchange for the ordinary shares of Hammer Ltd.

Required:

A table completed in the manner shown below, indicating the holdings of ordinary shares and debenture stock in Hammer (1979) Ltd if the proposed reconstruction is adopted.

	Holdings in Hammer (1979) Ltd	
Former security holders in Hammer Ltd:	15% debenture stock	Number of 50 pence ordinary shares
Preference shareholders		
Debenture stockholders		
Ordinary shareholders		

Note: Ignore taxation and any arrears or accrual of dividends or interest.

20 marks

3 MORTICE LTD AND TENON LTD

Summarised balance sheets of Mortice Ltd and Tenon Ltd at 21 April 1981 were:

	Mortice Ltd £	Tenon Ltd £
Issued share capital (£1 ordinary shares)	20,000	40,000
Profit and loss account	48,000	32,000
Current liabilities	22,000	18,000
	90,000	90,000
Property and equipment (at cost less depreciation)	50,000	57,000
Current assets	40,000	33,000
	90,000	90,000

On 22 April 1981, the two companies are to be amalgamated to form a new company, Joint Ltd, which will take over all assets and liabilities of Mortice Ltd and Tenon Ltd at that date.

Shares and debenture stock will be issued by Joint Ltd, as consideration, on the basis shown below:

(a) To shareholders in Mortice Ltd:

  (i) three £1 ordinary shares in Joint Ltd for each share held in Mortice Ltd; and

  (ii) £75 of 10% debenture stock for every 100 shares held in Mortice Ltd.

(b) To shareholders in Tenon Ltd:

  (i) three £1 ordinary shares in Joint Ltd for every two shares held in Tenon Ltd; and

  (ii) £100 of 10% debenture stock for every 100 shares held in Tenon Ltd.

Property and equipment, current assets and current liabilities acquired by Joint Ltd will be recorded in that company's books at the values at which they appear in the balance sheets of Mortice Ltd and Tenon Ltd.

Shareholders have made the following criticisms of the proposed scheme for amalgamation:

(a) Mortice's profit and loss account balance indicates that it will contribute three-fifths of the profits of the amalgamated company; therefore Mortice's shareholders should receive three-fifths of the capital to be issued by Joint.

(b) Tenon has twice as many issued shares as Mortice; therefore Tenon's shareholders should receive two-thirds of the capital to be issued by Joint.

(c) Mortice and Tenon contribute capital plus reserves (profit and loss account) to the amalgamated company in the proportion 68:72; therefore capital of Joint should be allocated to the shareholders of Mortice and Tenon in that proportion.

Required:

(a) Balance sheet of Joint Ltd at 22 April 1981 after the proposed amalgamation has taken place.

(b) Your views (with *brief* reasons) on whether you agree or disagree with each of the three criticisms made by shareholders.

20 marks

ANSWERS

1 FORM LTD

Holdings in Reform Ltd

	£1 ordinary shares	5% debenture stock
Form Ltd:		
Ordinary shareholders (W3)	72,500	–
Preference shareholders (W1)	37,500	£10,000
Debenture-holders (W2)	15,000	£32,000

Workings

1. Preference shareholders

    Present income: £50,000 × 7% = £3,500
    Debenture stock: (£50,000/100) × 20 = £10,000
    Income: £10,000 × 5% = £500
    Therefore balance from ordinary shares = £3,500 – £500 = £3,000
    Therefore number of ordinary shares = 3,000/0.08* = 37,500

2. Debenture-holders

    Intended income from Reform Ltd: £40,000 × 7% = £2,800
    Debenture stock: (£40,000/100) × 80 = £32,000
    Income: £32,000 × 5% = £1,600
    Therefore balance from ordinary shares = £2,800 – £1,600 = £1,200
    Therefore number of ordinary shares = 1,200/0.08* = 15,000

3. Ordinary shareholders

    Therefore balance of the £125,000 shares =
       125,000 – 37,500 – 15,000 = 72,500

*Dividend payable on ordinary shares: 10,000/125,000 = 8%

Tutorial note

The method of working to be followed is:

(a) Establish the income by reference to question.

(b) Determine amount of debenture stock to be issued and the income it will produce.

(c) Calculate the number of shares required to make up the balance of income: (a) – (b).

(d) The remaining shares are issued to Form Ltd's ordinary shareholders.

2 HAMMER LTD

Holdings in Hammer (1979) Ltd

Former security holders in Hammer Ltd:	15% debenture stock	No. of 50p shares
Preference shareholders (W1)	£18,000	42,000
Debenture-holders (W2)	£80,000	240,000
Ordinary shareholders (W3)	–	18,000

Workings

1 Preference shareholders

Previous income: 8% × £60,000 = £4,800
Debenture stock issued: (£60,000/10) × 3 = £18,000
  Income: £18,000 × 15% = £2,700
Therefore balance from ordinary shares = £4,800 – £2,700 = £2,100
Therefore number of ordinary shares = £2,100/0.05* = 42,000

2 Debenture holders

Previous income: £200,000 × 12% = £24,000
Debenture stock issued: (£200,000/100) × 40 = £80,000
  Income: £80,000 × 15% = £12,000
Therefore balance from ordinary shares = £24,000 – £12,000 = £12,000
Therefore number of ordinary shares = £12,000/0.05* = 240,000

3 Ordinary shareholders

Therefore the remaining shares are issued to the ordinary shareholders, i.e.
  300,000 – 42,000 – 240,000 = 18,000

*Future ordinary dividend = £15,000/300,000 = 5p per share (or 5%).

3 MORTICE LTD AND TENON LTD

(a) Balance sheet of Joint Ltd at 22 April 1981

		£
Goodwill (W2)		35,000
Property and equipment (50 + 57)		107,000
Current assets (40 + 33)	73,000	
Less: Current liabilities (22 + 18)	40,000	33,000
		175,000
10% debenture stock (W1)		55,000
		120,000
Issued share capital (W1)		120,000

(b) (i) An apportionment of shares on the basis of profitability is reasonable. However, the balances on the profit and loss accounts are balances of retained profits and do not, necessarily, reflect profitability now. Such balances cannot be considered appropriate.

(ii) The relative value of share capital provides a reasonable basis for apportionment. However, since the proportion stated relates to nominal share values, which differs considerably from real value, it cannot be considered appropriate.

(iii) An apportionment on the basis of 68:72 could be considered reasonable, on the grounds that the proportion does represent relative values. It suffers, however, from being based on book values which depend on accounting policies, which may not be the same for both companies.

None of the three statements allows for the fact that the purchase consideration is not being satisfied by share capital alone, but also by an issue of debentures.

Workings

1

	Shares £	Debentures £	Total £
To shareholders of Mortice Ltd:			
£20,000 × 3	60,000 (0.75)		
(£20,000/100) × 75		15,000	75,000
Tenon Ltd:			
£40,000/2 × 3	60,000 (1.00)		
(£40,000/100) × 100		40,000	100,000
	120,000	55,000	175,000

2 Goodwill

	£
Purchase consideration: Shares	120,000
Debentures	55,000
	175,000
Net value of assets	140,000
Goodwill	35,000

10 Group accounts

INTRODUCTION

The importance of this chapter is evidenced by the frequency of questions on this topic. Since the majority of companies have grown by acquisition and merger, the parent company's own balance sheet is inadequate to present the financial affairs of the group.

It is of particular importance that bankers understand the nature of a consolidated balance sheet because of their concern with the relationship between asset values and the equity in those assets, particularly where minority interests are significant. In this situation the consolidated balance sheet overstates the assets in relation to the parent company's equity interest in those assets.

This chapter requires knowledge of consolidated accounts, the Companies Act 1948, and SSAP 14.

A holding or parent company is required to produce a consolidated balance sheet as well as its own balance sheet. The two are the same in that they purport to state the assets and finance of the holding company, i.e., a legal entity with share capital. They differ in that the company's own balance sheet contains the item 'investment in subsidiary', whereas the consolidated balance sheet shows the net assets of the subsidiary representing that 'investment'.

A subsidiary is a company whose assets are controlled by the holding company. A consolidated balance sheet, therefore, includes *all* the assets and liabilities of the holding company and its subsidiaries. If the holding company does not own (or control) all of the subsidiary's shares, then it has not financed all of the net assets; the remainder must have been financed by the minority shareholders, whose interest appears in the consolidated balance sheet as external capital. It is important to note that this is not a liability but capital of the group which does not belong to the shareholders of the holding company.

A suitable procedure to follow to consolidate accounts is as follows:

(a)   Cancel internal indebtedness.

(b)   Eliminate unrealised profit from asset valuation and profit and loss account.

(c) Add assets and liabilities. Enter on balance sheet.

Associated companies – equity accounting: SSAP 1

The modern 'group' may include associated companies, i.e., companies in which the investing company has less than a controlling interest but one which ensures significant influence; the shareholding must be at least 20%.

Effect on the consolidated profit and loss account

The consolidated profit and loss account should include the following, whether or not they have been distributed as dividend:

(i) share of profits;
(ii) share of tax;
(iii) share of extraordinary items.

Effect on the consolidated balance sheet

Because the assets and liabilities of the associated company are not consolidated, the asset 'investment in associated company' will appear on the consolidated balance sheet, as follows:

	£
Share of net assets, excluding goodwill	XXX,XXX
Share of goodwill	XX,XXX
Premium/Discount paid on acquisition	XX,XXX
	XXX,XXX

Thus the consolidated reserves and the investment in the associated company may include a share of the associated company's post-acquisition profit.

This method of accounting is known as the equity method, since the balance sheet includes an investment representing a share of the net assets of the associated company and the profit and loss account includes a share of the profits for the year.

(d) Enter holding company's share capital on balance sheet.

(e) Apportion subsidiary's capital and reserves* into three elements:

(i) minority interest for balance sheet;
(ii) pre-acquisition, for comparison with cost of investment (stage f);
(iii) post-acquisition, for balance sheet (stage g).

(f) Deduct holding company's share of pre-acquisition capital and reserves, per e(ii), from investment cost to establish goodwill or capital reserve for balance sheet.

(g) Add holding company's share of subsidiary's *post-acquisition* reserves to its own reserves for the balance sheet.

*The apportionment of reserves may be illustrated as follows:

	Total reserves		
Goodwill calculation	Pre-acquisition profit	Minority interest	Balance sheet
Consolidated reserves	Post-acquisition profit		

SUGGESTED METHOD OF ANSWERING THE QUESTION

Method is of particular importance in preparing consolidated balance sheets since every item in the balance sheets of the individual companies has to appear on the consolidated balance sheet or in the workings. The substance of consolidation takes place in these three workings:

(a) Cost of control (goodwill, or exceptionally capital reserve).
(b) Minority interest.
(c) Post-acquisition profits.

Some questions require a pre-consolidation procedure for cancelling internal indebtedness, providing for unrealised profit and adjusting pre-acquisition dividends.

QUESTIONS

1 X LTD, Y LTD AND Z LTD

The following are the balance sheets of X Ltd, Y Ltd and Z Ltd as at 30.9.84:

	X Ltd £	Y Ltd £	Z Ltd £
Share capital	15,000	3,000	3,000
Reserves	6,000	4,000	(200)
10% debentures	6,500	–	1,000
Current liabilities	3,600	1,200	700
	31,100	8,200	4,500
Fixed assets	17,100	5,500	3,000
Investment, 1,800 shares in Y Ltd	4,000	–	–
Investment in Z Ltd	3,500	–	–
Current assets	6,500	2,700	1,500
	31,100	8,200	4,500

X Ltd, the holding company, acquired its shares in Y Ltd one year ago when Y Ltd's reserves stood at £1,600. X Ltd has only just bought its holding of 2,250 shares in Z Ltd.

Required:

The consolidated balance sheet of the group at 30.9.84, after the acquisition of Z Ltd.

20 marks

2 TREE, NUTMEG AND PEAR

The following are summarised balance sheets of Tree Ltd, Nutmeg Ltd and Pear Ltd at 31 December 1978:

	Tree Ltd £	Nutmeg Ltd £	Pear Ltd £
Issued share capital:			
£1 ordinary shares	180,000	35,000	50,000
£1 preference shares	–	–	10,000
Profit and loss account at 31 December 1976	93,200	24,300	13,400
Net profit (loss), 1977	20,400	(4,000)	5,400
Net profit (loss), 1978	15,800	(1,500)	6,700
Proposed preference dividend	–	–	700
Creditors	39,000	17,000	18,000
	348,400	70,800	104,200

	Tree Ltd £	Nutmeg Ltd £	Pear Ltd £
Fixed and current assets	245,600	70,800	104,200
35,000 ordinary shares in Nutmeg Ltd at cost	55,500	–	–
30,000 ordinary shares in Pear Ltd at cost	47,300	–	–
	348,400	70,800	104,200

Tree Ltd acquired:

(a) 35,000 ordinary shares in Nutmeg Ltd on 31 December 1976;
(b) 30,000 ordinary shares in Pear Ltd on 31 December 1977.

During 1978 Nutmeg Ltd sold goods to Tree Ltd for £3,600; these goods had cost Nutmeg Ltd £3,040. At 31 December 1978 one quarter of the goods remained in the stock of Tree Ltd and were included in current assets at the price paid by Tree Ltd.

The net profits of Pear Ltd for the years 1977 and 1978 are shown after deduction of £700 proposed preference dividend in each year. The dividend proposed in 1977 was paid in March 1978. No other dividends were paid or proposed by any of the companies in the relevant years.

Required:

The consolidated balance sheet of the group at 31 December 1978.

It is important that you submit your calculations of the items in the consolidated balance sheet.

Ignore taxation.

30 marks

3 ALE GROUP

The summarised balance sheets of Ale Ltd, Cakes Ltd, and Ginger Ltd at 31 December 1979 were:

	Ale Ltd £	Cakes Ltd £	Ginger Ltd £
Issued share capital (£1 ordinary shares)	150,000	60,000	50,000
Profit and loss account at 31 December 1977	43,000	18,000	22,800
Net profit (loss) 1978	4,400	(3,500)	7,200
Net profit (loss) 1979	4,100	(2,800)	10,600
6% debentures (redeemable 1981, secured by mortgage on freehold property)	–	50,000	–
Loan from Ale Ltd	–	30,000	20,000
Current liabilities	15,500	39,300	29,400
	217,000	191,000	140,000

	Ale Ltd £	Cakes Ltd £	Ginger Ltd £
Freehold property	13,000	65,000	43,000
Equipment (less depreciation)	10,000	54,000	47,000
Loan to Cakes Ltd	30,000	—	—
Loan to Ginger Ltd	25,000	—	—
36,000 shares in Cakes Ltd at cost	40,000	—	—
40,000 shares in Ginger Ltd at cost	75,000	—	—
Current assets	24,000	72,000	50,000
	217,000	191,000	140,000

Ale Ltd acquired:

(a) 36,000 shares in Cakes Ltd on 31 December 1977;
(b) 40,000 shares in Ginger Ltd on 31 December 1978.

On 31 December 1979 Ale Ltd increased its loan to Ginger Ltd; a cheque for £5,000 was despatched and entered in the books of Ale Ltd. The cheque was not received by Ginger Ltd until 2 January 1980, when it was recorded in the company's books.

Accrued debenture interest for 1979 has been included in the calculation of the net loss of Cakes Ltd for that year and in that company's current liabilities at 31 December 1979. Interest on the loan accounts was settled between the companies up to 31 December 1979.

No dividends were paid or proposed by any of the companies in the relevant years.

Required:

The consolidated balance sheet of the group at 31 December 1979.

It is important that you submit your calculations of the items in the consolidated balance sheet.

Note: Ignore taxation.

30 marks

4 DELTA GROUP

The following are summarised balance sheets of Delta Ltd, Easy Ltd and Fox Ltd at 30 June 1983:

	Delta Ltd £	Easy Ltd £	Fox Ltd £
Issued share capital (£1 shares)	150,000	50,000	30,000
Profit and loss account at 30 June 1982	41,200	27,000	15,300
Net profit, 1983	17,000	4,800	3,300
Current liabilities	69,300	30,200	22,400
	277,500	112,000	71,000
40,000 shares in Easy Ltd at cost	59,000	—	—
Sundry assets	218,500	112,000	71,000
	277,500	112,000	71,000

Delta Ltd acquired its shares in Easy Ltd on 30 June 1982.

On 30 June 1983, Delta Ltd acquired 20,000 shares in Fox Ltd at a price of £2 per share. The purchase price was entirely satisfied by the issue of 25,000 shares in Delta Ltd to former shareholders of Fox Ltd. The effect of the transaction has not yet been recorded in the relevant accounts.

No dividends were paid or proposed by any of the companies in the relevant years.

Required:

The consolidated balance sheet for the group at 30 June 1983, after the acquisition of Fox Ltd.

Note: Ignore taxation.

20 marks

5 NORTH GROUP

The following are the summarised balance sheets of North Ltd, South Ltd and West Ltd at 31.12.83:

	North £	South £	West £
Issued share capital	100,000	25,000	15,000
Profit and loss account at 31.12.81	44,000	7,000	6,000
Net profit (loss) 1982	16,500	2,400	(3,000)
Net profit (loss) 1983	18,000	3,600	(1,200)
6% debentures		5,000	
Current liabilities	11,500	4,000	2,600
	190,000	47,000	19,400
Fixed assets	115,000	27,000	14,000
25,000 ordinary shares in South at cost	39,000		
10,000 ordinary shares in West at cost		11,000	
£5,000, 6% debentures of South at cost	5,000		
Current assets	31,000	9,000	5,400
	190,000	47,000	19,400

North acquired its shares in South on 31 December 1981 and South its shares in West Ltd on 31 December 1982. The profit and loss account of South Ltd at 31 December 1981 had been debited with a proposed dividend of £2,500. The dividend was paid on 1 March 1982 and was included in the net profit of North Ltd for the year 1982. No other dividends have been paid or proposed by any of the companies in relevant years.

Required:

Prepare the consolidated balance sheet of the group at 31 December 1983.

Ignore taxation and interest on debentures.

30 marks

6 AIRE GROUP

The following are summarised balance sheets of Aire Ltd, Beal Ltd and Calder Ltd at 31 December 1979:

	Aire Ltd £	Beal Ltd £	Calder Ltd £
Issued share capital (£1 ordinary shares)	200,000	50,000	20,000
Profit and loss account at 31 December 1977	68,000	39,000	8,000
Net profit (loss) 1978	18,300	(3,200)	3,000
Net profit 1979	21,700	7,300	4,000
Current liabilities	72,000	16,900	5,000
	380,000	110,000	40,000
Fixed and current assets	310,000	86,200	40,000
40,000 ordinary shares in Beal Ltd at cost	70,000	–	–
15,000 ordinary shares in Calder Ltd at cost	–	23,800	–
	380,000	110,000	40,000

On 31 December 1977 Beal Ltd acquired its shares in Calder Ltd.

On 31 December 1978 Aire Ltd acquired its shares in Beal Ltd. No dividends were paid or proposed by any of the companies in the relevant years.

Required:

The consolidated balance sheet of the group at 31 December 1979.

It is important that you submit your calculations of the items in the consolidated balance sheet.

Ignore taxation.

30 marks

7 EXPANSION GROUP

The summarised balance sheets of Expansion Ltd, Flourish Ltd, and Growth Ltd at 31 December 1980 were:

	Expansion Ltd £	Flourish Ltd £	Growth Ltd £
Issued share capital (£1 ordinary shares)	120,000	200,000	300,000
Profit and loss account	63,000	13,000	59,000
Proposed final dividends	30,000	12,000	5,000
9% debentures	80,000	200,000	300,000
	293,000	425,000	664,000
200,000 shares in Flourish Ltd at cost	240,000	–	–
180,000 shares in Growth Ltd at cost	–	252,000	–
Sundry assets minus current liabilities	53,000	173,000	664,000
	293,000	425,000	664,000

Details of profits and dividends for 1979 and 1980 are shown below:

	Expansion Ltd £	Flourish Ltd £	Growth Ltd £
Profit and loss account 31.12.78	48,000	31,000	
Net profit 1979	23,000	18,000	(not relevant)
Less: Dividends for 1979:			
Interim paid July 1979:	–	(15,000)	
Final paid Feb. 1980	(15,000)	(5,000)	
Profit and loss account 31.12.79	56,000	29,000	83,000
Net profit 1980	37,000	34,000	21,000
Less: Dividends for 1980:			
Interim paid July 1980:	–	(38,000)	(40,000)
Final proposed	(30,000)	(12,000)	(5,000)
Profit and loss account 31.12.80	63,000	13,000	59,000

In the above statement, dividends have been credited to net profit of the relevant company when, and not before, the dividends were received.

All debenture interest has been appropriately deducted in the calculation of net profit and there were no share issues in the relevant years.

On 31 December 1978, Expansion Ltd acquired its shares in Flourish Ltd, and on 31 December 1979, Flourish Ltd acquired its shares in Growth Ltd. Both acquisitions were 'ex dividend', so that dividends declared prior to acquisition can be ignored.

Required:

(a) The consolidated balance sheet of the group at 31 December 1980.

It is important that you submit your calculations of all items in the consolidated balance sheet.

Ignore taxation.

(b) Brief comments on what you consider to be the advantages or disadvantages (to a user of the accounts) of the information which would be shown in the consolidated accounts, compared with accounts for Expansion Ltd alone.

30 marks

8 ABC GROUP

The summarised balance sheets of three companies at 30.9.84 are as follows:

	A £000	B £000	C £000
Ordinary share capital (£1)	100	50	200
Reserves 30.9.83	80	20	100
Profit for year ended 30.9.84	30	10	50
Liabilities	30	18	60
	240	98	410
Shares in B at cost	60		
Shares in C at cost	100		
Sundry assets	80	98	410
	240	98	410

A acquired 40,000 shares in B, and 60,000 shares in C on 1.10.83.

Required:

The consolidated balance sheet of A Ltd at 30.9.84.

20 marks

9 ANGLO LTD

Anglo Ltd is a well established private company which, over a number of years, built up a large balance of liquid resources surplus to operating requirements. The decision was taken, late in 1982, to use these resources to diversify the company's activities, and substantial shareholdings were subsequently acquired in Bangle Ltd and Carmen plc. The latter acquisition caused Anglo to arrange for a bank overdraft secured on its freehold property.

The following information is provided in respect of the three companies:

(a) **Summary of balances at 31 December 1983:**

	Anglo £000	Bangle £000	Carmen £000
Assets:			
Goodwill at cost	–	–	104
Freehold property at cost less depreciation	200	180	700
Plant and equipment at cost less depreciation	756	107	1,113
Investments: Bangle Ltd (180,000 shares)	440	–	–
Carmen plc (500,000 shares)	760	–	–
Current assets	521	351	976
	2,677	638	2,893
Share capital, reserves and liabilities:			
Issued share capital (£1 ordinary shares)	1,000	200	2,000
Retained profit at 1 January 1983	950	210	128
Net profit for 1983	247	90	236
Bank overdraft	374	–	–
Other current liabilities	106	138	529
	2,677	638	2,893

(b) The shares in Carmen were purchased on 1 January 1983 and in Bangle on 31 December 1983.

(c) Following the share acquisition, directors were appointed to the boards of both Bangle and Carmen to take an active part in their financial and operating decisions.

(d) The freehold property of Bangle possessed a fair value of £300,000 on 31 December; there were no other significant differences between the fair values and book values of the assets of Bangle and Carmen at the acquisition dates.

(e) Anglo's freehold property was recently valued at £230,000. This valuation is *not* to be written into the books.

Required:

A consolidated balance sheet of the group at 31 December 1983, not necessarily in a form for publication but complying, so far as the information permits, with the requirements of SSAPs 1 and 14.

30 marks

ANSWERS

1 X LTD, Y LTD AND Z LTD

Consolidated balance sheet of X Ltd and its subsidiaries Y Ltd and Z Ltd as at 30.9.84

	£
Issued share capital	15,000
Group reserves (W3)	7,440
Shareholders' funds	22,440
Minority interest (W2)	3,500
10% debentures	7,500
Current liabilities (£3,600 + £1,200 + £700)	5,500
	38,940
Fixed assets (£17,100 + £5,500 + £3,000)	25,600
Goodwill (W1)	2,640
Current assets (£6,500 + £2,700 + £1,500)	10,700
	38,940

Workings

1 Cost of control

		Y Ltd		Z Ltd
	£	£	£	£
Cost		4,000		3,500
Less: Shares	1,800		2,250	
Reserves:				
(18/30) × £1,600	960			
(225/300) × £200 (loss)			(150)	
		2,760		2,100
		1,240		1,400

Therefore goodwill = £1,240 + £1,400 = £2,640

2 Minority interest

		£
Y Ltd: (12/30) × (£4,000 + £3,000)	=	2,800
Z Ltd: (75/300) × (£3,000 − £200)	=	700
		3,500

3   Group reserves

	£
X Ltd	6,000
Y Ltd: (18/30) × (£4,000 − £1,600)	1,440
Z Ltd	Nil
	7,440

Notes

(a) Since the cost of the investments in subsidiaries exceeded the share of net assets (i.e., capital and reserves) acquired, the difference appears as 'goodwill' on the consolidated balance sheet.

(b) The minority interest is the minority shareholders' share of the net assets (capital + reserves) at *balance sheet date*.

(c) Although X owns 18/30 of Y's capital and reserves, only the *post-acquisition share* can appear in the reserves. Y's profit since the date of acquisition has been £2,400 of which £1,440 is attributable to X Ltd. Since X has only just acquired its share in Z, none of the loss is a post-acquisition loss.

2   TREE, NUTMEG AND PEAR

Tree group: consolidated balance sheet as at 31.12.78

	£
Issued share capital	180,000
Group reserves (W3)	127,780
Shareholders' funds	307,780
Minority interest (W2)	40,200
Creditors (£39,000 + £17,000 + £18,000)	74,000
Proposed minority dividend	700
	422,680
Fixed assets and current assets	
(£245,600 + £70,800 + £104,200 − £140)	420,460
Goodwill (W1)	2,220
	422,680

Workings

1   Goodwill

	Nutmeg £	Pear £
Cost of control	55,500	47,300
Less: Shares bought	(35,000)	(30,000)
Reserves bought:		
at 31.12.76 (35/35) × £24,300	(24,300)	
at 31.12.77 (30/50) × £18,800		(11,280)
	(3,800)	6,020

Therefore goodwill = £6,020 − £3,800 = £2,220

2   Minority interest

	£
Nutmeg: wholly owned	Nil
Pear: (20/50) × £75,500 net assets	30,200
Add: Preference shares	10,000
	40,200

3   Group reserves

	£
Tree	129,400
Nutmeg, since 31.12.76: (35/35) × (£5,500)	(5,500)
Pear, since 31.12.77: (30/50) × £6,700	4,020
	127,920
Less: Unrealised profit on inter-company stocks*	
(£3,600 − £3,040) × ¼	140
	127,780

*Also deducted from group current assets, i.e., reduction in the closing stock value of Tree Ltd.

3 ALE GROUP

Consolidated balance sheet as at 31.12.79

	£
Issued share capital	150,000
Group reserves (W3)	56,200
Shareholders' funds	206,200
Minority interest (W2)	46,800
6% debentures	50,000
Current liabilities (£15,500 + £39,300 + £29,400)	84,200
	387,200
Freehold property (£13,000 + £65,000 + £43,000)	121,000
Equipment (£10,000 + £54,000 + £47,000)	111,000
	232,000
Goodwill (W1)	4,200
Current assets (W4)	151,000
	387,200

Workings

1   Cost of control

	£	Cake £	£	Ginger £
Cost of shares		40,000		75,000
Less: Shares bought	36,000		40,000	
Reserves bought				
at 31.12.77				
(36/60) × £18,000	10,800			
at 31.12.78				
(40/50) × £30,000			24,000	
		46,800		64,000
		(6,800)		11,000

Therefore goodwill = £11,000 − £6,800 = £4,200

2   Minority interest

	£
Cake Ltd: 40% × £71,700	28,680
Ginger Ltd: 20% × £90,600	18,120
	46,800

3   Reserves

	£
Ale Ltd at 31.12.79, £(43,000 + 4,400 + 4,100)	51,500
Cake Ltd post 31.12.77, 60% × loss £(3,500 + 2,800)	(3,780)
Ginger Ltd post 31.12.78, 80% × £10,600	8,480
	56,200

4   Ginger's balance sheet adjusted

	£		£
Current assets in balance sheet	50,000	Loan from Ale	20,000
Cash in transit	5,000	Cash in transit	5,000
Current assets for consolidation	55,000	To be cancelled against loan from Ale	25,000

Therefore current assets = £24,000 + £72,000 + £55,000 = £151,000 for the group

Tutorial notes

(a)   No adjustment is required in respect of interest, which has been fully recorded.

(b)   Make any adjustments that are necessary in the books of Ale Ltd.

(c)   The minority interest is the appropriate proportion of the capital and reserves at balance sheet date.

4   DELTA GROUP

Consolidated balance sheet as at 30.6.83

	£	£
Issued share capital (W1)		175,000
Share premium (W1)	15,000	
Profit and loss account (W4)	62,040	
		77,040
Shareholders' funds		252,040
Minority interests (W3)		32,560
Current liabilities (£69,300 + £30,200 + £22,400)		121,900
		406,500
Sundry assets (£218,500 + £112,000 + £71,000)		401,500
Goodwill (W2)		5,000
		406,500

Workings

1. Share capital: £150,000 + £25,000 = £175,000

   Cost of shares in Fox Ltd = £40,000

   Therefore share premium = £40,000 − £25,000 = £15,000

2. Goodwill

	Easy £	Fox £
Cost of control	59,000	40,000
Less: Shares bought	(40,000)	(20,000)
Reserves bought:		
at 30.6.82 (4/5) × £27,000	(21,600)	
at 30.6.83 (2/3) × £18,600		(12,400)
	(2,600)	7,600

   Therefore goodwill = £7,600 − £2,600 = £5,000

3. Minority interest

	£
Easy: (1/5) × £81,800 net assets	16,360
Fix: (1/3) × £48,600 net assets	16,200
	32,560

4. Profit and loss account: distributable reserve

	£
Delta Ltd: £41,200 + £17,000	58,200
Easy Ltd: 4/5 × £4,800	3,840
	62,040

Tutorial notes

(a) Delta Ltd issued 25,000 shares worth £40,000, to buy control of Fox. Only the nominal value can be credited to the share capital account. The balance is a share premium.

(b) No part of Fox Ltd's profit can appear in the group's reserves, since only *post-acquisition* profits are available for distribution, and Delta Ltd did not acquire its interest in Fox Ltd until 30.6.83 (the consolidation date).

5 NORTH GROUP

Consolidated balance sheet at 31.12.83

	£	£
Fixed assets		156,000
Goodwill arising on consolidation (W1)		3,500
Current assets	45,400	
Less: Current liabilities	18,100	27,300
		186,800
Issued share capital		100,000
Profit and loss account (W2)		81,200
		181,200
Minority interest (W3)		5,600
		186,800

Workings

1 Goodwill

	£	South £	£	West £
Cost of shares purchased		39,000		11,000
Less: Dividend received out of pre-acquisition profit*		2,500		
		36,500		
Less: Shares purchased (100%)	25,000			
Profit at 31.12.81	7,000	32,000		
Shares purchased			10,000	
Profit at 31.12.82, (10/15) × £(6,000 − 3,000)			2,000	12,000
		4,500		(1,000)

Therefore goodwill = £4,500 − £1,000 = £3,500

2 Profit and loss account

	£
North:* £78,500 − £2,500	76,000
South: £2,400 + £3,600	6,000
West: (10/15) × (£1,200) loss	(800)
	81,200

3   Minority interest

   West: (5/15) × £16,800 (i.e. capital and reserves) = £5,600

*Dividends received out of pre-acquisition profit must be removed from the profit and loss account and treated as a reduction of the cost of the investment, i.e. although North paid £39,000 it almost immediately received £2,500 back, reducing the cost to £36,500.

6 AIRE GROUP

Consolidated balance sheet as at 31.12.79

	£
Issued share capital	200,000
Group reserves (W3)	116,240
Shareholders' funds	316,240
Minority interest (W2)	28,420
Current liabilities	93,900
	438,560
Fixed and current assets	436,200
Goodwill (W1)	2,360
	438,560

Workings

1   Goodwill

	£	£	£	£
		Beal Ltd		Calder Ltd
Cost at 31.12.77				23,800
Less: Shares purchased		15,000		
Reserves: (15/20) × £8,000		6,000		21,000
Cost at 31.12.78		70,000		
Less: Shares purchased	40,000			
Reserves Beal £35,800				
Add: *(15/20) × £3,000 2,250				
(40/50) ×	38,050	30,440	70,440	
		(440)		2,800

Therefore goodwill = £2,800 − £440 = £2,360

2   Minority interest

		£	£
Calder Ltd: (5/20) × £35,000 net assets			8,750
Beal Ltd:	Net assets	93,100	
	Add:* profit of Calder:		
	(15/20) × £7,000	5,250	
	(10/50) ×	98,350	19,670
			28,420

3   Group reserves

		£	£
Aire Ltd			108,000
Beal Ltd:	Beal's own profit	7,300	
	Add:* profit of Calder		
	(15/20) × £4,000	3,000	
	(40/50) ×	10,300	8,240
			116,240

*In these three workings a share of post-acquisition profit is being passed on to the next company up the chain; it is helpful to start the workings at the bottom of the chain.

7 EXPANSION GROUP

Consolidated balance sheet at 31.12.80

		£
Sundry net assets		890,000
Goodwill (W1)		31,200
		921,200

		£
Share capital		120,000
Profit and loss account (W2)		45,600
		165,600
Minority interest (W3)		143,600
9% debentures		580,000
Proposed dividends:	£	
Expansion Ltd	30,000	
Minority shareholders:		
40% × £5,000 (see note (c))	2,000	32,000
		921,200

Workings

1 Goodwill

		Flourish Ltd		Growth Ltd
	£	£	£	£
Cost of shares purchased		240,000		252,000
Less:				
Shares purchased	200,000			
Profits purchased, 31.12.78	31,000	231,000		
Shares purchased			180,000	
Profit purchased, 31.12.79				
(180/300) × £83,000			49,800	229,800
		9,000		22,200

Therefore goodwill = £9,000 + £22,200 = £31,200

2 Profit and loss accounts

	£	£
Expansion:	63,000	
Add: Dividend receivable from Flourish (Note (a))	12,000	75,000
Flourish: post-acquisition		
losses (note (b)) since 31.12.78		
(£13,000 − £31,000)	(18,000)	
Add: Dividend receivable from Growth	3,000	(15,000)
Growth: post-acquisition losses since 31.12.79,		
60% × (£59,000 − £83,000)		(14,400)
		45,600

3 Minority interest

Growth Ltd: (120/300) × (£300,000 + £59,000) = £143,600

Tutorial notes

(a) Since the proposed dividends had been appropriated from the subsidiaries' profit and loss accounts, the appropriate share has been brought into the accounts of their holding companies.

(b) The expression 'loss' has been used to indicate a reduction in the profit and loss account balance, e.g., at 31.12.79 it was £83,000 while at 31.12.80 it is only £59,000.

(c) Since a proposed dividend is a current liability, the £2,000 owing to the minority shareholders of Flourish Ltd, has been included under the heading proposed dividends, rather than in the minority interest.

8 ABC GROUP

Consolidated balance sheet as at 30.9.84

	£000
Sundry assets	178
Goodwill (W1)	4
Investment in C Ltd*	115
	297

Ordinary share capital	100
Reserves (W3)	133
Shareholders' funds	233
Minority interest (W2)	16
Liabilities	48
	297

*Investment in C Ltd at 30.9.84:

	£000
Share of net assets (W4)	105
Add: Premium paid on acquisition (W1)	10
	115

Workings

1

	Cost of control B £000	Premium on acquisition C £000
Cost	60	100
Less: Share of net assets, 1.10.83:		
$(40/50) \times (50 + 20)$	56	
$(60/200) \times (200 + 100)$		90
Goodwill	4	Premium 10

2   Minority interest in B (£000)

$(10/50) \times (50 + 20 + 10) = 16$

3   Consolidated reserves

	£000
A (80 + 30)	110
B 80% × 10 } see note below	8
C 30% × 50	15
	133

4   Share of C's net assets

	£000
30% × (200 + 100 + 50)	105

Note

Only post-acquisition profits may be included in reserves under the legally supported convention of acquisition accounting. There has been for many years a large body of opinion in favour of merger accounting. ED 31, on the possible use of merger accounting, has been modified but has not yet been published as a standard. It will allow merger accounting, i.e., the pooling of distributable reserves under certain strictly defined conditions.

9   ANGLO GROUP

Consolidated balance sheet at 31.12.83

	£000
Freehold property (note 1)	500
Plant and equipment at cost less depreciation	863
Investment in associated company (note 2)	819
Current assets	872
	3,054
Share capital	1,000
Reserve arising on consolidation (W1)	118
Reserves (W2)	1,256
	2,374
Minority interest (W3)	62
Bank overdraft	374
Current liabilities	244
	3,054

Notes

(1)   Freehold property is stated at cost less depreciation and revaluation. The property of Anglo Ltd has recently been valued at £230,000.

(2) Investment in associated company:

	£000
Share of net assets, excluding goodwill (W4)	565
Share of goodwill (W4)	26
Premium on acquisition (W1)	228
	819

Workings

1

		Cost of control: Bangle Ltd		Premium on acquisition: Carmen Ltd
	£000	£000	£000	£000
Investment at cost		440		760
Less: Shares purchased	180		500	
Reserves purchased 31.12.83 (180/200) × 300	270			
Revaluation reserve (180/200) × 120	108	558		
Reserves, 1.1.83 (500/2,000) × 128			32	532
	Capital reserve	118	Premium	228

2 Group reserves

	£000
Anglo	1,197
Bangle (all pre-acquisition)	Nil
Carmen: (500/2,000) × 236	59
	1,256

3 Minority interest (£000)

Bangle: (20/200) × (500 + 120) = 62

4 Associated company: Carmen Ltd

		¼-share
	£000	£000
Net assets (2,000 + 128 + 236)	2,364	591
Goodwill	104	26
Net assets, excluding goodwill	2,260	565

Tutorial note

SSAP 1 requires investments in associated companies to be shown at book value, i.e., the relevant proportion of the net assets plus the premium paid on acquisition. This is exactly the same as the goodwill calculation.

This 'equity' accounting brings a share of the associated company's profits into the consolidated profit and loss account.

11 Taxation in company accounts: SSAPs 8 and 15

INTRODUCTION

Since more than half of a company's profit may be payable as corporation tax, its relevance to the understanding of financial data is obvious. Of equal importance to those with a financial interest in a company, is the time of tax flows, since they are one of the major reasons for overdrafts reaching a peak.

The legal requirement to pay advance corporation tax almost immediately after paying dividends, places further demands on working capital, often causing a secondary peak demand for which temporary bank assistance may be required. While tax incentives are used as part of economic policy, their impact upon profits and related cash flows must be clearly understood, in order that those budgets, upon which financial management is based, can be prepared with reasonable confidence.

IMPUTATION TAX: SSAP 8

Advance corporation tax

When a company pays a dividend it must make a payment, 'on account' of its corporation tax, currently equivalent to 3/7 of the dividend. This advance corporation tax (ACT) is payable within 14 days of the end of the quarter; it can be set-off against the 'mainstream' corporation tax for the year, which is payable, in the case of companies incorporated since 5 April 1965, nine months after the financial year end.

Generally, ACT does not affect a company's profit and loss account but affects the liability on the balance sheet.

ACT set-off

The recipient of a dividend receives with the dividend a tax credit equal to 3/7 of the dividend. This tax credit can be used by individuals to pay income tax, and by companies to pay ACT.

Dividends from UK companies are known as franked investment income, since they are paid out of a fund which has suffered corporation tax. Remember that such income should be shown 'gross' in the profit and loss account, i.e., inclusive of the tax credit, which appears as part of the tax charge in the profit and loss account.

ACT is recovered by 'set-off' against corporation tax. Where the appropriate corporation tax has not yet been assessed as a liability, the ACT recoverable is carried forward as a deferred asset (included in the current assets), or deducted from any deferred tax balance the company is carrying. If the technical ability to recover ACT in the short term is lost, it should be written off as part of the tax charge in the profit and loss account. This may happen when companies pay high dividends relative to their tax liability, since set-off in any year is limited to 30% of the taxable profits.

Under- or over-provisions made in an earlier year should be incorporated in the tax charged in the profit and loss account.

DEFERRED TAXATION: SSAP 15, ED 33

Although corporation tax is charged on a company's profits, the actual tax payable for a year often bears little relationship to the year's disclosed profits. Some of the differences between disclosed profit and taxable profit are permanent, e.g., company expenditure on entertaining is not allowable for tax.

Timing differences

The majority, however, are timing differences which either will reverse in the short term (e.g., royalties and interest receivable may be calculated on an accruals basis in the accounts, whereas they are taxed on a cash basis) or which *may* reverse in later years, e.g., the timing of depreciation provisions in the accounts differs from the timing of capital allowances for taxation purposes.

Capital allowances

For many years businesses have been able to take 100% capital allowances on plant and machinery in the year of purchase, whereas writing off a long-term asset in the year of purchase would contravene a fundamental accounting concept. SSAP 15, modified by ED 33, requires a company to provide for deferred taxation where differences are likely to reverse, i.e., when the deferred tax provision is likely to crystallise as a real liability. Note that the 1984 Finance Act, in steadily reducing first-year capital allowances, poses a problem for companies which, anticipating ever-increasing first-year allowances appropriate to their capital expenditure, had not provided for deferred tax. It seems that provision should be made in this year's accounts, since the reversal is very likely, but can be treated as an extraordinary item, as it derives from an extraordinary event, i.e., a change of tax law.

SUGGESTED METHOD FOR ANSWERING THE QUESTION

Most questions on this topic require the candidate to produce the profit and loss account and excerpts from the balance sheet. These are based on a short list of transactions, such as profit, corporation tax on that profit, dividends paid, dividends proposed and dividends received. To gain good marks, therefore, one must put the items in the appropriate place, after doing the relevant calculation and remembering the relationship between: advance corporation tax; mainstream corporation tax; franked investment income and tax credits; and deferred taxation.

QUESTIONS

1 CHRISCRAIG LTD

Data for year ended 30.9.84

	£
Trading profit, after depreciation £20,000	100,000
Dividend received January 1984	14,000
Dividend paid April 1984	21,000
Proposed dividend	28,000
Profit on sale of property	20,000

The company wishes to provide for deferred taxation in respect of the capital allowances and uses a tax rate of 52%.

The corporation tax on the year's trading profits is £36,400, after using capital allowances of £50,000.

Tax on the property sale is £6,000.

Required:

The profit and loss account for the year ended 30.9.84, and the relevant extracts from the balance sheet at 30.9.84.

20 marks

2 TRANSIT LTD

Transit Ltd commenced trading in 1978. The following trial balance was extracted from the company's books for the preparation of its first annual accounts for the year ended 30 June 1979:

	£	£
Assets (all current)	192,500	
Franked investment income received (net of tax credit)		6,500
Operating profit (after bank interest of £4,000 but before investment income)		29,000
Share capital		20,000
Sundry creditors		150,000
Interim dividend paid 25 June 1979	13,000	
	205,500	205,500

It has been calculated that the company's corporation tax on its operating profit of £29,000 will be £12,000.

Assume an advance corporation tax rate of 35/65ths.

Required:

The profit and loss account of Transit Ltd for the year ended 30 June 1979 together with the balance sheet at that date, so far as the information permits. Show the dates on which tax liabilities will be payable, but in all other respects comply with standard accounting practice.

20 marks

3 IMPUTATION LTD

The following summarised trial balance was extracted from the books of Imputation Ltd in preparing the company's final accounts for the year ended 30 September 1984:

	£	£
Debenture interest paid (gross)	8,000	
Deferred taxation		68,000
Franked investment income received (net)		14,000
Reserves at 30 September 1983		110,000
Sales		600,000
Share capital		200,000
Sundry assets	592,000	
Sundry costs	512,000	
Sundry creditors		120,000
	1,112,000	1,112,000

Adjustments have yet to be made for the following items:

(a) Corporation tax on trading profit for 1984 is calculated at £44,000.

(b) A cash payment of £21,000 will be made to shareholders on 1 February 1985, in respect of a proposed dividend.

Imputation Ltd commenced trading in 1967.

Assume a basic rate of income tax of 30% and an advance corporation tax rate of three-sevenths. Ignore the effect of the current year's capital allowances on the deferred taxation account.

Required:

The profit and loss account of Imputation Ltd for the year ended 30 September 1984, and the balance sheet at that date, set out in good style.

Group current liabilities clearly in the balance sheet, and show dates on which tax liabilities will be payable, where possible. In all other respects comply with the recommendations of the Accounting Standards Committee so far as the information permits.

20 marks

4 LANCASTER LTD

Lancaster Ltd was incorporated and commenced business in January 1982. The following trial balance was extracted from the books at 31 December 1982:

	£	£
Share capital (ordinary shares of £1 each)		1,000,000
Trade creditors		264,500
Operating profit		315,000
Royalties		90,000
Dividends received		7,000
Fixed assets at cost (purchased January 1982)	200,000	
Provision for depreciation at 31 December 1982		40,000
Stock, debtors and cash	1,469,500	
Interim dividend paid	35,000	
Advance corporation tax	12,000	
	1,716,500	1,716,500

The following additional information is provided:

(a) Royalties consist of £65,000 received in cash and £25,000 outstanding at the year end.

(b) The royalties outstanding give rise to a 'short-term' timing difference as defined by SSAP 15 entitled 'Accounting for Deferred Taxation'.

(c) The directors intend to claim a first-year allowance of 100% on the fixed assets purchased in January 1982. No provision for deferred taxation will be made in respect of the resulting timing difference as the directors are in possession of reliable evidence which supports their opinion that it will not reverse in the foreseeable future.

(d) Corporation tax is payable at 52% on *taxable* profits of £220,000.

(e) The directors propose to pay a final dividend of 14p per share for 1982.

Required:

The profit and loss account of Lancaster Ltd for 1982 and balance sheet at 31 December 1982, not necessarily in a form for publication, but complying with the provision in SSAP 15.

Note: Advance corporation tax should be taken as 3/7ths for the purpose of your calculations.

20 marks

ANSWERS

1 CHRISCRAIG LTD

Profit and loss account for year ended 30.9.84

		£	Tutorial note
Trading profits after providing depreciation £20,000		100,000	
Investment income (14,000 + 6,000)		20,000	1
		120,000	
Taxation			
Corporation tax	£		
(mainstream)	36,400		2
Tax credit re franked investment income	6,000		1
Deferred tax	15,600	58,000	3
Profit after taxation		62,000	
Extraordinary item: profit on	£		
sale of property	20,000		
Less: Tax	6,000	14,000	4
		76,000	
Dividends: Paid	21,000		5
Proposed	28,000	49,000	7
Profits for year retained		27,000	

Extracts from balance sheet at 30.9.84

	£	Tutorial note
Current liabilities:		
Current tax	12,000	7
Corporation tax 30.6.85	39,400	6
Proposed dividend	28,000	7
Deferred liabilities:		
Deferred tax (15,600 − 12,000)	3,600	8

Tutorial notes

(1) Franked investment income is shown gross and the related tax credit included in the tax for the year.

(2) Mainstream corporation tax is payable nine months after year end.

(3) The provision for deferred tax is 52% × (£50,000 capital allowances less £20,000 depreciation). At some time in the future depreciation will exceed capital allowances and the timing difference will reverse.

(4) Extraordinary items are stated net of tax — usually at 30% applicable to capital gains.

(5) Shortly after the dividend was paid, the company had to pay ACT £9,000 (3/7 × £21,000), but used its tax credit of £6,000 and only paid £3,000.

(6) The mainstream corporation tax is £42,000, i.e., £36,400 on trading profits and £6,000 on the capital gain. Since ACT £3,000 *has already been paid*, the liability carried forward is £39,400, payable on 30.6.85.

(7) The company proposes to pay a dividend of £28,000, a current liability. It thus has an *additional* current liability of £12,000 ACT, i.e., 3/7 × £28,000. Since this ACT is recoverable against *future* corporation tax, it can be carried forward as a deferred asset.

(8) The deferred asset, £12,000, is netted off against the deferred liability, £15,600, leaving £3,600 to appear on the balance sheet.

It should be noted that the ACT of £12,000 cannot be set off against the corporation tax payable on 30.6.85, since this is tax for year ended 30.9.84, whereas the dividend in question is payable in the year ended 30.9.85.

Corporation tax — summary

	£
Mainstream corporation tax for year	42,400
ACT paid during year on £21,000 dividend paid	3,000
MCT remaining, paid 30.6.85 as normal	39,400
ACT paid next year on £28,000 dividend proposed	12,000

This must be shown as a liability at 30.9.84, and the ACT recoverable, £12,000, deducted from the deferred tax account.

If there is no deferred tax liability, or it is exceeded, a deferred asset (ACT recoverable) appears amongst the current assets.

2 TRANSIT LTD

Profit and loss account for year ended 30.6.79

	£	£
Operating profit		25,000
Add: Interest receivable		4,000
Investment income (6,500 + 3,500) (W1)		10,000
		39,000
Less: Taxation		
Corporation tax	12,000	
Tax credit on investment income (W1)	3,500	15,500
		23,500
Dividends paid		13,000
Profit for year, retained		10,500

Balance sheet at 30.6.79

	£	£
Current assets		192,500
Current liabilities	150,000	
Taxation 31.3.78 (W3)	8,500	
Current taxation 14.7.77 (W2)	3,500	162,000
		30,500
Share capital		20,000
Retained profits		10,500
		30,500

Workings

1 Tax credit on dividend received: 35/65 × £6,500 = £3,500

		£
2	ACT re dividend paid, 35/65 × £13,000 =	7,000
	Less: Tax credit	3,500
		3,500

		£
3	Corporation tax for year	12,000
	Less: ACT payable (W2)	3,500
		8,500

3 IMPUTATION LTD

Profit and loss account for year ended 30 September 1984

	£	£
Sales		600,000
Less: Sundry costs		512,000
		88,000
Add: Franked investment income (W1)		20,000
		108,000
Less: Interest paid		8,000
		100,000
Less: Taxation: Corporation tax	44,000	
Tax credit (W1)	6,000	50,000
		50,000
Dividend proposed (10½%) (W2)		21,000
Profit for year, retained		29,000

Balance sheet at 30 September 1984

	£	£
Sundry assets		592,000
Less:		
Sundry creditors	120,000	
Corporation tax, payable 30.6.85	44,000	
Current taxation, 14.4.85 (W2)	9,000	
Proposed dividend	21,000	194,000
		398,000
Share capital		200,000
Reserves (110,000 + 29,000)		139,000
		339,000
Deferred taxation (W3)		59,000
		398,000

Workings

1 Franked investment income:

   £14,000 + (3/7 × £14,000) = £20,000

2 ACT on proposed dividend:

   (3/7) × £21,000 = £9,000

   and to be paid on 14.4.85 if dividend is paid on 1.2.85 (i.e., 14 days after end of quarter – 31.3.85).

		£
3	Deferred tax liability	68,000
	Less: ACT recoverable	9,000
		59,000

Tutorial notes

(a) As the dividend will not be paid until 1985, the related ACT cannot be set off against the 1984 corporation tax.

(b) The ACT recoverable, £9,000, is a deferred asset and is set off against the deferred tax liability.

4 LANCASTER LTD

Profit and loss account for 1982

	£	£
Operating profit		315,000
Add: Royalties	90,000	
Investment income (7,000 + 3,000)	10,000	100,000
		415,000
Less: Taxation		
Corporation tax @ 52% (W1)	114,400	
Tax credit on investment	3,000	
*Deferred tax (W2), see note	13,000	130,400
		284,600
Dividends: Paid	35,000	
Proposed (14p per share)	140,000	175,000
		109,600

Balance sheet at 31.12.82

	£	£	£
Fixed assets at cost			200,000
Less: Depreciation			40,000
			160,000
Current assets			
Stock, debtors and cash		1,469,500	
Deferred asset, ACT recoverable (W2)		47,000	
		1,516,500	
Less: Current liabilities			
Trade creditors	264,500		
Corporation tax 1.10.83 (W3)	102,400		
Current tax	60,000		
Proposed dividend	140,000	566,900	949,600
			1,109,600
Share capital			1,000,000
Retained profit			109,600
			1,109,600

*Note: It has not been considered necessary to provide a further £83,200 in respect of £160,000 timing differences, since the directors have reliable evidence to support their view that they will not reverse in the foreseeable future.

Workings

1 Taxation account

	£		£
Tax credit re dividend received, 3/7 × £7,000	3,000*	Profit and loss account, corporation tax 52% × £220,000	114,400
ACT re dividend paid: 3/7 × £35,000 = £15,000 Less: Tax credit* £3,000	12,000	Tax re investment income	3,000
		ACT recoverable	60,000
Corporation tax: £114,400 (220,000 × 52%) Less: ACT paid 12,000	102,400		
ACT re proposed dividend: 3/7 × £140,000	60,000		
	177,400		177,400

2 Transfer to deferred taxation

52% × £25,000 = £13,000

Since ACT recoverable is and deferred taxation is	£60,000 (a deferred asset) £13,000
Net amount, amongst current assets	47,000

3 Mainstream corporation tax:

	£
Payable 1.10.83, i.e., 9 months after the accounting period	114,400
Against which can be set ACT paid	12,000
	102,400

Tutorial notes

(a) Since the company intends to pay a dividend early in 1983 it will have to pay ACT (3/7 × £140,000 = £60,000) shortly afterwards. This ACT is a current liablity directly related to the proposed dividend which is also a current liability.

(b) The ACT can be recovered by set-off against the corporation tax for 1983, i.e., the year in which the dividend is paid.

(c) 1983 corporation tax, the amount of which will not be known until the end of 1983, is not payable until 1.10.84. Thus the ACT which can be recovered is known as a deferred asset.

12 Published accounts

INTRODUCTION

Published accounts are relevant to bankers in two areas. Firstly, banks are large public companies, whose directors (who are bankers) must report to their shareholders through the media of published reports. Secondly, these accounts are the only comprehensive reports a company is obliged to produce in a standard form, and are thus the only source of audited information available to shareholders, potential investors, customers and creditors, including banks.

Published accounts refer to the accounts circulated to shareholders of public companies, particularly those with stock exchange listings. In one sense the final accounts of all companies are public documents, since they are filed, possibly in an abridged form, with the Registrar of Companies, to whom everyone has access.

Since the majority of shareholders of a public limited (liability) company (plc), do not have access to management, information about their investment has to be communicated through the medium of the published accounts, laid before the company at the annual general meeting, after prior circulation to all persons entitled to attend the meeting. The form and level of disclosure is prescribed by company law as stated in a number of Companies Acts, commencing with the Companies Act 1948, the main statutory source of company law, and most recently the Companies Act 1981, which implements for this country the requirements of the EEC's Fourth Directive on company law.

You must know the accounting policies upon which accounts should be based. These are developed by the Accounting Standards Committee and issued as Statements of Standard Accounting Practice with the overall requirement, in this country, that the accounts give a true and fair view.

The Companies Act 1981 permits a number of alternative presentations. In the examination, when the questions require accounts for publication the following format should be used.

ILLUSTRATION OF PROFIT AND LOSS ACCOUNT FOR 1984

Notes			£000	£000
(1)	Turnover			7,000
(2)	Cost of sales			4,000
	Gross profit			3,000
(2)	Distribution costs		1,200	
(2)	Administrative expenses		1,000	2,200
(3)	Operational profit			800
(4)	Income from investments			
		Subsidiaries	35	
		Associated companies	15	
		Other trade investments	10	60
				860
		Interest receivable		40
				900
(5)	Interest payable			200
				700
	Taxation on ordinary activities			300
	Profit on ordinary activities after tax			400
	Extraordinary items			
		Profit on sale of property	120	
		Less: Tax	36	84
				484
	Less: Transfer to reserve		20	
		Dividends paid	140	
		Dividends proposed	210	370
	Profit for year retained			114

Retained profits (for balance sheet)

	£000
Balance at 1.1.84	200
Retained profit for 1984	114
Prior year adjustment	90
	404

Supplementary information required

This data is usually given in notes to the relevant profit and loss account item.

Notes

(1) Turnover, i.e., sales net of trade discount and VAT:

    (a) sales and pre-tax profit for each class of business;
    (b) sales for each geographical market.

(2)   (a) Depreciation.

    (b) Hire of plant and machinery.

    (c) Directors' remuneration, classified as:

        (i) fees;
        (ii) salaries;
        (iii) pensions;
        (iv) compensation.

    If the total of (i) and (ii), excluding pension contributions, exceeds £40,000 the following must be shown:

        (i) chairman's emolument;
        (ii) highest paid director's emoluments;
        (iii) number of directors in each £5,000 income band;
        (iv) number who have waived remuneration and the amount.

    (d) Auditors' remuneration, including expenses.

    (e) Number of employees paid more than £40,000 p.a. in bands of £5,000.

    (f) Exceptional items.

(3) These six items may be relevant to the three classifications of operating expenditure: cost of sales, distribution, and administration; and therefore the relevant notes can be made to the operational profit figure using the expression 'this profit has been calculated after charging the following items': depreciation, etc.

(4) Investment income: details (name; country of incorporation; number, type and proportion of shares held) of subsidiaries and investments exceeding 10% of capital or total assets.

(5) Interest payable: this must distinguish between interest on bank loans and overdrafts, and other loans repayable within five years, and interest on all other loans.

ILLUSTRATION OF BALANCE SHEET PRESENTATION

	£	£	Notes
Fixed assets:			
Intangible			
Goodwill		X,XXX	(1)
Research and development expenditure		XXX	
Patent rights		X	
Tangible			
Land and buildings		XX,XXX	(2)
Plant and machinery		XX,XXX	
		XXX,XXX	
Current assets			
Stock	XX,XXX		(3)
Debtors	XX,XXX		
Cash at bank and in hand	XXX		
	XX,XXX		
Less: Creditors: amounts falling due within one year	£		
Trade creditors	XX,XXX		
Taxation	X,XXX		
Proposed dividend	XX,XXX	XX,XXX	
Net current assets		XX,XXX	
Total assets less current liabilities		XXX,XXX	
Creditors: amounts falling due after one year			
Debentures	XX,XXX		(4)
Deferred taxation	X,XXX	XX,XXX	
		XXX,XXX	
Capital and reserves			
Called-up share capital		XXX,XXX	(5)
Share premium account		XX	
Reserve arising on the revaluation of property		XX	
Profit and loss account		XXX	(6)
		XXX,XXX	

Notes

The notes will include:

(1) Intangible assets: a statement of the policy adopted in arriving at the balance sheet figures.

(2) Tangible assets: details of the cost at the beginning of year, additions, disposals and depreciation for the year and the related accumulated depreciation figures; statement of depreciation policy.

(3) Stock and work in progress: statement of accounting policy as to stock valuation; details of calculation of long-term work in progress.

(4) Debentures and loans: the nature of any security given to secured creditors. This could also apply to short-term liabilities.

(5) Share capital: details of the company's authorised, issued and paid-up capital; note that any share capital unpaid appears as one of the debtors.

(6) Movement on reserves: any movement on reserves not appearing in the profit and loss account must be explained.

SUGGESTED METHOD OF ANSWERING THE QUESTIONS

Method is as important as knowledge in attempting these long involved questions requiring the student to prepare balance sheet, profit and loss account and the notes to these accounts.

(a) The three should be done at the same time and thus three sheets of paper should be headed accordingly. In the accounts write on every second line, leaving space for the item which inevitably seems to be omitted.

(b) Place a number, referring to the relevant data in the question, against each item in the trial balance that requires adjustment.

(c) Take each item from the trial balance and place it in the appropriate position on the balance sheet or profit and loss account, after reference to the indicated question note, if any. If the Companies Acts require further detail or comment provide it in the notes.

(d) Difficult items of whose destination you are not sure, or which require further analysis, should be put into the workings. Do not take too long meditating (worrying); move on to the next item. The great majority of items are placed into the final accounts without alteration.

(e) When you have reached the end of the trial balance, check that all the question notes have been dealt with.

(f) Take the working balances into the balance sheet or profit and loss account if you are sure of their nature.

Note: Unless it is the last question you are attempting, do not spend any more than the appropriate time allocation, i.e., 1.8 minutes per mark, since the first 10 minutes on a question may yield 10 marks, whereas the last 10 minutes only 1 or 2 marks.

QUESTIONS

1 PENDANT LTD

The accounts of Pendant Ltd for the year ended 30 June 1979 are being prepared for publication. The following items appear in the draft accounts:

[*Italics indicate the actual words and figures appearing in the accounts.*]

Balance sheet items

		£
(A)	*Leasehold property at cost*	*150,000*
	Less: Accumulated depreciation	*39,000*
		111,000

The accounts do not reveal that the leasehold property consists of two leases. One has 91 years unexpired (cost £99,000, depreciation £8,000); the other has 10 years unexpired (cost £51,000, depreciation £31,000).

		£
(B)	*Plant and equipment at cost*	*200,000*
	Less: Accumulated depreciation	*70,000*
		130,000

The accounts do not reveal that the £200,000 includes £12,000 expenditure incurred on new plant and equipment during the year.

(C) *Unquoted shares at directors' valuation*   *13,000*

The accounts do not reveal that the shares involved are 4,000 ordinary shares in Crumble Ltd, representing 4% of that company's voting capital. Nor is there any reference to the fact that some shareholders in Crumble Ltd have recently been selling the shares for £2 each.

(D) *Contracts in progress at cost plus attributable profit, less foreseeable losses (cost includes a relevant proportion of operating overheads)*   *78,000*

The accounts show comparative figures for the previous year, in which contracts in progress were shown at cost (i.e., without attributable profit, less foreseeable losses). There is no explicit mention of this change in the accounts, nor is there any disclosure of the effect of the change in accounting basis on the current year's profit.

(E) *Trade debtors*   *176,000*

The accounts do not reveal that this figure was derived by deducting a bad and doubtful debts provision of £10,000 from gross debtors of £186,000.

(F) Contracts placed for future capital expenditure on fixed assets £49,000

This item does not appear in the balance sheet proper, but in a note to the accounts. The note does not mention a further £30,000 intended capital expenditure which the directors have sanctioned, but for which the company has not yet entered any contractual obligations.

Profit and loss account

(G) Operating profit (see note 4) £38,000

Note 4 to the accounts shows certain items deducted in the calculation of operating profit, but no mention is made of the following cost items:

	£
Audit fees	1,000
Cost of goods sold	350,000
Entertainment expenses	4,000
Rents paid	6,800

(H) Interest 18,600

The accounts do not reveal that this figure was made up of £14,000 interest on 14% debentures (redeemable 1990) and £4,600 interest on an overdraft carrying an interest rate of 13% at the end of the year.

Required:

(a) A list of those treatments which are *permissible* within the Companies Acts 1948 to 1981. Simply state the appropriate letters for each treatment (i.e., Permissible: letters . . . .). Marks may be lost for treatments incorrectly listed.

(b) A list of those treatments which are *not permissible* within the Companies Acts 1948 to 1981 (i.e., those which contravene the requirements of the Acts), and a brief explanation of why each treatment is not permissible. To gain marks you must give the correct explanations.

Note: You are asked to consider the Companies Acts' requirements only. You are not asked to consider whether the treatments satisfy accounting conventions (e.g., Statements of Standard Accounting Practice or Recommendations of the Institute of Chartered Accountants in England and Wales).

20 marks

2 BONZO LTD

The accounts of Bonzo Ltd for the year ended 31 March 1984 are being prepared for publication. The following items appear in the draft accounts; the first four items appear in the balance sheet, and the remainder in the profit and loss account. (Italics indicate words and figures appearing in the accounts.)

Balance sheet items

		£
(1)	*Stocks of raw materials, at replacement cost*	*137,000*
	Work in progress on long-term contracts, at cost plus attributable profit less foreseeable loss	*199,000*

The accounts do not show the original costs of either of these assets.

(2) *Trade debtors* — *201,000*

The accounts do not disclose that this figure was derived by deducting a bad and doubtful debts provision of £9,000 from gross debtors of £210,000

(3) *Freehold property, at valuation* — *150,000*

A note to the accounts shows that a 'revaluation reserve' of £30,000 was created during the year. However, the accounts do not mention that the revaluation was undertaken by A. Pointer, chartered surveyor, on 5 February 1984, nor is there any mention of tax liability which could arise on sale of the property.

(4) *Bank overdraft (secured)* — *47,000*

The basis on which the bank overdraft is secured is not mentioned in the accounts.

Profit and loss account items

(5) *Operating profit (see note 2)* — *79,000*

Note 2 to the accounts shows certain deductions made in determining operating profit, but does *not* disclose that the following were among deductions made in calculating operating profit:

	£
Advertising	7,500
Hire of machinery	12,000
Rent of offices	13,000
Research and development	15,000

		£
(6)	Share of profits less loss of associated companies	13,000

A note to the accounts shows that Bonzo Ltd holds investments in the following unquoted companies:

Associated companies	Total issued share capital £	Percentage holding of Bonzo Ltd
Retriever Ltd	24,000	30%
Setter Ltd	10,000	40%

		£
(7)	Interest	37,100

The accounts do not disclose that this amount was made up of £35,000 interest on 10% debentures (redeemable 1997) and £2,100 bank overdraft interest.

(8)	Taxation	40,000

The accounts do not reveal that this figure was made up as follows:

	£
UK corporation tax on profits of year	26,000
Underprovision for UK corporation tax on profits of previous year	6,000
Overseas taxation	3,000
Taxation on share of profits of associated companies	5,000
	40,000

Required:

(a) A list of those treatments which are *permissible* within the Companies Acts 1948 to 1981. Simply state the appropriate numbers for each treatment (i.e., Permissible: numbers . . . .). Marks may be lost for treatments incorrectly listed.

(b) A list of those treatments which are *not permissible* within the Companies Acts 1948 to 1981 (i.e., those which contravene the requirements of the Acts), and a brief explanation of why each treatment is not permissible. To gain marks you must give the correct explanation.

Note: You are asked to consider the Companies Act requirements only. You are not asked to consider whether the treatments satisfy accounting conventions (e.g., Statements of Standard Accounting Practice or Recommendations of the Institute of Chartered Accountants in England and Wales).

20 marks

3 ANNERY LTD

The following trial balance was extracted from the books of Annery Ltd at 31 December 1983:

	£	£
Issued ordinary share capital (£1 shares)		600,000
Reserves at 1 January 1983		372,500
Deferred taxation		65,900
Taxation due 1 January 1984		206,000
Creditors and accruals		317,500
Bank overdraft		97,700
Stock and work in progress valued at total cost of production	626,800	
Debtors and prepayments	495,200	
Turnover		3,160,200
Cost of goods sold	2,475,600	
Research and development expenditure	73,500	
Salaries and staff bonuses	316,800	
Directors' emoluments	53,400	
Rent and rates	32,000	
Telephone, postage and stationery	17,100	
Lighting and heating	32,000	
Travel and entertainment expenses	5,900	
Audit fee	20,000	
Bad debts	2,600	
Hire charges	5,400	
Subscriptions and donations	1,500	
Dividends received, net of ACT 3/7		7,000
Investments		16,000
Plant and machinery at cost	960,000	
Provision for depreciation, 1 January 1983		275,000
	5,117,800	5,117,800

You are provided with the following additional information:

(a) The company began to undertake research and development of new products on 1 January 1983. The balance on the research and development account is made up as follows:

	£
Pure research	22,000
Applied research	35,000
Development expenditure	16,500
	73,500

The development expenditure relates to a new product which will come on to the market in January 1984. Management is confident that the new product will earn a substantial profit for the company.

(b) The figure for directors' emoluments includes directors' fees of £2,000 paid to each of the company's five directors.

(c) Plant and machinery at cost £960,000 includes purchases of £60,000 made on 1 July 1983.

(d) Depreciation is to be provided at the rate of 10% p.a. on the cost of plant and machinery.

(e) On 30 November 1983 Annery Ltd sold its investments, which had cost £29,000 many years ago, for £45,000. The cash received from the sale was credited to the investments account. The directors estimate a tax liability of £4,800 on the gain arising.

(f) A provision for tax on the current year's trading profits of £10,000 is to be made. In addition, £8,000 is to be transferred to the deferred taxation account as representing the estimated increase in tax liability which may arise on timing differences in the foreseeable future.

(g) The following expenses may be apportioned:

	Production	Distribution	Administration
Salaries and staff bonuses		£200,000	£116,800
Rent and rates	½	¼	¼
Light and heat	½	¼	¼

Required:

The profit and loss account of Annery Ltd for the year to 31 December 1983, the balance sheet at 31 December 1983 and notes attached thereto. The accounts should comply with the requirements of the Companies Acts 1948 to 1981 and best accounting practice, so far as the information permits.

30 marks

4 MELODY LTD

The following is a trial balance prepared from the accounting records of Melody Ltd at 31 March 1982:

	£	£
Authorised and issued share capital (£1 ordinary shares fully paid)		25,000
Bank		3,620
Bank and loan interest	1,270	
Cost of goods sold	105,800	
Creditors		14,790
Debtors	12,920	
Disposal of fixtures and fittings		2,600
Fixtures and fittings at cost	23,170	
Freehold property at valuation	36,000	
Mortgage loan		10,000
Profit and loss account at 31 March 1981		20,860
Provision for depreciation of fixtures and fittings		9,530
Sales		146,000
Stock in trade at 31 March 1982	20,760	
Sundry expenses	32,480	
	232,400	232,400

Some of the following information is relevant:

(a) Sundry expenses consisted of:

	£	£
Directors: salaries:		
Chairman	3,000	
Director A	5,000	
Director B	2,000	
		10,000
Depreciation of fixtures and fittings for year to 31 March 1982		2,050
Entertainment expenses		430
Travel expenses		1,270
Other expenses		18,730
		32,480

All directors perform their duties within the United Kingdom.

(b) The mortgage loan is secured by a mortgage over the company's freehold property: the company entered into the loan on 31 December 1979, and the loan is redeemable by 10 annual instalments of £1,000 commencing 1 January 1984. The loan carries an interest rate of 9% p.a. and £900 interest paid for the current year has been included in bank and loan interest.

(c) The company's bank overdraft is secured in two ways: by a debenture giving a floating charge over the company's assets, and by the personal guarantee of the company's chairman.

(d) The greater part of stock in trade is recorded at cost but certain specific items have been reduced to net realisable value.

(e) The directors have authorised an extension to the company's premises at an estimated cost of £13,000 but contracts are still being negotiated.

(f) The freehold property cost £26,000 in 1970. On 1 December 1979 the property was valued at a realisable value of £36,000 by I. Price, professional valuer: the asset was revalued in the company's accounts and the surplus on revaluation was immediately converted into a bonus issue of shares to shareholders.

(g) Fixtures and fittings at cost £23,170 include:

    (i) The items sold during the year for £2,600, which are still recorded at cost £5,000, with corresponding provision for depreciation £3,800.

    (ii) Items purchased during year; recorded at cost £4,950, with corresponding provision for depreciation £495.

(h) Provision is to be made for corporation tax at 40% on chargeable profits of £6,000 for the year to 31 March 1982.

(i) Provision is to be made for a proposed dividend of 10% on share capital.

Required:

The profit and loss account for the year ended 31 March 1982, and the balance sheet at 31 March 1982, set out in good style to provide the information required by the Companies Acts 1948 to 1981, so far as the above information permits. Disclosure by notes to the accounts may be adopted where appropriate. Ignore comparative figures for previous year, directors' and auditors' reports.

Note: Marks will be deducted for disclosing information which is not specifically required by the Acts.

30 marks

5 VERONA LTD

The following trial balance of Verona Ltd, a company whose principal activity is the manufacture of aluminium foil, has been prepared:

Trial balance as at 30 June 1981

	£000s	£000s
Ordinary share capital (£1 shares)		2,000
Reserves at 1 July 1980		1,654
12% debentures, 1990		1,000
Provision for deferred taxation		157
Trade creditors and accruals		1,756
Bank balance	822	
Freehold properties at cost	400	
Plant and machinery, etc. at cost	2,523	
Provision for depreciation of plant and machinery, etc. 30 June 1981		1,068
Investments at cost	200	
Stock and work in progress	3,164	
Trade debtors and prepayments	2,935	
Turnover		37,146
Cost of goods sold	28,614	
Administration and distribution costs	6,123	
Interim dividend paid	280	
Dividends received		70
Advance corporation tax	90	
Proceeds from the sale of freehold property		300
	45,151	45,151

You are given the following additional information:

(a) The figure for turnover includes exports to other European countries amounting to £2,168,000.

(b) The administration and distribution costs are made up as follows:

	£000s
Hire of plant	365
Salaries of staff	1,420
Printing and stationery	97
Interest paid	120
Directors' remuneration	143
Audit fee and expenses	80
Lighting and heating	341
Political contributions	50
Depreciation of furniture and fittings	73
Other expenses	3,434
	6,123

They may be apportioned one-third to administration and two-thirds to distribution, apart from the interest paid.

(c) The corporation tax payable on trading profits for the year has been estimated at £809,000 and in addition a transfer of £65,000 is to be made to the deferred tax account.

(d) Included in the cost of goods sold are manufacturing wages amounting to £3,135,000 and depreciation of plant and machinery of £206,000. The average number of employees, per week, during the year was 960.

(e) Included in the balance of trade debtors and prepayments is £410,000 owing from one of Verona Ltd's principal customers which has recently gone into liquidation. It is estimated that a dividend of 20p in the £ will eventually be paid to unsecured creditors.

(f) In June 1981, the company sold one of its freehold properties, which had cost £160,000 some years ago, for £300,000. It is estimated that the corporation tax liability arising in respect of this capital gain will be £42,000. B. Thomas & Co, a firm of chartered surveyors, has valued the remaining property at £520,000. The directors have decided to include the property in the accounts at that figure.

(g) The company's investments consist of 50,000 shares in Florence Ltd which were quoted on the stock exchange at £3.50 each on 30 June 1981.

(h) The directors propose to pay a final dividend for the year of 17.5 pence per share.

Required:

The profit and loss account of Verona Ltd for the year ending 30 June 1981 and the balance sheet at 30 June 1981. The accounts should be presented in vertical format containing the information required by the Companies Acts 1948 to 1981 and, where relevant, Statements of Standard Accounting Practice so far as the information permits.

Notes:

1 Ignore comparative figures for the previous year and the auditors' report.

2 Assume all amounts are 'material' for the purpose of disclosure.

3 Assume an advance corporation tax rate of 3/7 for the purpose of your calculations.

30 marks

6 MILFORD LTD

The final accounts of Milford Ltd are in the course of preparation, and it is intended to publish them in accordance with the formats prescribed by the Companies Act 1981. The draft profit and loss account and balance sheet, both of which comply with format 1, are set out below.

Profit and loss account for the year ended 31 December 1982

	£	£
Turnover		862,150
Less: Cost of sales		484,500
Gross profit		377,650
Less: Distribution costs	25,000	
Administration expenses	185,700	210,700
Operating profit		166,950
Less: Interest payable		12,000
Profit on ordinary activities before taxation		154,950
Tax on profit on ordinary activities		77,000
Profit on ordinary activities after taxation		77,950
Retained profit as at 1 January 1982		96,800
Retained profit as at 31 December 1982		174,750

Balance sheet as at 31 December 1982

	£	£
Fixed assets		
Intangible assets: Development costs	24,100	
Goodwill	33,000	57,100
Tangible assets: Land and buildings	85,000	
Plant and machinery	126,600	211,600
		268,700
Current assets		
Stocks	139,400	
Debtors	91,200	
Cash at bank and in hand	14,000	
	244,600	
Creditors: amounts falling due within one year		
Trade creditors	57,100	
Current corporation tax	77,000	
	134,100	
Net current assets		110,500
Total assets less current liabilities		379,200
Creditors: amount falling due after more than one year		
12% debenture		100,000
		279,200
Capital and reserves		
Called-up share capital		100,000
Share premium account		4,450
Profit and loss account		174,750
		279,200

The following *additional information* is provided:

(1) Development costs £24,100 are made up of:

	£
Research costs	15,000
Development expenditure	9,100
	24,100

The development expenditure relates to a separately identifiable project which will undoubtedly produce a significant improvement in the quality of one of the company's product lines.

(2) The figure for goodwill is stated at cost, and arose as the result of purchasing the business of a former competitor on 1 January 1982. It is thought that the goodwill possesses an economic life of five years.

(3) Stock is valued at 'total' cost in the balance sheet set out above. Stock was valued at 'prime' cost, £75,000, for the purpose of the 1981 accounts, and this amount was used when computing the cost of sales figure appearing in the profit and loss account. The corresponding total cost valuation of stock at 31 December 1981 is £98,300 made up as follows:

	£
Prime cost	75,000
Production overheads	23,300
	98,300

(4) It has recently come to light that an invoice for £4,900, received from a supplier, has been erroneously omitted from the books. The goods referred to in the invoice were included in the physical stock-take.

(5) The company's land and buildings are stated in the balance sheet at cost less depreciation. They were professionally revalued at £120,000 on 1 January 1982. It has now been decided to use this figure for the purpose of the accounts. Administration expenses include a depreciation charge of £2,000 which should be revised to £3,500 to take account of the revaluation.

Required:

(a) The profit and loss account of Milford Ltd for 1982 and the balance sheet at 31 December 1982 redrafted, as necessary, to take account of the *additional information*. The revised accounts should comply, so far as the information permits, with the requirements of the Companies Act 1981 and Statements of Standard Accounting Practice. *26 marks*

(b) A calculation of the profit available for distribution according to the requirements of the Companies Act 1980. *4 marks*

Notes:
Show all adjustments clearly.
Assume that the adjustments you make do not alter tax payable.

Total 30 marks

ANSWERS

1 PENDANT LTD

(a) Permissible: (C), (E)

(b) Not permissible:

- (A) Property held on long lease has not been distinguished from that held on a short lease.

- (B) Additions and disposals have not been disclosed.

- (D) Nature, details and reasons for the change of accounting policy have not been given nor the treatment of the resulting prior-year adjustment.

    Also, there is no note giving the grounds for adopting a valuation policy not sanctioned by the 1981 Companies Act.

- (F) Capital expenditure authorised but not yet subject to contract has not been disclosed.

- (G) The list is inappropriate, since cost of goods sold either appears in the profit and loss account as a separate item, or its components appear in a different form. Audit fees and expenses should be disclosed.

- (H) Analysis of interest into that payable on overdrafts, and loans repayable within and outside five years is not given.

Tutorial notes

(1) Re (C), unquoted shares may be shown at directors' valuation, and since the holding is less than 10%, details are not required. If they are treated as fixed assets, the rules require a note of the year of revaluation, or if in present year the name or qualification of valuer and basis of valuation.

(2) Re (E), unexceptional provisions against current assets do not require separate disclosure.

2 BONZO LTD

(a) Permissible treatment: (1), (2), (6).

(b) Non-permissible treatment:

- (3) When assets are revalued during the year, the name and qualification of the valuer and the basis used should be disclosed.

- (4) The nature of the security should be disclosed as well as the total of secured liabilities.

(5) Hire of plant and machinery is a disclosable item.

(7) Notes should distinguish interest on bank borrowings, interest on loans repayable within five years, and interest on other (longer-term) borrowing.

(8) An analysis of the tax charge is required, distinguishing particularly between corporation tax and other tax charges.

Tutorial notes

(a) Re (1), the 1981 Companies Act in allowing current cost accounting presumably endorses replacement cost. Including attributable profit in long-term work in progress is not prohibited, and is encouraged if the accounts give a true and fair view.

(b) Re (2), current assets do not require to be stated at book value less provisions; the net figure is adequate.

(c) Re (6), the inclusion of a share of associated company profit is allowed in the group accounts. Presumably, the balance sheet shows the investment in the form required by SSAP 1 as revised.

3   ANNERY LTD

Profit and loss account for the year ended 31 December 1983

Notes			£
(1)	Turnover		3,160,200
	Less: Cost of sales (W1)		2,663,000
			497,200
	Less: Distribution costs (W2)	221,900	
	Administrative expenses (W3)	227,400	449,300
(2)	Profit on trading		47,900
	Income from quoted investments (£7,000 + £3,000)		10,000
	Profit on ordinary activities		57,900
(3)	Less: Tax on profit on ordinary activities		21,000
			36,900
(4)	Add: Extraordinary profit after tax		11,200
	Profit for year retained		48,100

Notes

(1) Turnover is the sales net of trade discount and excluding VAT.

(2) Profit on trading 47,900 has been calculated after charging:

	£
Depreciation	93,000
Directors emoluments: fees	10,000
other	43,400
Research and development	57,000
Audit fee	20,000
Hire of plant and machinery	5,400

(3) Tax on ordinary activities:

	£
UK corporation tax on profits for the year at X%	10,000
Tax credit on franked investment income	3,000
Deferred taxation	8,000
	21,000

(4) Extraordinary profit

	£
Profit on the sale of investments (£45,000 – £29,000)	16,000
Tax liability	4,800
	11,200

Balance sheet as at 31 December 1983

Notes	Fixed assets		£	£
(1)	Intangible			16,500
(2)	Tangible			592,000
				608,500
	Current assets			
(3)	Stock and work in progress		626,800	
	Debtors and prepayments		495,200	
			1,122,000	
	Creditors falling due within one year	£		
	Bank overdraft	97,700		
	Creditors and accruals	317,500		
	Corporation tax due 1.1.84	206,000	621,200	
	Net current assets			500,800
	Total assets less current liabilities			1,109,300
	Creditors falling due after one year:			
	Corporation tax 1.1.85		14,800	
	Provision for deferred taxation			
	(£65,900 + £8,000)		73,900	(88,700)
				1,020,600

	£	£
Capital and reserves		
Called-up share capital:		
Authorised: 600,000 ordinary shares of £1 each		
Issued and fully paid, 600,000		600,000
Profit and loss account		
Retained profit at 1.1.83	372,500	
Profit for year retained	48,100	420,600
		1,020,600

Notes

(1) Intangible fixed asset

Development expenditure, £16,500, relating to a new product, to be marketed in 1984; the directors are confident that it will earn a substantial profit.

(2) Tangible fixed assets

Plant and machinery:

	£	£
Cost at 1.1.83	900,000	
Additions during year	60,000	
Cost at 31.12.83		960,000
Depreciation:		
Balance at 1.1.83	275,000	
Depreciation for year*	93,000	
		368,000
Net book value		592,000

*Depreciation has been provided at 10% on cost, on a strict time basis.

(3) Stock and work in progress has been valued at total cost of production £626,800, which is less than the net realisable value.

Workings	W1 £	W2 £	W3 £
Cost of sales	2,475,600		
Research and development (£73,500 – £16,500)	57,000		
Salaries: £316,800		200,000	116,800
Directors' emoluments			53,400
Rent and rates: £32,000	16,000	8,000	8,000
Telephone, etc.			17,100
Light and heat: £32,000	16,000	8,000	8,000
Travel and entertaining		5,900	
Audit			20,000
Bad debts			2,600
Hire charge	5,400		
Subscriptions and donations			1,500
Depreciation	93,000		
	2,663,000	221,900	227,400

4 MELODY LTD

Profit and loss account for year ended 31.3.82

	Notes	£
Turnover	(1)	146,000
Cost of goods sold		(105,800)
Gross profit		40,200
Distribution costs	XX,XXX	
Administrative expenses	XX,XXX	(31,080)
		9,120
Interest payable	(2)	(1,270)
Profits before tax	(3)	7,850
Tax	(4)	(2,400)
Profits after tax		5,450
Dividends paid and proposed	(5)	(2,500)
Profit for year retained		2,950

Notes

(1) Turnover

Analysis of business and geographical markets — no information given.

(2) Interest payable £
On bank loans and overdraft payable within five years   370
On mortgage repayment loan by 10 instalments of
£1,000 commencing 1.1.84   900

(3) Profits on ordinary activities before tax after charging:

	£	
Staff costs	4,000	
Directors' emoluments	10,000	(if more than £40,000 then more details would have to be given.)
Provision for depreciation	650	

(Where available, information re number of employees should be given.)

(4) Tax on ordinary activities

40% on chargeable profits £6,000 = £2,400

(5) Dividends paid and proposed

Dividend 10p per share: 10p × 25,000 = £2,500.

Balance sheet at 31.3.82

	Notes	£	£
Fixed assets			
Tangible assets	(1)		48,440
			48,440
Current assets			
Stocks	(2)	20,760	
Debtors	(3)	12,920	
		33,680	
Creditors: amount falling due within one year	(4)	23,310	
Net current assets			10,370
Total assets less current liabilities			58,810
Creditors: amount due after one year	(5)		10,000
Net assets			48,810
Capital and reserves			
Called-up share capital	(6)	25,000	
Profit and loss account	(7)	23,810	48,810

Notes

(1) Tangible fixed assets

(a)

	Freehold property	Fixtures and fittings	Total
Cost or valuation at 31.3.81	36,000	18,220	54,220
Additions at cost	—	4,950	4,950
Disposals at cost	—	(5,000)	(5,000)
Cost or valuation at 31.3.82	36,000	18,170	54,170
Total depreciation at 31.3.81	—	7,480	7,480
Provision for year	—	2,050	2,050
Disposals	—	(3,800)	(3,800)
Total depreciation at 31.3.82	—	5,730	5,730
Net book value at 31.3.82	36,000	12,440	48,440
Net book value at 31.3.81	36,000	10,740	46,740

(b) The freehold property was revalued in 1979.

(2) Stocks

Stock in trade has been valued at cost except for some specific items which have been reduced to net realisable value.

(3) Debtors

Falling due within one year: trade debtors, £12,920

(4) Creditors: amounts falling due within one year

 (a)
		£
Trade creditors		14,790
Corporation tax payable 1.1.83		2,400
Bank loans and overdrafts		3,620
Proposed ordinary dividend		2,500
		23,310

 (b) The bank overdraft is secured by a floating charge over the company's assets and by guarantee.

(5) Creditors: amounts falling due after more than one year

9% mortgage loan: £10,000
Repayable by 10 instalments commencing 1 January 1984.
Secured by mortgage over freehold property.

(6) Called-up share capital

Authorised and issued share capital:
25,000 ordinary shares of £1 each fully paid, £25,000

(7) Profit and loss account

	£
Balance at 31.3.81	20,860
Retained profit for the year	2,950
Balance at 31.3.82	23,810

Tutorial notes

(a) Directors' remuneration: if more than £40,000, more detail would be required.

(b) Depreciation:

	£
The figure £650 comprises	2,050 depreciation for the year
Less: Overprovision in respect of fixtures and fittings sold during the year	1,400
	650

5 VERONA LTD

Profit and loss account for the year ended 30.6.81

Notes			£000
	Turnover, i.e., sales net of trade discount and ex VAT		37,146
	Less: Cost of sales		28,614
	Gross profit		8,532
	Less: Distribution costs (W1)	4,002	
	Administrative expenses (W2)	2,329	6,331
			2,201
	Dividends received: (70 + 30)		100
(1)			2,301
	Less: Interest payable		120
	Profit on ordinary activities		2,181
(2)	Tax on profit on ordinary activities		904
(3)			1,277
	Extraordinary item: Profit on sales of property (W3)	140	
	Less: Tax on gain	42	98
			1,375
	Dividends: (280 + 350)		630
	Profit for year, retained		745

Notes

(1) Profit, £2,301, is calculated after charging:

	£000
Depreciation (206 + 73)	279
Hire of plant	365
Directors' remuneration	143
Audit fee	80

960 employees earned on average £4,750 p.a. (W4)

(2) Taxation

	£000
Corporation tax on year's profit	809
Tax credit on franked investment income	30
Transfer to deferred tax account	65
	904

(3) Earnings per share

63.8p, based on earnings of £1,277,000 and 2,000,000 ordinary shares of £1 each.

Balance sheet at 30.6.81

	£000	£000
Fixed assets		
Freehold properties at valuation per B. Thomas & Co		520
Plant and machinery at cost	2,523	
Less: Depreciation	1,068	1,455
		1,975
Investments at cost (market value @ 30.6.81, £175,000)		200
Current assets		
Stock and work in progress	3,164	
Debtors (2,935 – 328)	2,607	
Cash at bank	822	
	6,593	

Less: Creditors payable within one year	£000		
Trade creditors and accruals	1,756		
Current taxation (W5)	911		
Proposed dividend	350	3,017	

		£000
Net current assets		3,576
Total assets less current liabilities		5,751
Creditors: amounts payable in more than one year		
12% debentures 1990	1,000	
Deferred taxation (W6)	72	1,072
		4,679
Capital and reserves		
Ordinary share capital: 2,000 shares of £1, authorised, issued and paid		2,000
Reserve: revaluation of properties (W7)		280
Other reserves: Balance at 1.7.80	1,654	
Add: Profit retained for year ended 30.6.81	745	2,399
		4,679

Workings

1. Distribution expenses (£000)

Costs	6,123	
Less: Interest	120	
	———	
2/3 ×	6,003	= 4,002

2. Administrative expenses (£000)

1/3 ×	6,003	= 2,001
Add: Bad debt: (80p/100) ×	410	= 328
		———
		2,329

3. Profit on sale of property (£000)

   (Proceeds) 300 − (cost) 160 =   140

4. Average remuneration

   (3,135,000 + 1,420,000)/960 =   £4,750

5. Current tax liability

	£000
Corporation tax on profits	809
Less: ACT re dividend paid (per trial balance)	90
	———
	719
Tax on capital gain	42
ACT on proposed dividend (3/7 × 350)	150
	———
	911

6. Deferred tax

	£000
Balance at 30.6.80	157
Transfer from profit and loss account	65
	———
	222
Less: ACT recoverable (a deferred asset)	150
	———
	72

7 Revaluation reserve

Properties:	£000
Balance (cost) 30.6.80	400
Disposal, cost	160
	240
Surplus on revaluation	280
Value, per Balance Sheet	520

Tutorial notes

(a) It is no longer necessary to state the value of exports, though if the information were available an analysis of turnover and profitability by geographical area and activity would be required.

(b) Since the director's remuneration exceeds £40,000, an analysis is required; the question did not provide the data to make this analysis.

(c) Since examiners in this and other accountancy examinations appear to be no longer asking for accounts showing the *minimum* information required by the Companies Acts, the 'workings' and 'notes' are very similar. A reasonable policy in tackling such questions would be to disclose rather than conceal.

6 MILFORD LTD

Profit and loss account for the year ended 31.12.82

	£	£
Turnover, i.e., sales excluding VAT		862,150
Cost of sales (W1)		527,700
Gross profit		334,450
Distribution costs	25,000	
Administrative expenses (W2)	193,800	218,800
Operating profit		115,650
Interest payable		12,000
Profit on ordinary activities before taxation		103,650
Tax on profit on ordinary activities		77,000
Profit on ordinary activities, after tax, retained		26,650
Earnings per share		26.7p

Balance sheet at 31.12.82

Notes	Fixed assets		£	£
(1)	Intangible assets: Development expenditure		9,100	
	Goodwill		26,400	
				35,500
(2)	Tangible assets: Land and buildings		116,500	
	Plant and machinery		126,600	
				243,100
				278,600
	Current assets			
(3)	Stock		139,400	
	Debtors		91,200	
	Cash at bank and in hand		14,000	
			244,600	
	Creditors: amounts falling due within one year			
	Trade creditors (57,100 + 4,900)	62,000		
	Corporation tax	77,000	139,000	
	Net current assets			105,600
	Total assets less current liabilities			384,200
	Creditors: amounts falling due after one year			
	12% debentures			100,000
				284,200
	Capital and reserves			
	Called-up share capital – 100,000 shares of £1 each, fully paid			100,000
	Share premium account			4,450
(4)	Revaluation reserve			33,000
(5)	Profit and loss account			146,750
				284,200

Notes

(1) Intangible assets

	Research and development	Goodwill
Cost	24,100	33,000
Less: amounts written off	15,000	6,600
	9,100	26,400

Research and development:

This expenditure, £9,100, has been carried forward as the development costs of *improving* the quality and contribution of one of the company's product lines (SSAP 13).

Goodwill is being written off over its estimated economic life of 5 years (ED 30).

(2) Land and buildings, valued by 1.1.82   £120,000
   Less: Depreciation (SSAP 12)   £3,500
    £116,500

Plant and machinery: information not available.

(3) Stocks are valued at total cost of production, including overheads (SSAP 9). Reinstatement of the opening stocks on the same basis has given rise to a prior-year adjustment (SSAP 6).

(4) Revaluation reserve

	£
Value of property	120,000
Less: Balance, 1.1.82 (85 + 2)	87,000
Profit on revaluation	33,000

(5) Profit and loss account

	£
Balance at 1.1.82	96,800
Prior-year adjustment – revaluation of opening stock at total cost	23,300
Retained profit for 1982	26,650
	146,750

Workings

1
	£
Cost of sales	484,500
R & D written-off	15,000
Adjustment re opening stock	23,300
Accrual re purchases	4,900
	527,700

2
	£
Administrative expenses	185,700
Goodwill written off	6,600
Depreciation re land and buildings	1,500
	193,800

13 Current cost accounting: SSAP 16

INTRODUCTION

Though inflation, an increase in the general price level, may be relatively low in 1984, companies with substantial imports may still be suffering from the financial effects of high price level changes, namely, cash flow problems, even though apparent profitability may be good and dividends high.

Current cost accounting demonstrates to bankers, and other providers of finance, the extent to which real capital can be eroded by high distributions of historic profits, out of which inadequate provisions have been made for fixed and current asset replacement.

Profit and loss account

Current cost profit is the result of charging against income the cost of replacing the resources consumed in producing that income, i.e., the costs of maintaining the operating capital.

You must be familiar with its calculation: deduct from the historic profit, per the profit and loss account, provisions representing the additional cost of replacing the resources used up during the year. These include adjustment for:

(a)   cost of sales;
(b)   depreciation;
(c)   monetary working capital.

If the business is financed by loan (or similar) capital, the current cost profit is modified by a gearing adjustment to determine the current cost profit attributable to the shareholders.

Balance sheet

The current cost balance sheet states assets at their value to the business, i.e., current cost, which is usually replacement cost, which may be determined by observation (catalogues and price lists), indexation or valuation.

THE CURRENT COST ADJUSTMENTS

The cost of sales adjustment (COSA)

To avoid the tedious and expensive calculations of determining the actual cost of replacing stocks at all stages, consumed during the year, the Sandilands Committee, which proposed this method of accounting for UK companies, suggested an 'averaging' method of calculation.

COSA = Stock increase,   less   Stock increase,
       at historical cost   at average price for year

Example

Opening stock £140,000 (index at beginning 280)
Closing stock £176,000 (index at end 320)

Calculation of COSA

	HC £		Stock at average price £
Opening stock	140,000	× 300*/280 =	150,000
Closing stock	176,000	× 300/320 =	165,000
COSA =	36,000	less	15,000 = £21,000

*In the absence of any specified figure, 300 has been taken as the average price for the year.

You must be clear about the following distinction: the stock increase of £36,000 comprises two elements, a real quantity increase of £15,000 and a price increase of £21,000, which is treated as a holding gain and transferred to current cost reserve, with the other adjustments.

Balance sheet adjustment: stock is shown on the current cost balance sheet at replacement cost and, therefore, usually requires revaluation from historical cost, e.g., if the stock turn is 4 times a year and 3 months before the year end the index had been 310, the current cost of the stock at the year end is £176,000 × (320/315*) = £178,794, i.e., £2,794 more, which should be credited to current cost reserve.

*It is assumed that stock is acquired steadily over the three-month period and that (320 + 310)/2 = 315 reasonably represents the average price.

The depreciation adjustment

This is the additional amount required to provide for depreciation on an asset's replacement cost as compared with its historical cost. The calculation is usually based on the average replacement cost for the year, giving rise to a back-log adjustment in the current cost reserve on the balance sheet.

Example

Machinery, which cost £100,000 in January 1981, and is being depreciated at 20% on cost, appears as follows in the balance sheets:

	31.12.82 £000	31.12.83 £000
Cost	100	100
Less: Depreciation	40	60
	60	40

The charge for 1983 is 20, i.e., 20% × 100

The appropriate indices were:

January 1981	200
31 December 1982	260
31 December 1983	290
Average 1983	276

Current cost depreciation adjustment

Depreciation, per profit and loss account, $20 \times \dfrac{276}{200}$ = 27.6

Less: Provision, per profit and loss account   20.0

Additional charge for year   7.6

The current cost balance sheet show:

		31.12.82 £000			31.12.83 £000
Cost:	$100 \times \dfrac{260}{200}$	130	$100 \times \dfrac{290}{200}$	=	145
Depreciation:	$40 \times \dfrac{260}{200}$	52	$60 \times \dfrac{290}{200}$	=	87
	60	78	40		58

Bank-log depreciation

Alternatives

		(i) £000	(ii) £000
Provision required for CC balance sheet		87.0	87.0
Less: Provided per HC accounts	60.0		60.0
Additional charge for 1982	7.6	67.6	
		19.4	27.0

If all CC adjustments are credited to CC reserve, use alternative (ii).

Monetary working capital adjustment

This adjustment, introduced as the Exposure Draft developed, applies a COSA type averaging calculation to the other components of the working capital, i.e., debtors, creditors, and even cash/overdraft, when these vary in direct sympathy with the other net current assets.

GEARING ADJUSTMENT

To the extent that net operating assets (fixed assets, stock and monetary working capital) are financed by borrowing, the current cost adjustments need not be provided from shareholders' funds.

The gearing adjustment is, therefore:

$$\text{Current cost adjustments} \times \frac{\text{Average borrowings}}{\text{Average net operating assets*}}$$

*This figure should be based on the current cost balance sheets.

Example

The current cost adjustments above, excluding a monetary working capital adjustment, total £28,600, i.e., £21,000 + £7,600. If loan capital, and similar borrowing not entering into the MWCA, amounted on average to 1/5 of total finance, the gearing adjustment = 1/5 × £28,600 = £5,720. This amount is effectively credited to the CC profit and loss account and debited to the CC reserve.

THE CURRENT COST RESERVE
(Previously called capital maintenance reserve)

A current cost balance sheet shows assets at replacement cost rather than historical cost; the CC reserve absorbs the revaluation surpluses. It is credited with CC adjustments and debited with the gearing adjustment and possibly back-log depreciation.

Example

Using the figures calculated above, the CC reserve would appear as follows:

Current cost reserve

	£			£
Back-log depreciation	*27,000	Stock revaluation		
Gearing adjustment	5,720	(178,794 − 176,000)		2,794
Balance, a capital reserve on		Fixed assets		
balance sheet	43,674	(145,000 − 100,000)		45,000
		Current cost		
		adjustments	21,000	
			*7,600	28,600
	76,394			76,394

*The two CC adjustments have been credited to the CC reserve. If the depreciation figure of £7,600 had not been so credited, the back-log depreciation would have been only £19,400.

Illustration of current cost profit and loss account

(using above figures)

			£
Profit before interest per historic profit and loss account, say			127,000
Less: Current cost adjustments			
Cost of sales		21,000	
Depreciation		7,600	28,600
Current cost profit			98,400
Less: Interest, say		20,000	
Gearing adjustment		(5,720)	14,280
Current cost profit, before tax, attributable to shareholders			84,120
Taxation, say			41,000
			43,120
Dividends, say			35,000
CC profit for year retained			8,120

Current cost balance sheet

Remember that this differs from the historic balance sheet in the following aspects:

(a) Fixed assets are valued at current cost, less depreciation based on that cost.
(b) Stock is valued at current cost.
(c) The reserves include a current cost reserve.

SUGGESTED METHOD OF ANSWERING THE QUESTION

Having memorised the lay-out of the current cost profit and loss account, which is fairly easy, prepare the pro-forma accounts inserting those items that can be lifted directly from the historic statement given.

In the workings, calculate:

(a) the *cost of sales adjustment* and balance sheet *stock* figures;
(b) *depreciation adjustment* and balance sheet *fixed asset* figures;
(c) *monetary working capital adjustment*.

Remember the completion of the double entry is in the current cost reserve. Calculate the *gearing* adjustment using the current cost balance sheet values. Complete the profit and loss account and take the retained profit figures to the balance sheet, which with the current cost reserve completes that statement.

QUESTIONS

1 ROCIETY LTD

The summarised profit and loss account and balance sheet of Rociety Ltd, a trading company, prepared under the historical cost convention, were as follows:

Profit and loss account for 1980

	£000	£000
Sales		1,400
Less: Opening stock	156	
Purchases	1,024	
Closing stock	(196)	
Cost of goods sold		984
Gross profit		416
Less: Depreciation	50	
Other running costs	300	350
Net profit		66

Balance sheet at 31 December 1980

	£000	£000
Fixed assets purchased 1 January 1979		500
Less: Depreciation (10% straight-line)		100
		400
Stock	196	
Debtors	160	
Bank	20	
	376	
Less: Creditors	136	240
		640
Share capital		300
Reserves at 1 January 1980	274	
Profit for 1980	66	340
		640

The following price indices are provided for the company's stock and fixed assets:

	Stock	Fixed assets
1 January 1979	*	80
Average for November/December 1979	120	*
31 December 1979	*	90
Average for 1980	130	96
Average for November/December 1980	140	*
31 December 1980	142	104

Stock turns over, on average, once every two months.

*Indices not provided.

Required:

A summarised profit and loss account for 1980 and balance sheet at 31 December 1980, prepared on the *current cost basis*. The profit and loss account should contain a cost of sales adjustment and a depreciation adjustment, whilst the balance sheet should contain a current cost reserve.

Notes:

1. Ignore (i) the monetary working capital adjustment, (ii) the gearing adjustment, (iii) taxation, (iv) dividends.
2. Calculations to nearest £000.

20 marks

2 HOLFORD PLC

The summarised profit and loss account for Holford plc for 1982, prepared under the historical cost convention, was as follows:

Profit and loss account for 1982

	£000	£000
Turnover		360,000
Less: Opening stock	35,000	
Purchases	200,000	
Closing stock	(50,000)	
Cost of goods sold		185,000
Gross profit		175,000
Less: Depreciation	20,000	
Other running costs	126,000	146,000
Operating profit		29,000
Less: Interest payable		5,000
Profit on ordinary activities before taxation		24,000
Taxation		10,000
Profit after tax		14,000
Less: Dividends		7,000
Retained profit for the year		7,000

The following additional information is provided:

(a) Relevant indices for stocks are as follows:

Average for October/December 1981	120
At 31 December 1981	124
Average for 1982	135
Average for October/December 1982	142
At 31 December 1982	145

On average the company holds stock for three months.

(b) All the company's fixed assets were purchased when the company was incorporated in January 1976. Their original cost was £200,000,000 and they are being depreciated over a 10-year period assuming a nil residual value. The original estimate of these assets' lives is still considered appropriate. The following current cost valuations are provided:

	£000
At 1 January 1982	310,000
Average for 1982	330,000
At 31 December 1982	355,000

(c) Net borrowings were approximately one-third of net operating assets throughout 1982.

Required:

A summarised profit and loss account for 1982 prepared on the current cost basis in accordance, so far as the information permits, with the principles contained in Statement of Standard Accounting Practice 16.

Notes:

(i) All calculations are to be made to the nearest £000.
(ii) Ignore the monetary working capital adjustment.

20 marks

3 TISCH PLC

The summarised accounts of Tisch plc for 1981, prepared on the historical cost basis, are as follows:

Profit and loss account, year ended 31 December 1981

	£000
Operating profit	355
Less: Interest payable	60
Net profit before taxation	295
Less: Corporation tax	150
Net profit after taxation	145
Add: Retained profit at 1 January 1981	180
Retained profit at 31 December 1981	325

Balance sheet at 31 December 1981

1980 £000	£000		£000	£000
1,000		Fixed assets at cost		1,000
250		Less: Deprecaition		375
750				625
		Current assets		
	600	Stock (December purchases)	900	
	30	Cash	50	
	630		950	
		Less: Current liability		
	100	Corporation tax payable	150	
530		Net current assets		800
1,280				1,425
		Financed by:		
700		Share capital (£1 ordinary shares)		700
180		Reserves		325
880				1,025
400		15% Debenture repayable 1990		400
1,280				1,425

The directors intend to publish supplementary accounts based on the provisions contained in Statement of Standard Accounting Practice No. 16 entitled 'Current Cost Accounting'.

The following additional information is provided:

(a) Sales, purchases and other expenses accrue evenly during the year.

(b) The company purchases and sells all goods on an immediate cash basis.

(c) The fixed assets were purchased on 1 January 1979 and are being depreciated on the straight-line basis over a period of eight years assuming a nil residual value. The depreciation charge in the 1981 accounts was, accordingly, £125,000.

(d) The following price indices are provided for the company's stock and fixed assets:

	Stock	Fixed assets
1 January 1979	*	100
Average for December 1980	130	*
31 December 1980	132	120
Average for 1981	136	124
Average for December 1981	144	*
31 December 1981	145	132

*Indices not provided.

(e) The company's stocks turn over, on average, once a month.

Required:

The current cost profit and loss account and balance sheet of Tisch plc for 1981 (1980 comparatives need not be given), in accordance, so far as the information permits, with the principles contained in Statement of Standard Accounting Practice No. 16. The profit and loss account should contain a depreciation adjustment, a cost of sales adjustment and a gearing adjustment. The balance sheet should contain a current cost reserve.

Notes:

(i) The monetary working capital adjustment is not applicable to the affairs of Tisch plc.

(ii) All calculations to the nearest £000.

30 marks

ANSWERS

1 ROCIETY LTD

Current cost profit and loss account for year ended 31.12.80

	£000	£000
Profit, before interest, per historical profit and loss account		66
Less: Current cost adjustments:		
Cost of sales (W1)	27	
Depreciation (W2)	10	37
Current cost profit		29

Current cost balance sheet at 31.12.80

	£000	£000
Fixed assets at current cost (W2)		650
Less: Depreciation (W2)		130
		520
Stock (W1)	199	
Debtors	160	
Bank	20	
	379	
Less: Creditors	136	243
		763
Share capital		300
Current cost reserve (W3)		160
Reserves (274 + 29)		303
		763

Workings

1 Cost of sales adjustment

$$\text{Stock 1.1.80} \quad 156 \times \frac{130}{120} = 169$$

$$\text{Stock 31.12.80} \quad 196 \times \frac{130}{140} = 182$$

$$40 \quad \text{Less} \quad 13 = 27$$

Balance sheet adjustment

stock 31.12.80   196 × $\dfrac{142}{140}$ =   199, i.e., increase = 3

2   Depreciation adjustment

$50 \times \dfrac{96}{80} = 60$ (i.e., current cost charge)

Historical charge = 50, therefore extra = 10

Balance sheet adjustment

Cost	500 ×	$\dfrac{104}{80}$	=	650, i.e., increase = 150	
Depreciation	100 ×	$\dfrac{104}{80}$	=	130	
	400			520	

Back-log depreciation

Provision per CC balance sheet		130
Less: Balance 31.12.80	100	
Additional, per above	10	110
		20

3   Current cost reserve

Back-log depreciation (W2)	20	Fixed assets (W2): (650 − 500)	150
Balance	160	Stock (W1)	3
		COSA (W1)	27
	180		180

Tutorial note

If the depreciation adjustment were based on year-end values, it would be $(\dfrac{104}{80} \times 50)$ − 50 = 15, i.e., 5 more than calculated above. The back-log would be 5 less at 15, and the CC reserve 5 more, compensating for a lower profit of 24, i.e., 5 less than 29.

2 HOLFORD PLC

Current cost profit and loss account for 1982

	£000	£000
Profit before charging interest, per historical profit and loss account		29,000
Less: Current cost adjustments:		
Cost of sales (W1)	6,840	
Depreciation (W2)	13,000	19,840
		9,160
Less: Interest	5,000	
Gearing adjustment (W3)	(4,683)	317
		8,843
Less: Taxation		10,000
Current cost loss, attributable to shareholders		(1,157)
Dividends		10,000
Current cost loss, carried forward		(11,157)

Workings

1 COSA

	HC		Stock at average price
	£000		£000
Stock 31.12.81	35,000	$\times \dfrac{135}{120} =$	39,375
Stock 31.12.82	50,000	$\times \dfrac{135}{142} =$	47,535
	15,000		8,160

Adjustment = 15,000 − 8,160 = 6,840

2 Depreciation

	£000	
10% × 330,000 =	33,000	Replacement cost
Less: 10% × 200,000 =	20,000	Historic cost
Additional provision =	13,000	

3   Gearing adjustment

	31.12.81		31.12.82	
	HC £000	CC £000	HC £000	CC £000
Fixed assets	200,000	310,000	200,000	355,000
Less: Depreciation	120,000*	186,000*	140,000+	248,500+
	80,000	124,000	60,000	106,500
Stock	35,000 × 124/120 =	36,167	50,000 × 145/142 =	51,056
Net operating assets	115,000	160,167	110,000	157,556
Net borrowing (1/3)	38,333	38,333	36,667	36,667
Equity (2/3)	76,667	121,834	73,333	120,889
	115,000	160,167	110,000	157,556

*6 years   +7 years

Average net borrowing: $\dfrac{(38{,}333 + 36{,}667)}{(160{,}167 + 157{,}556)}$ = 23.6%

Gearing adjustment: 23.6% × 19,840 = 4,683

the gearing adjustment being a proportion of the current cost adjustments.

Tutorial notes

(1) The COSA is the stock increase due to price increases. There has been a £15,000 quantity and price increase. Since £8,160 represents a quantity increase, because opening and closing stocks have been evaluated at a standard price, the balance, £6,840, represents a price increase.

(2) The depreciation adjustment represents the additional charge necessary to provide for the replacement cost of fixed assets.

(3) The gearing adjustment represents that proportion of the current cost adjustments attributable to the loan capital (or net borrowing). This proportion is based on the current cost balance sheet, as shown in W3.

3 TISCH PLC

Current cost profit and loss account for 1981

		£000
Profit per historical cost profit and loss account, before interest		355
Less: Current cost adjustments:		
Cost of sales (W1)	78	
Depreciation (W2)	30	108
Current cost profit on trading		247
Less: Interest	60	
Gearing adjustment (W3)	(32)	28
		219
Less: Taxation		150
Current cost profit, attributable to shareholders		69

Current cost balance sheet at 31.12.81

	£000	£000
Fixed assets at current cost		1,320
Less: Depreciation		495
		825
Current assets		
Stocks (W1)	906	
Cash	50	
	956	
Less: Current liability		
Corporation tax	150	806
		1,631
Share capital		700
Current cost reserve (W4)		282
Retained profits (180 + 69)		249
		1,231
15% debentures, 1990		400
		1,631

Workings

1 Cost of sales adjustment

	HC £000		Stock at average price £000		
Stock 31.12.80	600	× $\frac{136}{130}$ =	628		
Stock 31.12.81	900	× $\frac{136}{144}$ =	850		
	300	Less	222	=	78

Balance sheet adjustment

| Stock 31.12.80 at HC | 600 | × $\frac{132}{130}$ = | 609, i.e., 9 increase |
| Stock 31.12.81 at HC | 900 | × $\frac{145}{144}$ = | 906, i.e., 6 increase, − per CC reserve |

2 Depreciation adjustment

		£000
Depreciation per profit and loss account (375 − 250)	125 × $\frac{124}{100}$ =	155
Less: Depreciation provided		125
Additional depreciation in profit and loss account		30

Balance sheet adjustment

	31.12.80			31.12.81		
	HC £000		CC £000	HC £000		CC £000
Fixed assets	1,000	× $\frac{120}{100}$ =	1,200	1,000	× $\frac{132}{100}$ =	1,320
Depreciation	250	× $\frac{120}{100}$ =	300	375	× $\frac{132}{100}$ =	495
Net book value	750		900	625		825

Back-log depreciation

	£000	£000
Provision for depreciation at 31.12.81		495
Less: Provision at 31.12.80	250	
Provided for year, HC	125	
Additional	30	405
Additional provision: debit to current cost reserve		90

3 Gearing adjustment

	31.12.80		31.12.81
Assets at current cost	£000		£000
Fixed assets	900		825
Stock	609		906
	1,509		1,731
Financed by:			
Debentures	400		400
Tax	100		150
Bank	(30)		(50)
		Average	
	470	485	500
Equity	1,039	1,135	1,231
	1,509	1,620	1,731

Gearing adjustment (£000): $\dfrac{485}{1,620} \times 108 = 32$

4 Current cost reserve

	£000		£000
Back-log depreciation (W2)	90	Plant and machinery (W2):	
Gearing adjustment (W3)	32	(1,320 − 1,000)	320
		Stock (W1): (906 − 900)	6
Balance	282	Cost of sales adjustment (W1)	78
	404		404

14 Statements of Standard Accounting Practice

INTRODUCTION

Since the accounting conventions and policies acceptable in the UK are determined by the Accounting Standards Committee, the Statements of Standard Accounting Practice are very relevant to the producers and users of financial data.

The greater their impact on the earnings and capital figure, the more significant the standards are. Most of those with direct relevance have been covered in earlier chapters. Of the remainder, probably the following are the most important and thus the most examinable, though not necessarily as free standing questions, but as integral parts of questions on published accounts (see Chapter 12):

SSAP 6   Prior year adjustments and extraordinary items
SSAP 9   Stock and work in progress
SSAP 12 Depreciation
SSAP 19 Investment companies
SSAP 13 Research and development expenditure

These standards produced by a joint committee of the major accountancy bodies have strong moral if not legal persuasion, mainly because the Stock Exchange requires companies seeking a stock exchange listing to prepare their accounts in conformance with them.

The following summarises those points which students must be aware of.

SSAP 1   Associated Companies

See Chapter 10.

SSAP 2   Policies

The standard considered four fundamental concepts, now embodied in the 1981 Companies Act:

(a)   going-concern basis;
(b)   accruals basis;
(c)   prudence basis;
(d)   consistency basis.

305

Going concern: in preparing accounts one assumes that the business is continuing, i.e., it is a going concern, and assets are valued accordingly.

Accruals: in calculating profit, income is compared with expenditure, not receipts with payments, as in a cashflow statement. It is often called the matching concept.

Prudence: income and profit are not recognised (recorded) until represented by an asset that is realisable with a fair degree of certainty. Expenditure and losses are recognised (recorded) immediately they are apparent.

Consistency: once chosen, an accounting basis should not be changed unless it is necessary to conform to the prudence concept which is paramount.

Accounting bases are the various ways of implementing the fundamental concepts, usually to achieve the 'matching' of the accruals concept.

Accounting policies are the actual bases chosen by the directors in the preparation of the accounts. They must appear as notes to the accounts.

SSAP 3   Earnings per share

$$\text{Earnings per share} = \frac{\text{Earnings}}{\text{No. of equity shares}}$$

Earnings = Profits after: tax
                         minority interest
                         preference dividend
                    but before extraordinary items

Where more shares are issued at market value during the year, the calculation is based on the weighted average number of shares. In the case of a rights issue, the number of shares is modified by the bonus element.

SSAP 4   Government Grants

Capital grants can be absorbed into the profit and loss account as the asset, recorded at full price, is depreciated.

SSAP 5   VAT

Generally VAT does not affect the profit and loss account—turnover, as disclosed in the accounts, excludes VAT. Any difference between VAT charged on outputs and that claimed on inputs is payable quarterly to Customs and Excise, appearing as a current liability until paid.

SSAP 6   Prior-year Adjustments and Extraordinary Items

Prior-year adjustments are material amounts resulting from:

(a)   a change of accounting policy; or
(b)   a fundamental error.

A common example of (a) is changing stock valuations from marginal cost to full absorption cost. In calculating the cost of sales for the year of change, the increase in the valuation of the opening stock is credited to reserves, as a prior-year adjustment, since it has not been generated by this year's activities.

Extraordinary items are profits or losses which derive from transactions or events outside the ordinary activities of the business. Such an item, which includes its own tax, is shown in the profit and loss account after the earnings figure.

Exceptional items derive from the ordinary activities of the firm but merit separate disclosure because of their size or incidence, e.g., abnormally high bad debts.

PSSAP 7

This was the provisional standard on Current Purchasing Power Accounting.

SSAP 8 Imputation Tax

See Chapter 12.

SSAP 9 Stock and Work in Progress

Stock and work in progress should be valued at the lower of cost including overheads, and net realisable value.

Long-term (i.e., longer than a year) work in progress may include an element of profit, and thus appears amongst the current assets as follows:

	£
Long-term work in progress at cost	XXX,XXX
Add: Attributable profit	XX,XXX
Less: Full provision for loss	(X,XXX)
	XXX,XXX
Less: Amounts received and receivable on account	XX,XXX
	XX,XXX

Attributable profit is a fair proportion of the expected profit on contracts, the outcome of which can be assessed with reasonable certainty. Following the prudence concept of SSAP 2, if a loss is expected it should be provided for immediately. Fair proportion relates to the work done, which may be measured at cost or at selling price, i.e., work certified.

SSAP 10 Source and Application of Funds

See Chapter 2.

SSAP 11

Replaced by SSAP 15.

SSAP 12 Depreciation

Provision must be made for depreciation on all fixed assets with a finite life — this includes freehold buildings.

Where assets are revalued, provision for depreciation should be made on the new valuation.

No specific method is supported. Notes to the accounts should indicate the method or rate being used.

Investment properties are excluded and considered in SSAP 19.

SSAP 13 Research and development expenditure

All R & D expenditure should be written off in the year it is incurred except development costs which are specific to a project or product, the commercial viability of which is assured. Such expenditure can be carried forward and amortised in proportion to the sales as they materialise.

SSAP 14 Group Accounts

See Chapter 10.

SSAP 15 Deferred Taxation

See Chapter 12.

SSAP 16 Current Cost Accounting

See Chapter 13.

SSAP 17 Accounting for Post Balance Sheet Events

The accounts should only be adjusted if the post balance sheet event provides evidence of the situation at balance sheet date, e.g., liquidation proceedings are evidence of a bad debt. Post balance sheet events affecting an understanding of the accounts should be noted, e.g., substantial damage to property.

SSAP 18 Accounting for Contingencies

The company should provide for contingent liabilities which are likely to materialise. Others should be noted, as should contingent assets.

SSAP 19 Treatment of Investment Properties

Investment properties, i.e., property producing rent, should not be depreciated but revalued, profits being taken to a revaluation reserve. Losses are debited to the reserve unless the balance is inadequate, when the excess should be charged to the profit and loss account.

SSAP 20 Foreign Currency Transactions

Transactions in foreign currency should be converted using the temporal method, i.e., historical rates. Profits/losses on exchange should be passed through the profit and loss account as ordinary items.

The balance sheets of foreign subsidiaries and autonomous decision-making branches should be converted using the closing rate. Differences should be passed through reserves.

SSAP 21 Leasing and Hire-purchase

Financial leases: assets should be shown on the balance sheet of the lessee and depreciated in the usual way. The interest element of the rental payments should be charged to the profit and loss account. The balance sheet shows a liability to the lessor. Hire-purchase transactions are treated in the same way.

Operational leases: the lessee's use of the asset is considered only temporary, and hence it does not appear on the balance sheet. The full rental is charged to the profit and loss account.

SSAP 22 Goodwill

(Previously ED 30).

Goodwill, the difference between the fair value of the purchase consideration and the fair value of the net separable assets, should be eliminated from the balance sheet either:

(a) immediately by writing off against reserves; or

(b) by write-off in the profit and loss account over the estimated economic life — not to exceed 20 years.

Negative goodwill, a capital reserve, should be transferred to distributable reserves as assets to which it relates are realised. If the low purchase price incorporates a provision for expected losses, the negative goodwill may be credited to the profit and loss account as the anticipated losses are made.

ED 31 Merger Accounting – 'Pooling'

This exposure draft seeks to allow merging companies to pool their capital and reserves so that on completion of the merger the nature of the reserves is not changed. The major condition for this controversial form of accounting is that substantially the greater part of the purchase consideration is satisfied by the issue of shares, i.e., the merger is accomplished by a 'swopping' of shares. Note that conventional acquisition accounting, per SSAP 14, capitalises the pre-acquisition reserve of the subsidiary and only post-acquisition profits may appear in the consolidated reserves.

QUESTIONS

1 CAVOUR LTD

Cavour Ltd is a firm of building contractors. The following information is provided relating to their uncompleted contracts at 31 December 1980:

Contract	A	B	C	D
Date contract commenced	1.1.80	1.2.80	1.8.80	1.10.80
Expected completion date	30.4.81	31.3.81	31.1.81	31.3.82
	£	£	£	£
Cost of work to 31 December 1980	159,000	57,000	15,000	4,000
Estimated further costs to completion	36,000	15,000	2,000	62,000
Value of work certified to 31 December 1980	200,000	50,000	18,000	–
Contract price	260,000	65,000	21,000	75,000
Progress payments received and receivable at 31 December 1980	175,000	40,000	–	–

Required:

(a) A statement showing your calculations of the separate values to be placed on each contract at 31 December 1980. The statement should show the profit or loss, if any, included in each of the valuations. You should include in the statement appropriate narratives to explain the treatments chosen.

(b) A statement of the information in respect of the four contracts which would appear in the balance sheet of Cavour Ltd at 31 December 1980.

Note:

Your calculations should take account of the requirements contained in Statement of Standard Accounting Practice 9.

20 marks

2 ELECTRONICS LTD

Electronics Ltd manufactures the 'Electron' component and undertakes contract building of electronic display units.

In the 'Electron' *components division* of the company costs for the year ended 31 August 1984, were:

	£
Materials	10,000
Labour	21,000
Depreciation	8,000
Factory rent	6,000
Sundry factory expenses	9,000
Head office administration	5,000
Selling expenses	7,000
	66,000

1,000 'Electron' components were manufactured during the year, of which 100 were held in stock at 31 August 1984.

A substantial reduction in material prices occurred recently and the directors estimate that, at 31 August 1984, the replacement cost of the materials used during the year would have been £7,000.

The most recent sale of 'Electron' components was made on 15 July 1984, at a price of £70 per unit.

In the *contracts division* of the company the contracts in progress at 31 August 1984 were:

Contract	Date commenced	Cost incurred to 31 August	Estimated completion date	Estimated total cost	Contract price
A	20 Mar 1984	£48,000	15 Sep 1985	£50,000	£40,000
B	4 May 1984	£27,000	1 Oct 1985	£36,000	£44,000
C	22 Aug 1984	£2,000	31 Jan 1986	£25,000	£30,000

No payments on account have been received for any of the contracts.

The following have been suggested as possible values at which the stocks of finished components and work in progress on long-term contracts might be shown in the balance sheet at 31 August 1984:

No.	'Electron' components £
1	3,100
2	5,100
3	5,400
4	6,300
5	6,000

	Work in progress on long-term contracts			Total amount for
	Contract A	Contract B	Contract C	balance sheet
6	38,000	27,000	2,000	67,000
7	48,000	33,000	2,400	83,400
8	38,000	33,000	2,000	73,000
9	38,000	35,000	7,000	80,000
10	38,000	35,000	2,000	75,000

Required:

A statement showing whether or not each suggested amount is acceptable within Statement of Standard Accounting Practice No. 9.

Consider each amount independently and state your answer in the form:

Acceptable. . . . . (Nos.)
Not acceptable . . . . (Nos.)

(For the long-term contracts, consider in each case the acceptability of the total amount for the balance sheet — the individual items are shown in the question to reveal the composition of that total.)

You are *not* required to present a balance sheet.

20 marks

3 LARCHMONT LTD

Larchmont Ltd was established on 1 January 1983 to manufacture a single product using a machine which cost £400,000. The machine is expected to last for four years and then have a scrap value of £52,000. The machine will produce a similar number of goods each year and annual profits before depreciation are expected to be in the region of £200,000. The financial controller has suggested that the machine should be depreciated using either the straight-line method or the reducing balance method. If the latter method is used, it has been estimated that an annual depreciation rate of 40% would be appropriate.

Required:

(a) Calculations of the annual depreciation charges and the net book values of the fixed asset at the end of 1983, 1984, 1985 and 1986 using:

  (i)   the straight-line method;
  (ii) the reducing balance method.   *10 marks*

(b) A discussion of the differing implications of these two methods for the financial information published by Larchmont Ltd for the years 1983-1986 inclusive. You should also advise management which method you consider more appropriate bearing in mind expected profit levels.   *10 marks*

Note: Ignore taxation.

Total 20 marks

4 PORTLAND LTD

The financial director of Portland Ltd has prepared the following information with a view to drawing up the company's profit and loss account for the year to 30 June 1983:

	£000
Retained profit at 1 July 1982	7,200
Turnover	17,500
Cost of sales (Note 1)	10,800
Loss on closure of factory in Scotland	760
Administration expenses (Note 2)	3,660
Distribution costs	1,200
Taxation (Note 3)	635
Dividends paid and proposed	100

Notes:

1. The calculation of cost of sales includes opening stock of £1,000,000 and closing stock of £1,200,000, each valued on the marginal cost basis. The directors have since decided that the total cost basis gives a fairer presentation of the company's results and financial position, and the auditors agree with this assessment. Using the total cost basis, opening stock should be valued at £1,425,000 and closing stock at £1,840,000. You may ignore the effect on tax payable of this change in the method of stock valuation.

2. Administration expenses include bad debts of £850,000. Bad debts are normally in the region of £100,000 p.a., whereas the figure for the current year includes a loss of £750,000 incurred when a major customer went into liquidation.

3. The figure for taxation is made up of the following items:

	£000	£000
Tax payable on 'normal' trading profit		1,180
Less: Tax relief on bad debt arising from liquidation of a major customer	375	
Tax relief arising from loss on closure of factory in Scotland	170	545
		635

Required:

(a) Define exceptional items and extraordinary items in accordance with the provisions of Statement of Standard Accounting Practice 6. Give two examples of each. *8 marks*

(b) Prepare the profit and loss account and statement of retained earnings of Portland Ltd, not necessarily in a form suitable for publication but in accordance with good accounting practice and complying with the provisions of Statement of Standard Accounting Practice 6. *22 marks*

Total 30 marks

ANSWERS

1 CAVOUR LTD

(a)
Contracts	A	B	C	D
Contract price (£000)	260	65	21	75
Cost to date	159	57	15	4
Further costs	36	15	2	62
Total costs	195	72	17	66
Expected profit	65	(7)	4	9
Work certified	200	50	N/A	N/A
Contract price	260	65		
Attributable profit*	50	(7)		
Value placed on contract	(159 + 50) 209	(57−7) 50	15	4

*Attributable profit means a fair share of the expected profit, provided the final outcome is reasonably certain, i.e., the contract is in an advanced state. 'Fair share' has been calculated here in terms of work certified relative to sale (contract) price. An acceptable, though less sound, interpretation of fair share could be:

$$\frac{\text{Cost incurred to date}}{\text{Total cost of contract}}$$

(b) Long-term *work in progress* (appearing amongst the current assets)

	£
Cost (A + B + D)	220,000
Add: Attributable profit	50,000
	270,000
Less: Full provision for expected loss	(7,000)
	263,000
Less: Progress payments	215,000
	48,000
Other work in progress at cost*	15,000

*Contract C is a short-term contract, i.e., less than one year and should be valued at cost, unless a loss is anticipated.

A note appearing in the company's statement of policies would indicate that long-term work in progress is valued at cost including overheads, and that profit is only taken when a contract is sufficiently advanced for the final outcome to be relatively certain.

2 ELECTRONICS LTD

Stocks of finished goods (electron components)

Acceptable

3   i.e., cost including production overheads

Not acceptable

1   i.e., prime cost, excluding overheads

2   i.e., replacement cost; there is no need to provide for a loss since the goods will be sold at a profit

4   i.e., net realisable value (selling price less selling expenses)

5   i.e., cost including elements of administration and selling expenses.

Work in progress on long-term contracts (electronic display units)

Acceptable

6   i.e., cost less provision for loss on A

8   i.e., cost plus 'attributable profit' less provision for loss

Not acceptable

7   i.e., A at cost; C at cost plus profit; A should not be valued at cost, since its net realisable value is only £38,000; C is not sufficiently advanced to incorporate any profit in its valuation.

10   i.e., B is valued at net realisable value

9   i.e., B at net realisable value and C at cost and anticipated profit

Note: SSAP 9 requires that work in progress be valued at cost (including overheads absorbed on a normal basis), or net realisable value, whichever is the lower. Long-term work in progress may include 'attributable profit', i.e., a fair proportion of the expected profit provided the contract is sufficiently well advanced for the outcome to be ascertained with reasonable certainty.

Workings

Components	1,000 units £	100 units £
Prime cost	31,000	3,100
Production overheads	23,000	2,300
Production cost	54,000	5,400 (correct valuation)
Administration	5,000	500
	59,000	5,900
Selling price	70,000	7,000
Less: 'Selling expenses'	7,000	700*
	63,000	6,300

*These expenses relate to costs of selling the goods, and are therefore unlikely to be $1/10 \times £7,000$.

Long-term work in progress

	A	B	C
Cost to date,	48,000	27,000	2,000
Attributable profit	$\frac{27}{36} \times 8,000 =$	6,000	Nil**
Full provision for loss	(10,000)		
	38,000	33,000	2,000
Contract (selling price)	40,000	44,000	30,000
Less: Further costs	2,000	9,000	23,000
	38,000	35,000	7,000

**Since only 8% (i.e., 2/25) of contract C is completed, its outcome is not at all certain, and the attributable profit is thus nil.

3 LARCHMONT LTD

(a) Cost of machine £400,000
    Less: Residual value 52,000

    348,000

Annual provision for depreciation

Straight-line: 25% × £348,000 = £87,000

Reducing balance: 40% × balance at beginning of year

(Calculation to nearest £1,000.)

	(i)		(ii)	
	Net book value	Depreciation	Net book value	Depreciation
1.1.83 Cost	400		400	
1983 Depreciation	87	87	160	160
31.12.83	313		240	
1984 Depreciation	87	87	96	96
31.12.84	226		144	
1985 Depreciation	87	87	58	58
31.12.85	139		86	
1986 Depreciation	87	87	34	34
31.12.86	52		52	

(b)   The purposes of depreciation are to charge against profits the cost of using up fixed assets, and thus to show on the balance sheet the value of the assets to the business in terms of their unexpired cost. There is the associated objective of providing funds for the replacement of fixed assets by the retention of an appropriate amount of the annual cash flow.

Depreciation is a charge made against profit for the use of fixed assets. If assets 'contribute' equal amounts annually to the business profits, it would seem reasonable to make equal provision for depreciation using the straight-line (fixed instalment) method. Possibly, the running and maintenance costs will be higher in later years, in which case, the higher charges produced by the reducing balance method, would appear to be more appropriate, in the earlier years. Unless assets are old and are being run continuously close to full capacity, running and maintenance costs are not likely to be so much higher in the later years. Since the scrap value will be 13% of original cost, there is little evidence of the intention to exhaust the machine. It is true that some fixed assets are valued at their approximate resale value, using the reducing balance method, but these are assets such as motor vehicles, which are often sold well before the end of their useful lives, and thus their resale value is of significance.

SSAP 12, the accounting standard on depreciation, does not prescribe any particular method of providing for depreciation, and therefore one should consider the impact of the alternative methods on the disclosed profits. Whereas method (i) absorbs a steady 43% (87/200) of the expected profit, method (ii) takes a staggering 80% (160/200) of the first year's profit. Since it is acceptable accounting policy to equalise profits, i.e., remove variability, which is the basis of business risk, method (i) seems more appropriate for depreciating the majority of fixed assets. Note that the use of method (ii) could produce results that might be misleading:

	Profits after depreciation
Year 1	40
2	104
3	142
4	166

The related return on investment would show:

Year 1	40/240	=	17%
2	104/144	=	72%
3	142/86	=	165%
4	166/52	=	319%

4 PORTLAND LTD

(a) Exceptional items are those items deriving from a company's ordinary activities which require separate disclosure in the final accounts because they are abnormal in size or incidence, e.g., abnormal bad debts or stock write-offs; redundancy costs (provided the business is continuing).

Extraordinary items are substantial items which derive from events or transactions outside the ordinary activities of the business, e.g., profit or loss on the sale of investments; redundancy and other costs related to discontinued businesses (see tutorial note).

(b) **Profit and loss account for the year ended 30.6.83**

		£000
Turnover		17,500
Less: Cost of sales (W)		10,585
Gross profit		6,915
Less: Distribution costs	1,200	
Administrative expenses including bad debts £850,000	3,660	
		4,860
Profit on ordinary activities		2,055
Tax on ordinary activities (1,180 − 375)		805
		1,250
Less: Extraordinary loss on closure of factory	760	
Less: Tax relief	170	590
Profit for year		660
Dividends paid and proposed		100
Retained profit for year		560
Retained profit at 1.7.82	7,200	
Add: Prior-year adjustment	425	7,625
Profits retained for balance sheet at 30.6.83		8,185

Workings

	£000
Cost of sales	10,800
Add: Increase in opening valuation (1,425 − 1,000) (see tutorial note)	425
	11,225
Less: Increase in valuation of closing stock (1,840 − 1,200)	640
	10,585

Tutorial note

In a review of SSAP 6 in 1983, the Accounting Standards Committee suggested that the words 'expected not to recur frequently or regularly' be dropped from the original definition, because of difficulty of interpretation and significance in practice.

A prior-year adjustment is a substantial item deriving from a change in accounting policy or the correction of a fundamental error. In this case the profits of earlier years should be increased by £425,000.

15 Capital project appraisal

INTRODUCTION

Although a banker's more immediate interest is in a company's working capital policy, fixed asset (capital) policy and decisions are the more important since investment is the real substance of business, and in a major sense is what banking is all about. The relevance of investment appraisal to the banker is well illustrated by the regularity and frequency of questions on this fundamental element of financial management in examination papers.

TECHNIQUES

Students must be familiar with the following terms and techniques:

(a) **Pay-back period**

This is the time required for the original investment to be recovered. Its major limitation is that profit is ignored.

(b) **Accounting rate of return**

This is: $\dfrac{\text{Average profit}}{\text{Average capital employed}}$, i.e., a project's rate of return.

Although this technique is concerned with profitability, it ignores the time value of money, which is a major principle of investment.

(c) **Net present value (NPV)**

In this method, a project's cash flows (payments and receipts), are discounted by applying factors determined by the company's cost of capital or target rate of return.

(d) **Internal rate of return (IRR)**

This is also known as the true rate of return or discounted cash flow yield.

A project's internal rate of return is the rate of interest which discounts the cash flows to zero.

(e) **Sensitivity analysis**

All investment appraisal is based upon estimates. Sensitivity analysis is an approach to the problem of uncertainty which considers the margin of error in making these estimates.

DISCOUNTED CASH FLOW

NPV and IRR techniques are superior to the others because they take into account the timing as well as the value of cash flows. In order that cash flows in earlier and later years may be compared, they should be expressed in common units, present value £1, which can be read from discount tables.

ILLUSTRATION

Calculate the pay-back period, the accounting rate of return, the net present value and the internal rate of return of the following proposal, if the company's cost of capital is 10%:

Cost	£100,000
Working capital	£ 40,000
Life	4 yrs
Residual value	£ 20,000
Annual earnings*	£ 30,000

*Earnings means cash flow and is therefore profit before charging depreciation.

Pay-back period

3 years 4 months, i.e., 100,000/30,000.

Note that only the fixed asset is included in this calculation, since working capital is not consumed and therefore does not have to be recovered.

Accounting rate of return

$$\frac{\text{Average profit}}{\text{Average investment}} = \frac{10,000}{100,000} = 10\%$$

Working

	£
Profit:	
Income = 4 × 30,000	120,000
Less: Expenditure: depreciation (£100,000 − £20,000)	80,000
	40,000

Therefore average profit is £10,000

Investment:
At beginning (£100,000 + £40,000)   £
At end (£20,000 + £40,000)   140,000
    60,000

    200,000

Therefore average investment (capital employed) is   100,000

This figure of 10%, which is a reasonable first estimate, should be compared with the internal rate of return.

Net present value

	Year	Cash flow	Factor	PV or DCF
Cost	0	100,000	1.0	(100,000)
Working capital	0	40,000	1.0	(40,000)
Earnings	1-4	30,000	3.17	95,100
Residual value	4	20,000		
Working capital released	4	40,000 60,000	0.68	40,800
				(4,100)

Since the NPV is negative, the project does not give a 10% return; it will be rejected as not meeting the target return.

Internal rate of return

This is estimated by trial and error. Since the project does not yield 10%, try a lower rate, e.g., 5%.

	Year	Cash flow	Factor	DCF
Cost	0			(100,000)
Working capital	0			(40,000)
Earnings	1-4	30,000	3.54	106,200
Residual value	4	20,000	0.82	16,400
Working capital	4	40,000	0.82	32,800
				15,400

The project's IRR lies somewhere between 5% and 10% (closer to 10%), as illustrated below:

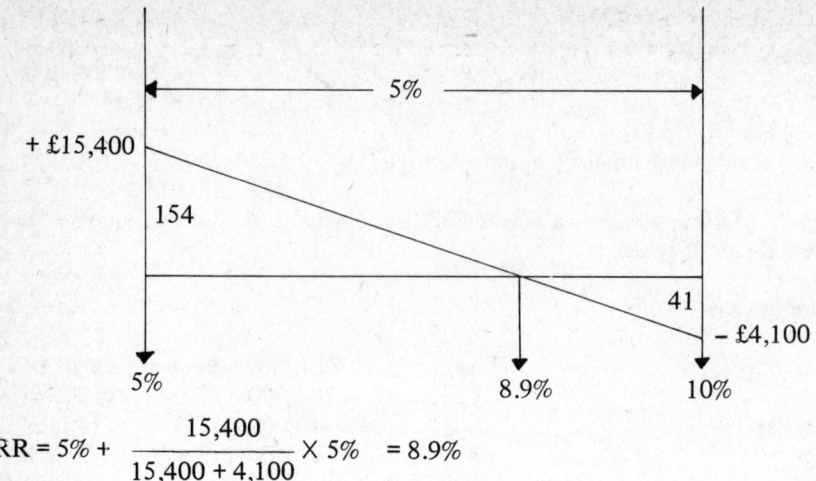

$$\text{IRR} = 5\% + \frac{15,400}{15,400 + 4,100} \times 5\% = 8.9\%$$

DCF conventions

It is important that you remember that the following are conventions of DCF, unless otherwise stated:

(a) Investment takes place at the beginning of the year, i.e., year 0.

(b) Income and expenditure occur at the end of each year.

(c) Taxation (usually corporation tax) is payable one year after the end of the year to which it relates — in reality it is payable only nine months after the financial year end.

COST OF CAPITAL

This is the cost to a firm of having assets on the balance sheet. All assets have been financed by someone who, apart from trade and expense creditors, requires a return. The major forms of finance are equity, debt, and bank finance. Since they provide a pool of capital, investment appraisal techniques use the weighted average cost of capital, estimated as follows:

$$\text{WACC} = \frac{\text{Interest and dividends payable}}{\text{Market value of capital}}$$

Interest payments are allowed for tax purposes so that gearing reduces a company's cost of capital. Investment undertaken at 'target' rates lower than the cost of capital will reduce a firm's value, since the (present) value added by future profits is less than the value lost in servicing the capital.

INFLATION

Where all expenses, and selling prices, are subject to the same rate of inflation (r), calculation of net present value can be simplified by using the real cost of capital (i) instead of the money cost of capital (m).

They are related by the formula:

$$i = \frac{m - r}{1 + r}$$

For example, a money cost of capital of 21%, subject to 10% inflation, produces a real cost of:

$$\frac{0.21 - 0.10}{1.10}$$

i.e., 10%.

SUGGESTED METHOD OF ANSWERING THE QUESTION

Since these questions are concerned with the evaluation of alternatives, state what the alternatives are, and list the cash flows attributable to them.

As timing is of the essence of finance, the cash flows must be discounted in order that different streams of cash flow may be compared. Do not reject the marks usually awarded for a short commentary on the chosen alternative, which can include a criticism of the technique and mention of other matters that must be taken into account when making decisions. Note, these marks can be earned even if the actual figure work has gone awry.

QUESTIONS

1 TURNER

Turner wants a new machine for his workshop. He comes to you with the following problem:

> I have to decide whether to buy or lease the machine. In either case it will have a useful life of six years. The alternatives are:
>
> (i) Buy for £6,600. The machine is very specialised, so its resale value at any time after acquisition can be ignored.
>
> (ii) Contract to lease the machine for a fixed period of three years at £2,000 per year. I would then have the option of renewing the lease annually at a cost of £1,000 per year (for a further three years).
>
> The machine will give a net saving (after running costs) of £5,000 per year in labour costs and material wastage, so there is no doubt that I should have it.
>
> I can find the money to purchase outright, but is it worth it? I estimate that my cost of capital is 14% p.a., because I could always earn that much on other projects.

All receipts and payments (unless immediate) occur end-year.

Required:

(a) A numerical analysis (confined to aspects specified in the above information) which will assist Turner in his decision.

(b) Comment briefly on any other aspects which might need to be considered in a practical situation.

Table of factors for r = 14%

Years n	Future value of £1 $(1+r)^n$	Present value of £1 $(1+r)^{-n}$	Present value of £1 received per year $\dfrac{1-(1+r)^{-n}}{r}$	Annual value of £1 received now $\dfrac{r}{1-(1+r)^{-n}}$
1	1.140	0.877	0.877	1.140
2	1.300	.769	1.647	;607
3	1.482	.675	2.322	.431
4	1.689	.592	2.914	.343
5	1.925	.519	3.433	.291
6	2.195	.456	3.889	.257
7	2.502	.400	4.288	.233
8	2.853	.351	4.639	.216
9	3.252	.308	4.946	.202
10	3.707	.270	5.216	.192

20 marks

2 JOHNS (MANUFACTURING)

John owns a manufacturing firm. He is considering the replacement of some old equipment used in the manufacture of widgets. He believes that replacement will be very profitable, but he asks your assistance in reviewing his analysis, which follows:

	£	£
Old equipment:		
Cost in 1966	20,000	
Less: Accumulated depreciation	12,000	
Current book value		8,000
Working capital		2,000
Value invested		10,000
Annual revenue from sale of widgets		8,000
Less: Labour, materials, running costs		6,800
Net revenue per year		1,200
New equipment:		
Cash purchase price	13,000	
Less: Trade-in allowance on old equipment	8,000	
Net purchase price		5,000
Working capital		6,000
Value invested		11,000
Annual revenue from sale of widgets		16,000
Less: Labour, materials, running costs		12,000
Net revenue per year		4,000

Return on investment: calculated as (Net revenue/Value invested) × 100

Old equipment: (£1,200/£10,000) × 100 = 12%

New equipment: (£4,000/£11,000) × 100 = 36%

John informs you that he would get only £7,300 cash for the old equipment if he sold it independently now instead of trading it for new equipment.

Both old and new equipment have an economic life of four years: at the end of that time there will be no market for the sale of widgets and neither old nor new equipment will have any salvage value.

Working capital consists of the total amounts required to finance stocks and debtors associated with widgets under each alternative; under either alternative the full amount shown as working capital would be recovered when production of widgets ceased.

John's cost of capital is 10% p.a. in all relevant years. Assume that annual revenues and costs occur end-year.

Ignore taxation.

Required:

Your own analysis of the choices available to John. State briefly which choice you would recommend on the basis of the information available.

Table of factors for r = 10%

Years n	Future value of £1 $(1+r)^n$	Present value of £1 $(1+r)^{-n}$	Present value of £1 received per year $\dfrac{1-(1+r)^{-n}}{r}$	Annual value of £1 received now $\dfrac{r}{1-(1+r)^{-n}}$
1	1.100	0.909	0.909	1.100
2	1.210	.826	1.736	0.576
3	1.331	.751	2.487	.402
4	1.464	.683	3.170	.315
5	1.611	.621	3.791	.264
6	1.772	.564	4.355	.230
7	1.949	.513	4.868	.205
8	2.144	.467	5.335	.187
9	2.358	.424	5.759	.174
10	2.594	.386	6.145	.163

20 marks

3 DEXTER

Dexter is a businessman who has invented a plastic tin-opener. He has patented the device, and he is considering whether he should dispose of the patent or exploit it himself.

Octopus Ltd has offered to buy the patent outright for an immediate payment of £20,000, or to acquire sole use of the patent in exchange for a royalty on each tin-opener manufactured. In the latter case Dexter estimates that he would receive £5,000 per year for five years, after which Octopus Ltd would drop the product and the patent would be valueless.

Dexter believes he could derive an income from the patent for a longer period by exploiting it himself. He could do either of the following:

(a) Subcontract the manufacture of the tin-opener and engage agents to sell the product. Dexter estimates sales would be £50,000 per year for seven years; his total costs would be £40,000 each year, in addition to which he would require a 'salary' of £4,000 per year to compensate him for effort diverted from other activities and for risk. Thus his net receipts after personal compensation would be £6,000 per year. The patent would be valueless at the end of the seven years.

(b) Rent a factory to manufacture the tin-opener and other products. This would require an immediate capital outlay of £36,000 on equipment; it can be assumed that production would commence immediately. Estimated sales would be £100,000 per year for nine years. Total costs (excluding depreciation of equipment) would be £84,000 each year; in addition Dexter would require a 'salary' of £6,000 per year for effort and risk. Thus his net receipts after personal compensation would be £10,000 per year. At the end of nine years the patent and equipment would be valueless and the factory would be closed.

Dexter's cost of capital is 10% p.a. All forecasted figures can be accepted as accurate. All receipts and payments (unless immediate) occur end-year.

Required:

A numerical analysis which will assist Dexter in his decision. Comment briefly on your results.

Ignore taxation and investment in working capital.

Please refer to Table of factors r = 10% given in Question 2, on page 328.

30 marks

4 HI-FI LTD

Hi-Fi Ltd manufactures sound reproduction equipment. Some of its employees have discovered a method of improving the performance of cassette tapes, and the company has patented the invention.

The company's operations do not at present include the processing of tapes, and it is therefore faced with a decision on how it might best exploit the invention.

Hi-Fi Ltd has received two offers from other companies. Splice Ltd is prepared to buy the patent for £30,000, whereas Mainbrace Ltd seeks exclusive use of the process in exchange for a royalty on the tapes produced. In the latter case, Hi-Fi Ltd has estimated that £9,000 per year would be received for seven years, by which time the patent would be valueless.

Two other possibilities are being considered by Hi-Fi Ltd:

(I) Processing and marketing could be subcontracted to a tape manufacturer. If this approach is taken, it is estimated that net receipts, after meeting all costs, will be £8,000 per year. However, these amounts could be maintained for eight years, after which the patent would be valueless.

(II) Hi-Fi Ltd could acquire equipment to undertake the process itself, and market the tapes with its other products. The company could lease premises and some equipment, and it is estimated that net receipts after meeting annual outlay costs would amount to £17,000 per year for nine years. However, the company would also have to purchase items of equipment for £45,000, and would have to tie up working capital of £15,000. The equipment would be valueless at the end of the nine years, but the working capital would be run down in the normal course of business at the end of the project's life.

Assume that:

(i) The cost of capital for Hi-Fi Ltd in all relevant years is 10% p.a.

(ii) The payment from Splice Ltd would be received immediately; the outlay on equipment and investment in working capital would be made immediately; and all annual amounts would occur at the end of the appropriate years.

Required:

(a) A numerical analysis of the options available to Hi-Fi Ltd.

(b) A discussion (based on the results of the numerical analysis) of the factors to be taken into account by the company in their deliberations.

Note: Ignore taxation.

Please refer to Table of factors r = 10% given in Question 2, on page 328.

30 marks

5 CAMPBELL AND McCARTHY

Campbell and McCarthy own an engineering firm. They have asked your financial advice regarding the replacement of their existing equipment for the manufacture of flibbets. Campbell explains:

I am not keen on the idea. The new equipment would cost £25,000, but it will be worthwhile using for only five years. It should yield a net revenue (after all costs except depreciation) of £25,000 in the first year, declining by £5,000 per year thereafter. We would have to keep higher stocks of raw materials and finance more debtors, so about £6,000 additional working capital would be needed above the present level of £4,000 required with our existing equipment.

If we bought the new equipment we could sell the existing equipment for only £5,000, although it has a written-down value of £15,000 in the firm's books. It is still serviceable and would yield a net revenue (after all costs except depreciation) of £5,000 per year if we did not replace. After five years the market for flibbets will almost certainly be negligible, and whatever equipment we have then will not be worth anything, even as scrap.

Taking the current realisable value of the existing equipment as the basis for depreciation, the status quo offers us a net profit of £4,000 per year:

	£
Net revenue before depreciation	5,000
Depreciation (straight-line)	1,000
Net profit	4,000

As a return on capital, that is pretty good; £4,000 per year on the current realisable value of £5,000 is 80%.

Compare the new equipment. That will involve a £10,000 loss on the sale of the old equipment, which we cannot charge in our accounts against reserves because we have no reserves. So £2,000 per year will have to be charged against future profits, which added to straight-line depreciation of £5,000 per year on the new equipment, gives an outlay cost equivalent to £7,000 per year.

Thus:

	£000				
End of year	1	2	3	4	5
Net revenue before depreciation	25	20	15	10	5
Less: Outlay cost	7	7	7	7	7
	18	13	8	3	(2)
Less: Annual profit forgone on existing equipment	4	4	4	4	4
Net profit (loss)	14	9	4	(1)	(6)

Averaged over the five years those net profit figures come to £4,000 per year. On an investment of £31,000 (new equipment £25,000 plus working capital £6,000) that yields a return of about 13%. We have access to ample funds, but we estimate out cost of capital at 14% p.a., so the new equipment is unattractive.

McCarthy objects:

Although I agree with Campbell's basic figures and forecasts, I cannot accept his juggling. The new equipment will pay for itself in the first year; that is good enough for me, and I want to go ahead.

Assume that the working capital levels mentioned by Campbell would apply throughout the five years, that the cash outlay on the new equipment (less the amount received for the existing equipment) would occur immediately, and that all other receipts and payments would occur end-year.

Required:

(a) Your own numerical analysis of the alternatives (calculate to the nearest £100).

(b) Comments on your results in relation to the views expressed by Campbell and McCarthy.

Ignore taxation.

Please refer to table of factors r = 14% given in Question 1, on page 326.

30 marks

6   GOLDSMITH

Goldsmith requires some equipment for his firm. The following methods of acquisition are available:

(i)   purchase of the equipment for cash;

(ii) purchase of the equipment under a hire-purchase contract. involving an initial deposit and two annual payments;

(iii) hire of the equipment.

You are given the following information:

Cash price of equipment	£10,000
Period of use in Goldsmith's firm	5 years
Sale value at end of use	£1,000
Initial deposit under hire-purchase contract	£4,000
Two subsequent payments under hire-purchase contract, one year and two years after initial deposit	£4,000 per year
Annual rental under hire-contract, payable at the end of each year of (5 years) service	£2,500 per year

In all cases maintenance and running expenses would be borne by Goldsmith.

Goldsmith's estimated cost of capital over the 5-year period is 10% p.a.,

Required:

(a) Calculate which is the best method of acquisition, on the basis of the available information (ignore taxation).

(b) Comment very briefly on any further aspects which may be relevant to the decision.

Please refer to table of factors r = 10% given in Question 2, on page 328.

20 marks

7 SORTER LTD

Sorter Ltd requires some new equipment to help to manufacture a product for a period of four years, commencing 1 January 1983. The accounts of Sorter Ltd are prepared on the calendar year basis. At the end of four years, demand for the product will collapse and the company will be unable to make any further use of the equipment.

The equipment required by Sorter Ltd can be obtained in any one of three ways:

(i) It could be purchased for cash on 1 January 1983.

(ii) It could be acquired under a hire-purchase contract which requires a deposit to be paid on 1 January 1983, and three further instalments at annual intervals following the date of the initial deposit.

(iii) It could be rented, commencing 1 January 1983.

You are given the following financial information and facts relevant to an assessment of the three alternatives:

(1) The cash price of the equipment is £50,000.

(2) The equipment will have no resale value at the end of the four-year period.

(3) The deposit required under the hire-purchase contract is £26,000.

(4) The annual instalments payable under the hire-purchase contract are £13,000, and each payment includes an interest element of £5,000.

(5) The annual rental of the equipment, payable in arrears each year, is £20,000.

(6) You may assume that Sorter Ltd is subject to corporation tax at the rate of 50% and that the tax is payable one year following the end of the accounting period to which the assessment relates.

(7) The company will be entitled to claim a 100% first-year allowance on the cash price of the equipment under options (i) and (ii), and it is the company's policy to claim maximum capital allowances as soon as they become available.

(8) Sorter Ltd's estimated cost of capital over the four-year period is 15% p.a.

Required:

(a) Calculations showing the best method of acquisition on the basis of the available information. *16 marks*

(b) A brief discussion of any further matters which might be taken into consideration when making a decision. *4 marks*

Factors for the present value of £1 applying a discount rate of 15%

Year	15%
1	0.870
2	0.756
3	0.658
4	0.572
5	0.497

Total 20 marks

8 MERCURY LTD

The directors of Mercury Ltd are considering whether to replace the company's equipment for the manufacture of pobbles.

Pobbles are currently made on equipment which cost £20,000 14 years ago. The equipment's remaining useful life is estimated at six years and the net receipts from manufacturing pobbles can be assumed to continue at £12,000 per year for that period. The net receipts comprise sales minus costs of production, but no deductions have been made for depreciation or tax.

A leading company has approached Mercury Ltd with an offer of new equipment. The equipment would be leased to Mercury Ltd for £9,000 per year, payable at the *beginning* of each year in which the equipment is leased. The leasing contract would be effective for six years. The directors of Mercury Ltd estimate that the equipment would produce £21,000 per year in net receipts (defined as above, but before lease payments).

The manager of Mercury's pobble-making department has discovered that new equipment identical to that offered by the leasing company can be purchased for £40,000. The purchased equipment would have a useful life of six years. Annual net receipts would be the same as if the equipment were leased, except that £1,000 per year would have to be spent on maintenance – which in the leasing arrangement would be covered by the actual leasing charge.

If either leasing or purchase were undertaken the old equipment would be sold for £2,000. No tax would be payable on that receipt.

Assume the following:

(1) In any sale or purchase of equipment the appropriate payment would be received or made immediately, and annual amounts would occur at the end of the appropriate years except where specifically stated to the contrary.

(2) Working capital is provided by creditors, and can therefore be ignored in the options open to the company.

(3) Mercury Ltd will be subject to 50% corporation tax and will pay tax on taxable profits one year after those profits are earned. Taxable profits will be the company's net receipts after deduction of leasing charges or maintenance

costs where appropriate. If the new equipment is purchased the company will get a 100% capital allowance on the purchase price to set against taxable profits. The company's profits from other sources would be sufficient to ensure that relief is received in full for the year in which the equipment is acquired (i.e., the tax relief can be treated as a receipt at the end of the second year).

(4) Mercury's cost of capital after tax in all relevant years is 12% per year.

Required:

(a) A numerical analysis of the options available to Mercury Ltd.

(b) Brief comments on the implications of your results, including reservations where necessary.

Table of factors for r = 12%

Years n	Future value of £1 $(1 + r)^n$	Present value of £1 $(1 + r)^{-n}$	Present value of £1 received per year $\dfrac{1 - (1 + r)^{-n}}{r}$	Annual value of £1 received now $\dfrac{r}{1 - (1 + r)^{-n}}$
1	1.120	0.893	0.893	1.120
2	1.254	0.797	1.690	0.592
3	1.405	0.712	2.402	0.416
4	1.574	0.636	3.037	0.329
5	1.762	0.567	3.605	0.277
6	1.974	0.507	4.111	0.243
7	2.211	0.452	4.564	0.219
8	2.476	0.404	4.968	0.201
9	2.773	0.361	5.328	0.188
10	3.106	0.322	5.650	0.177

30 marks

9 MERCURY (1984) LTD

Mercury (1984) Ltd has decided to replace its old machinery with new equipment costing £40,000, with an expected life of six years. It requires regular maintenance costing £1,000 p.a.

An alternative is to lease the equipment for six years at £9,000 p.a., payable in advance, which includes full maintenance. The company's cost of capital is 12%.

You are required to provide calculations showing that:

(a) Leasing is less expensive than purchase.

(b) A 15% residual value of the machine would be sufficient to make purchase cheaper than leasing.

Take tax at 50% and assume that 100% capital allowances are available on the purchase of the equipment.

Please refer to table of factors r = 10% given in question 8, on page 328.

20 marks

10 BURLEY LTD

The directors of Burley Ltd are considering two mutually exclusive investment projects in respect of which the following information is provided:

	Project A £	Project B £
Initial capital outlay	80,000	100,000
Net cash inflows, year: 1	40,000	20,000
2	60,000	30,000
3	10,000	50,000
4	5,000	50,000
5	5,000	50,000

The initial capital outlay will occur immediately and you may assume that the net cash inflows will arise at the end of each year.

Burley's estimated cost of capital over the five-year period is 12%.

Required:

(a) Numerical assessments of the two projects based on the following methods of investment project appraisal:

    (i) pay-back;
    (ii) net present value (NPV).

12 marks

(b) Comment on the relative merits of the two methods of investment project appraisal in the light of your findings under (a). *8 marks*

Note: Ignore taxation.

Factors for the present value of £1 applying a discount rate of 12%

Year	Factor
1	0.893
2	0.797
3	0.712
4	0.636
5	0.567

Total 20 marks

11 CARTER LTD

The directors of Carter Ltd have decided to undertake a programme of expansion. They have under consideration two mutually exclusive five-year projects and intend to invest in the project which offers the greater financial gain. Project I requires an initial capital investment of £140,000 and Project II an initial capital investment of £280,000. The annual net cash flows which are expected to arise from the project are as follows:

Year	Project I	Project II
1	£30,000	£100,000
2	£60,000	£90,000
3	£60,000	£90,000
4	£60,000	£90,000
5	£24,155	£53,706

Required:

(a) Calculations of the net present value of each of the two projects, assuming a 12% cost of capital.

(b) Calculations of the discounted cash flow yield (internal rate of return) of each of the two projects.

(c) Compare and comment on the results of your calculations under (a) and (b). You should support your analysis with relevant numerical calculations.

Notes:

1 The capital investment will be undertaken immediately and the annual cash flows may be assumed to arise at the year end.

2 Ignore taxation.

Table of factors for the present value of £1

Years	12%	13%	14%	15%	16%	17%	18%	19%	20%	21%	22%
1	0.893	0.885	0.877	0.870	0.862	0.855	0.847	0.840	0.833	0.826	0.820
2	0.797	0.783	0.769	0.756	0.743	0.731	0.718	0.706	0.694	0.683	0.671
3	0.712	0.693	0.675	0.658	0.641	0.624	0.609	0.593	0.579	0.564	0.551
4	0.636	0.613	0.592	0.572	0.552	0.534	0.516	0.499	0.482	0.467	0.451
5	0.567	0.543	0.519	0.497	0.476	0.456	0.437	0.419	0.402	0.386	0.370

30 marks

12 STAMFORD LTD

Stamford Ltd specialises in the production of plastic sports equipment. The company has recently developed a new machine for automatically producing plastic cricket bats. The machine cost £150,000 to develop and install, and production is to commence at the beginning of next week. It is planned to depreciate the £150,000 cost evenly over four years after which time production of plastic cricket bats will cease. Production and sales will amount to 30,000 bats each year. Annual revenues and operating costs, at April 1983 prices, are estimated as follows:

	£
Sales (£9.60 each)	288,000
Variable manufacturing costs	200,000

This morning a salesman has called and described to the directors of Stamford Ltd a new machine ideally suited to the production of plastic cricket bats. This item of equipment is distinctly superior to Stamford's own machine, reducing variable costs by 30% and producing an identical product. The cost of the machine, which is also capable of producing 30,000 cricket bats p.a. is £190,000.

Assume the following:

(1) Annual revenues and operating costs arise at the year end.
(2) The general rate of inflation is 10% p.a.
(3) The company's *money* cost of capital is 21%.
(4) The existing machine could be sold immediately for £12,000.
(5) If purchased, the new machine could be installed immediately.
(6) Either machine would possess a zero residual value at the end of four years.

Required:

(a) Calculations of the net present value of the two options open to management using the *real* cost of capital.   *22 marks*

(b) Advice to the management as to which course should be followed, and an explanation of the significance of your calculations under (a).   *8 marks*

Note: Ignore taxation.

Total 30 marks

Table of factors for n = 4 years

Interest rate (per cent) r	Present value of £1 $(1+r)^{-n}$	Present value of £1 received per year $\dfrac{1-(1+r)^{-n}}{r}$
10	0.68	3.17
11	0.66	3.10
12	0.64	3.04
13	0.61	2.97
14	0.59	2.91
15	0.57	2.85
16	0.55	2.80
17	0.53	2.74
18	0.52	2.69
19	0.50	2.64
20	0.48	2.59
21	0.47	2.54
22	0.45	2.49

13 SENSITIVITY LTD

A firm's target rate of return for investment appraisal is 10%. The appropriate discounting calculations have been carried out indicating acceptance of the project. However, the managing director is concerned about the degree of uncertainty in each of the figures and has asked you to estimate the margin of error in each of the estimates, i.e., the % by which the estimate can be incorrect without making the project unacceptable.

Estimates:
Cost	£100,000
Life	4 years
Sales p.a.	10,000 units
Selling price	£10
Cost	£6
Cost of capital	10%

Required:

(a) Calculate the margin of error in each of the six estimated figures.

(b) Comment on those to which the decision is most sensitive.

	Years	1	2	3	4
Annuity values	(10%)	0.91	1.74	2.49	3.17
	(20%)	0.83	1.52	2.10	2.58
	(25%)	0.80	1.44	1.95	2.36

30 marks

ANSWERS

1 TURNER

(a) Option (i): Buy

Years		Net cash flow £	X	Factor	=	PV £
0	Cost of machine	6,600	X	1.0	=	6,600

Option (ii): Lease at 14% p.a.

Years		Net cash flow £	X	Factor	=	PV £
1-3	Fixed period (annuity)	2,000	X	2.322	=	4,644
4	Optional years	1,000	X	0.592	=	592
5	Optional years	1,000	X	0.519	=	519
6	Optional years	1,000	X	0.456	=	456
						6,211

(b) Leasing works out cheaper and 'after sales' service is virtually guaranteed. While lease repayments, charged in the profit and loss account, reduce net profit and thus taxation, only buying for cash or on hire-purchase would enable Turner to obtain capital allowances.

He should also consider maintenance costs if he buys the machine; these tend to increase in later years.

2 JOHNS (MANUFACTURING)

Option A: Continue using old equipment

Years		Net cash flow £	X	Factor	=	PV £
1-4	Net revenue (annuity)	1,200	X	3.170	=	3,804
4	Working capital released	2,000	X	0.683	=	1,366
				Net present value		5,170

Option B: Buy new equipment

Years		Net cash flow £	X	Factor	=	PV £
1-4	Net revenue (annuity)	4,000	X	3.170	=	12,680
0	Less: Capital expenditure	5,000				
	Extra working capital	4,000				
		9,000	X	1.0	=	9,000
						3,680
4	Working capital released	6,000	X	0.683	=	4,098
				Net present value		7,778

Option C: Sell up; cease manufacture

Years		Net cash flow £	X	Factor	=	PV £
0	Sale of equipment	7,300	X	1.0	=	7,300
0	Working capital released	2,000	X	1.0	=	2,000
						9,300

On the basis of these figures John should be advised to sell the equipment and release the working capital, provided he can find an alternative use for the £9,300 yielding 10%, e.g., investment outside the business, or better still an alternative product.

3 DEXTER

Option A: Sell the rights to the patent

Years		Net cash flow £	X	Factor	=	PV £
0	Bought by Octopus	20,000	X	1.0	=	20,000

Option B: Royalties from the invention

1-5	Octopus pay royalties (annuity)	5,000	X	3.791	=	18,955

Option C: Subcontract the manufacture

1-7	Salary (annuity) £4,000 Profit (annuity) £6,000	10,000	X	4.868	=	48,680

Option D: Dexter manufactures

0	Equipment		36,000	X	1.0	=	(36,000)
1-9	Salary (annuity)	£ 6,000					
	Profit (annuity)						
	(100 – 84 – 6)	£10,000	16,000	X	5.759	=	92,144
							56,144

Options C and D seem to completely outweigh A and B, but with A and B Dexter would be free to earn a salary. Thus we should deduct the 'salary' element from C and D for comparison:

341

Option C:

Years		Net cash flow £	X Factor	= PV £
1-7	Profit (annuity)	6,000	X 4.868	= 29,208

Option D:

1-9	Profit (annuity)	10,000	X 5.759	= 57,590
0	Equipment	36,000	X 1.0	= (36,000)
				21,590

4 HI-FI LTD

(a) Option (i): Sell the patent

Years		Net cash flow £	X Factor	= PV £
0	Receipt from Splice	30,000	X 1.0	= 30,000

Option (ii): Sell the royalties

1-7	Cash from Mainbrace (annuity)	9,000	X 4.868	= 43,812

Option (iii): Subcontract the manufacture

1-8	Subcontract receipts (annuity)	8,000	X 5.335	= 42,680

Option (iv): Hi-Fi manufactures

1-9	Net receipts (annuity)	17,000	X 5.759	= 97,903
0	Less: Working capital injected	15,000		
	Equipment	45,000	X 1.0	= 60,000
				37,903
9	Add: Working capital released	15,000	X 0.424	= 6,360
				44,263

(b) There is little to choose between options (ii), (iii), and (iv), though (iv), manufacturing, is marginally the best on the basis of the net present value calculated above. It is, therefore, preferable to the others, provided there is little risk and not too much effort is required. Since these two conditions are unlikely to be met, option (ii), selling the royalties, involving little risk and no management problems, yet providing almost the same net present value, becomes the most preferable option.

Clearly Hi-Fi Ltd should not be advised to sell the patent rights, unless they can find an alternative use for £30,000 which will yield well over 10% and thus be worth at least £44,263.

5 CAMPBELL AND McCARTHY

(a) Option (i): Continue using old equipment

Years		Net cash flow £	X	Factor	=	PV £
1-5	Net revenue (annuity)	5,000	X	3.433	=	17,165
5	Working capital released	4,000	X	0.519	=	2,076
				Net present value		19,241

Option (ii): Purchase new equipment

1		25,000	X	0.877	=	21,925
2		20,000	X	0.769	=	15,380
3	Net revenue for year	15,000	X	0.675	=	10,125
4		10,000	X	0.592	=	5,920
5		5,000	X	0.519	=	2,595
						55,945
0	Less: Net cost of new equipment	20,000				
	Extra working capital	6,000				
		26,000	X	1.0	=	26,000
						29,945
5	Working capital released	10,000	X	0.519	=	5,190
				Net present value		35,135

Option (iii): Cease manufacture of flibbets

	£
Sale of equipment	5,000
Working capital released	4,000
	9,000

(b) Based upon these figures, option (ii), purchasing new equipment, is clearly the most beneficial, though not for the reason advanced by McCarthy. He is basing his decision on the payback method,* an investment appraisal technique which considers only the time required to recover the initial cost of the fixed asset. As a sole method of investment appraisal it is seriously defective, since it ignores profitability, the key principle of investment, and capital tied up in working capital.

Campbell is right in suggesting that the profitability of the present equipment must be considered (the calculation in (a) considered two options); however, he has confused profits with cash flow and ignored the time value of money, in using average profits rather than considering the timing of the profits.

*See later questions.

6 GOLDSMITH

(a) Option (i): Buy equipment now

Year		Net cash flow £	×	Factor	=	PV £
0	Purchase of equipment	10,000	×	1.0	=	10,000
5	Less: Scrap value proceeds	1,000	×	0.621	=	621
				Net present cost		9,379

Option (ii): Buy equipment on hire-purchase

			×		=	
0	Initial deposit	4,000	×	1.0	=	4,000
1	1st instalment	4,000	×	0.909	=	3,636
2	2nd instalment	4,000	×	0.826	=	3,304
						10,940
5	Less: Scrap value proceeds	1,000	×	0.621	=	621
				Net present cost		10,319

Option (iii): Hire equipment over the 5 years

1-5	Rental in arrears (annuity)	2,500	×	3.791	=	9,478

(b) On the basis of these figures, option (i), purchasing the equipment, appears the best. However, the taxation implications have not been considered; A company purchasing an asset or acquiring it on hire-purchase is entitled to capital allowances, currently 100% first-year allowance.

Since the purchase price is allowable for tax, only the interest element of hire-purchase repayments is also allowable via the reduction of net profit in the profit and loss account. On the other hand, rental payments are fully allowable for tax purposes, via the profit and loss account. If the company is not making adequate profits, tax relief is of no benefit to its cash flow.

Another consideration is the sales back-up and service usually available to the lessee in a rental and hire-purchase contract, which is often not available to the outright purchaser.

7 SORTER LTD

(a) Option (i): Buy for cash

Year		Net cash flow £	X	Factor	=	PV £
0	Cost	50,000	X	1.0	=	50,000
2	Tax relief on capital allowance: (50,000 × 50%)	25,000	X	0.756	=	(18,900)
						31,100

Option (ii): Buy on hire-purchase

0	Deposit	26,000	X	1.0	=	26,000
1-3	Instalments	13,000	X	2.284	=	29,692
2	Relief on capital allowances (50,000 × 50%)	25,000	X	0.756	=	(18,900)
3-5	Tax relief on interest (5,000 × 50%)	2,500	X	1.727	=	(4,318)
						32,474

Option (iii): Lease

1-4	Rentals, in arrears	20,000	X	2.856	=	57,120
2-5	Tax relief on rentals (20,000 × 50%)	10,000	X	2.483	=	(24,830)
						32,290

Notes

Annuity values are found by adding the successive elements of a present value table, e.g., an annual receipt of £1 at the end of years 3, 4, 5 is worth, at 15%:

Year 3	.658
4	.572
5	.497
3-5	1.727

This value is applied to the interest in the hire-purchase payments, since the first instalment is paid at the beginning of year 2 and is thus allowed in the year 2 tax computation, the tax on which is not paid until the end of year 3.

(b) Based on the above calculations, option (i), purchase for cash, is best; however, it requires an immediate payment of £50,000, as against option (ii) which requires only £26,000 and option (iii) which requires no immediate payment. Under option (i) the purchaser has complete responsibility for the property whereas under the other two options the lessor may accept some responsibility in order to protect his interest.

Although leasing, option (iii), has a higher present value cost, it may give the opportunity of returning the equipment to the lender, particularly if it were on operational lease, rather than a financial lease.

A danger of buying outright is that all maintenance falls immediately on Sorter. This is not so with option (iii) where maintenance may fall on the lessor.

8 MERCURY LTD

(a) Option (i): Continue with existing equipment

Years		Net cash flow £	X	Factor	=	PV £
1-6	Net receipts (annuity)	12,000	X	4.111	=	49,332
2-7	Less: Corporation tax at 50%	6,000	X	3.671*	=	22,026

Net present value 27,306

*4.564 − 0.893

Option (ii): Lease new equipment

0	Sale of old equipment	2,000	X	1.00	=	2,000
1-6	Receipts (annuity)	21,000	X	4.111	=	86,331
0	Less: First lease payment	9,000	X	1.0	=	(9,000)
1-5	Less: Remaining payments	9,000	X	3.605	=	(32,445)
						46,886
2-7	Less: Corporation tax at 50% net profits (21,000 − 9,000)	6,000	X	3.671	=	(22,026)

Net present value 24,860

Option (iii): Buy new equipment

Years		Net cash flow £	X Factor	= PV £
0	Sale of old equipment	2,000	X 1.0	= 2,000
1-6	Receipts (21,000 – 1,000) (annuity)	20,000	X 4.111	= 82,222
0	Cost of new equipment	40,000	X 1.000	= (40,000)
2	Tax relief at 50% on capital allowances	20,000	X 0.797	= 15,940
2-7	Corporation tax at 50% X 20,000 annuity	10,000	X 3.671	= (36,710)

Net present value 23,452

(b) It would appear that the best option open to the firm, is to run the old equipment for another six years, though one should consider the marketing aspects of the decision as well as production and financial aspects.

Further information is required about the £21,000 receipts, e.g., whether they are based on larger sales and a better market, or on cost reduction, and, if the latter, what is the nature of the costs.

In time the equipment has to be replaced. Competitors who have replaced their old equipment, may endanger the anticipated net receipts of £21,000 p.a.

The decision should be broken into two parts: (a) Continue with or replace old machines; and (b), if the latter, whether to finance it by purchase or leasing. Although leasing appears to be the less expensive, presumably because of the built-in maintenance cost, a reasonable residual value of, say, 15% may be sufficient to change the decision in favour of purchase.

9 MERCURY (1984) LTD

(a) Purchase the machine

Year		£	Factor	PV £
0	Cost £40,000	40,000	X 1.0	40,000
1-6	Maintenance £1,000 p.a. (annuity)	1,000	X 4.111	4,111
2-7	Tax relief on maintenance at 50%	500	X 3.671	(1,835)
2	Tax relief on capital allowance 50%	20,000	X 0.797	(15,940)
	Discounted cost			26,336

Lease the machine

0	Rentals, first year	9,000	X 1.0	9,000
1-5	Rentals (annuity)	9,000	X 3.605	32,445
2-7	Tax relief (50% X 9,000 annuity)	4,500	X 3.671	(16,519)
	Discounted cost			24,926

Note: the present value cost of leasing is £1,408 less than purchasing, i.e., the same difference as between options (ii) and (iii) in question 8.

(b) If the present value of the net proceeds of sale exceeded £1,408, purchase becomes cheaper than leasing.

Let R = required residual value.

Year		Cash flow £	× Factor	= PV £
6	i.e., end of life of machine, proceeds	R	× 0.507	= 0.507R
7	i.e., one year later, 50% tax	R/2	× 0.452	= (0.226R)
			Net present value	0.281R

0.281R = £1,408 to make NPV of leasing equal that of purchase.

Therefore R = £1,408/0.281 = £5,010

If the residual value were £6,000 (15% × £40,000), purchase would be clearly cheaper than leasing.

10 BURLEY LTD

(a)

Year	Factor			A £		B £
0		Initial outlay	80,000	(80,000)	100,000	(100,000)
1	0.893		40,000	35,720	20,000	17,860
2	0.797		60,000	47,820	30,000	23,910
3	0.712		10,000	7,120	50,000	35,600
4	0.636		5,000	3,180	50,000	31,800
5	0.567		5,000	2,835	50,000	28,350
				16,675		37,520

(i) Pay-back period — $1\frac{2}{3}$* years — 3 years

*i.e., 1st year 40
2nd year 40 after 8 months

(ii) Net present value — £16,675 — £37,520

(b) Although it is claimed that the pay-back method is used extensively as a method of investment appraisal, it would appear to have severe limitations if used as the sole criterion for investment decisions; as a final screening for profitable projects it may have considerable merit.

In the figures shown above, A recovers its outlay very quickly — in less than two years. Even in discounted terms the investment has been recovered in less than two years. However, once the outlay has been recovered it produces relatively little cash flow.

Project B on the other hand, is much slower in recovering the original outlay. Its pay-back period is three years. This is not untypical of capital expenditure, particularly on new products which often produce little cash flow in the early years. However, project B, unlike A, continues to produce substantial cash flows after the initial cost has been recovered, or in the final analysis, increases the company's value by £37,520, compared with the £16,675 increase produced by A.

It is true that B requires more initial capital than A, but even taking that into account, B performs better than A, with a profitability index of 1.37 (i.e., 137,520/100,000) compared to 1.21 (i.e., 96,675/80,000) for A.

There may be circumstances in which A, because of its better pay-back period, could be considered better than B. Such circumstances would include those of serious cash shortage and difficulty in forecasting cash flows for more than a couple of years ahead.

11 CARTER LTD

(a)

	Year	Factor		Project I		Project II	
Cost	0	1.0		(140,000)		(280,000)	
Receipts	1	0.893	30,000	26,790	100,000	89,300	
	2	0.797	60,000	47,820	90,000	71,730	
	3	0.712	60,000	42,720	90,000	64,080	
	4	0.636	60,000	38,160	90,000	57,240	
	5	0.567	24,155	13,696	53,706	30,451	
Net present value				29,186		32,801	

(b) Repeat calculations using a higher %, say 20%

				Project I		Project II	
Cost			0	(140,000)		(280,000)	
Receipts	1		0.833	30,000	24,990	100,000	83,300
	2		0.694	60,000		90,000	
	3		0.579	60,000		90,000	
	4		0.482	60,000		90,000	
			1.755		105,300		157,950
	5		0.402	24,155	9,710	53,706	21,590
Net present value					–		(17,160)

Internal rate of return

Project I: 20%

Project II: $12\% + \dfrac{32{,}801}{32{,}801 + 17{,}160} \times (20\% - 12\%) = 17.2\%$

(c) The internal rate of return is considered to be more easily understood by managers who are looking for a return on their investments. Project I is better than Project II using this criterion. This superiority can be supported by calculating a profitability index (present value/investment) for each.

Project I has an index of 1.208, i.e., 169,186/140,000 compared with Project II which has an index of 1.117, i.e., 312,801/280,000.

However, choice of I rather than II produces £3,615 less wealth or value for the company, (£32,801 less £29,186). The choice, because they are mutually exclusive, is between a small, high-yielding investment and a much larger but lower yielding investment, i.e., £140,000 yielding 20% compared with £280,000 yielding 17.2%. Project II, using the net present value technique is better than Project I by £3,615 in present value terms. Unless the company is finding difficulty in raising the funds at the present cost of capital — a situation known as capital rationing — the NPV technique is generally better.

Further attempts to reconcile the difference between the results of the two techniques could include an estimate of the internal rate of return of the difference between the two cash flows, i.e., what is the IRR implicit in the figures?

0	(140,000)
1	70,000
2	30,000
3	30,000
4	30,000
5	29,551

12 STAMFORD LTD

(a)

	Option 1 Present machine £		Option 2 New machine £
Annual sales	288,000		288,000
		200,000	
		60,000	
Variable costs	200,000		140,000
Annual contribution	88,000		148,000

	Option 1 Present machine £		Option 2 New machine £
4-year annuity (10%) (see tutorial note)	3.17		3.17
Present value	278,960		469,160
Less: Cost of new machine Less: Sale proceeds		190,000 12,000	(178,000)
Net present value			291,160

Tutorial note

The cash flows have been discounted at 10%, the real cost of capital, since the money cost of capital is 21% and all money flows will inflate at 10%. Since the relationship between the real cost of capital (i), the money cost of capital (m) and the rate of inflation (r) are related as follows:

$$i = \frac{m - r}{1 + r}$$

in this example;

$$i = \frac{0.21 - 0.10}{1 + 0.10} = \frac{0.11}{1.10} = 0.10$$

(b) On the basis of the figures, purchase of the new machine is better. However it requires another £190,000 less £12,000 = £178,000 (£190,000 - £12,060). The company could be short of funds particularly as it has only just finished paying £150,000 for the development of its own machine.

Emotionally it is difficult to part with an asset costing £150,000 for a mere £12,000 and to commit a further £178,000 to a machine which, on paper, can cut costs by 30%.

Only if the two factors making the new machine a better proposition (the 30% savings in variable costs, and the 10% rate of inflation), *can be substantiated*, should the firm be advised to proceed with the purchase of the new machine. If the cost saving were only 25%, the net present value of the new machine would be only £259,460 (i.e., £10,000 × 3.17 less than in the calculations). To help management it would be possible to carry out a simple sensitivity analysis to see what margin of error there is in the estimates.

13 SENSITIVITY LTD

(a) Project cost

Years		£		£
0	Cost	100,000 × 1.00	=	(100,000)
1-4	Annuity	40,000* × 3.17	=	126,800
				26,800

Margin of error: 26,800/100,000 = 26.8%

*Annual profit contribution = 10,000 × (10 − 6) = £40,000

Life

Cost (present value) to be recovered	£100,000
Annual contribution	£40,000
Annuity factor required: 100,000/40,000	2.50

Annuity factor at 10% for 3 years is 2.49 (approximately 2.50).

Minimum life required: 3 years

Margin of safety 1/4, i.e., 1 year less than the engineer's estimate of 4 years = 25%.

Sales quantity

Cost to be recovered	£100,000
Annuity value, four years at 10%	3.17
Annual cash flow required: 100,000/3.17	£31,546
Contribution per unit: 10 − 6	£4

Minimum sales required: 31,546/4 = 7,887 units

Margin of safety: (10,000 − 7,887)/10,000 = 21.1%

Selling price

Annual contribution required (see above): £31,546

Minimum contribution per unit: 31,546/10,000 =	£3.16
Add: Cost per unit	£6.00
Minimum selling price	£9.16

Margin of error: (10.00 - 9.16)/10.00 =   8.4%

Unit cost price

	£
Selling price	10.00
Less: Minimum contribution	3.16
	6.84

Margin of error: 6.84 - 6.00/6.00 = 14%

Cost of capital

4 years annuity factor = 100,000/40,000 = 2.50

From table, 4 years annuity factors:

At 20% = 2.58

At 25% = 2.36

$$\text{Required rate of interest*} = 20\% + \frac{2.58 - 2.50}{2.58 - 2.36} \times 5\%$$
$$= 20\% + 1.8\%$$
$$= 21.8\%$$

The project is only required to give a return of 10%; the margin of error in estimating the cost of capital is:

$$\frac{21.8 - 10.0}{10.0} = \frac{11.8}{10.0} = 118\%$$

*This estimate is based on the following diagram.

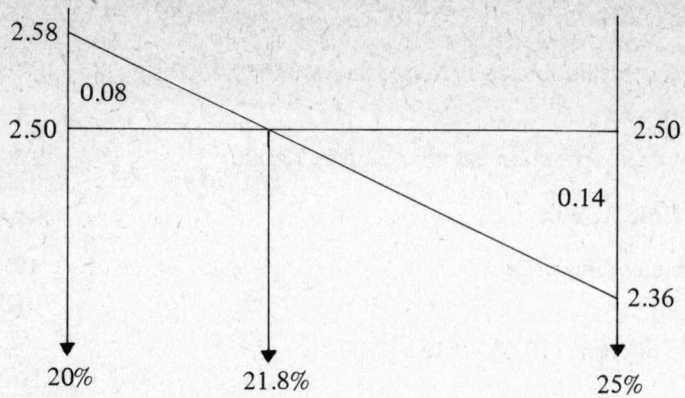

At 20% the annuity factor is 2.58, i.e., 0.08 more than 2.50.
At 25% the annuity factor is 2.36, i.e., 0.14 less than 2.50.

Therefore the estimated rate of interest (IRR) is:

$$20\% + \left(\frac{8}{8+14} \times 5\%\right) = 21.8\%$$

(b) The decision to purchase the fixed assets is clearly far more sensitive to variations in the product's selling price (8.4%) and cost (14%) than to any other factor.

Unfortunately, fixing a new product's selling price and forecasting movements in that selling price are among management's most difficult financial decisions, for which they can obtain little absolutely dependable advice. Similarly, product costs are difficult to forecast over the four-year period, though management has more control over some components of cost than it has over selling price.

The investment decision is far less sensitive to the four other factors, which can be estimated with more certainty. Engineers can advise as to the cost, life and output of machinery, while market researchers can advise as to likely sales once the price has been established.

Index

Page numbers in **bold** type refer to the introductory sections of each chapter; those in roman type are to questions, and those in *italics* are to answers.

Accounting bases **306**
Accounting policies **305-6**
Accounting rate of return **321**, *322*
Accounting Standards Committee **21**
Accruals basis **305, 306**
Accrued debenture interest 222
Acquisition
   best method of 332, 333, 334, 335, *344-5, 345-6, 346-7, 347-8*
Acquisition accounting **239**
Activity **42-3**, *58-9*
Adjustments **232**, *272, 285*
   cost of sales **287, 288**, 293, 296, *297, 299, 300, 302*
   current cost **287, 288-90**
   depreciation **287, 288**, 293, 296, *297-8, 299, 300, 302-3*
   gearing **287, 290**, 296, *300, 303*
   monetary working capital **287, 290**
   prior year **306-7**, *319*
   see also SSAP 6
Advance corporation tax **243**, *249, 253*
   and dividend paid 250, 251, *253*
   in published accounts *282*
   set-off **243-4**
Annuity values **339**, *345, 351, 352*
Asset cover ratio **44**
Asset turnover ratio **43**
Asset values **217**
Assets
   deferred *249*
      ACT as *253*
   equity in **217**
   in published balance sheet notes **259**, *276, 278, 284*
   rate of return on 47, *55-6*
   see also Net assets valuation
Associated companies
   equity accounting **218**
   in published accounts 264, *274*
   investment in *240, 241*
   see also SSAP 1
Attributable profit **307**, *314*
Auditors' remuneration 257

Bad debts provision 9, *18, 19*
Bad publicity 201, *204*
Balance sheets **1-3**, 5-9, *10-12, 17-19*, **61-2**
   budgeted 65, 67, 69, 71, *85, 88, 92, 93, 95-6, 110*, 116, 117, 120, 125, *126, 129, 137, 147*
   preparation 65, *82-3*
   showing share capital 68, *90*
   consolidated *see* Consolidated balance sheet

Balance sheet — *continued*
   current cost **287, 291**, 293, 296, *297, 301*
   adjustment **288**, *298, 302*
   date *229*
   forecast 30, *38*, **62**, 72, *97*, 118, 121, *132, 140*
   including tax 245, 246, 247, *248, 250, 252*
   published 261-2, 263, 266, 268, 270, *275, 278, 281, 284*
   illustration of **258**
   summarised 77, *106*
Bank balance **62**
   calculation of 63, *81-2*
   calculation of minimum 117-18, *131-2*
   effect of change in credit period 71, *96*
   forecast 122, *141-2*
   not in line with profit 27, *33-4*
Bonus issue **32**, 154, 156, *161*
Book value **164**, 169, 173, *176, 177, 180, 181*
Borrowing limit 68
Break-even point
   additional sales 77, *107-8*
   margin of safety 102, *105*
   quantity *104*
Break-up value
   see Liquidation value
Budgeting **61-2**, 63-80, *81-112*
   using given cost behaviour 72-8, *99-108*
   using ratios 63-72, 79-80, *81-99, 109-12*
Business valuation **163-4**, 165-74, *175-82*

COSA *see* Cost of sales adjustment
Capital
   in published balance sheet *281*
Capital allowances **244**, 245, 336, *344*
Capital expenditure 262, *273*
Capital injection 156, *161*
Capital intensive operation 74-5, *102, 105*
Capital maintenance reserve *see* Current cost reserve
Capital project appraisal **321-5**, 326-39, *340-54*
Capital reconstruction **188**, 191, 194, *199, 201-2, 205*, 208, 209-11, *213-14*
   shareholders criticism of scheme 211-12, *214-15*
Capital redemption 207
Capital redemption reserve *37*
Capital reduction 207
Capital reserve *240*
Capital turnover **59**
Capital turnover ratio **42**
Capitalisation 154, 156, *161*

Cash in working capital 149
Cash budgets   99, *113-14*, 116-25, *126-48*
Cash discounts and working capital   153, 160
Cash flow   32, *58-9*, *129*
  discounted   **322-4**, *351*
  estimated   *98*
  statement *see* Cash budgets
  expected, valuations based on   173-4, *180*
Cash forecasts *see* Cash budgets
Cash operating cycle   43, 47, *54*
Cash receipts and payments   25, *32-3*
Closing stock   *16*
Collateral valuation of shares   165-6, *175*, *183*
  see also Valuation
Companies Acts   262, 264, 266, 268, 270, 273-4
  1948   207, 209, *210*, **217**, 255
  1980   272
  1981   **3, 255,** 270, 272, **305**
Company accounts
  taxation in   **243-4,** 245-7, *248-54*
Consistency basis   **305, 306**
Consolidated accounts   *217*
  see also Group accounts
Consolidated balance sheets   **217, 218,** 220-4, 226, *228*, 229, 231, 232, *234-6*, *238*, *239*
Consolidated profit and loss accounts   218
Consolidated reserves   **218,** *239*
Cost structure   61
Credit periods   28, *35*, **62**
  effect on balance of changes in   71, *96*
  effect on working capital   151, 154, 156, *158*, *159*, *160*, *161*
Creditors   **62**
  in published balance sheet   *279*, *281*
  rate of payment calculation   46, *54*
Current assets in balance sheet   2
Current cost accounting   **287-91,** 292-6, 297-305, **308**
Current cost balance sheet   **287, 291,** 293, 296, *297*, *301*
  adjustment   **288,** *298*, *302*
Current cost profit and loss account **287, 291,** 293, 296, *297*, *299*, *301*
Current cost reserve   **290,** 293, 296, *297*, *298*, *303*
Current liabilities   246, *250*
  ACT and dividends   *249*, *253*
  in balance sheet   3
  in working capital   149
Current purchasing power accounting   **307**
Contingencies   **308**
Contracts in progress   **307,** 310, 311, *314-15*
  in published accounts   261, 263, *273*, *274*
  see also SSAP 9

Corporation tax   98, 249, 250, 252, 253
  ACT *see* Advanced corporation tax
  cash balance at payment   **113**
  in published accounts   *282*
  mainstream   243, 245, *248*, *249*, *253*
  on trading profit   270
Cost behaviour   **61**
Cost of capital   **324**
  margin of error   *353*
Cost of control   **219,** *228*, *230*, *231*, *233*, *238*, *240*
Cost of materials used   9, *19*
Cost of sales   9, *16*, *19*, *59*, **63**, *82*, *285*
  purchases equal to   *129*
Cost of sales adjustment   **287, 288,** 293, 296, *297*, *299*, *300*, *302*
Cost of shares   *234*, *235*, *237*
Current ratio   **43,** *58*, *59-60*, 68, 70, *94-5*, *98*, 152, 153, 154-5, *158*, *159*, *160*
  lowest   70, *94-5*

Debenture interest   225, 246
  accrued   222
Debenture stock   166, *176*
  in proposed reconstruction   209-11, *213-14*
Debentures   68, *92-3*, *95*
  notes to published balance sheet   **259**
Debtors
  in published accounts   261, 263, 270, *273*, *274*, *279*
  in working capital   **149,** 153, 154, *159-60*
  order of priority for repayment   **183-4,** 185-6, *197-7*, *198*, *200*, *201*, *203*, *204*
  rate of collection   46, *54*
Deferred taxation   **244,** 245, 246, *248*, *249*, *251*, *253*, *266*, *275*, *282*, **308**
Depreciation   28, *32*, *35*, 171, *179*, 252, 267, 270, **308,** 312, *316-18*
  adjustment   **287, 288-9,** 293, 296, *297*, *298*, *299*, *300*, *302-3*
  and capital allowances   **244,** *248*
  and working capital   151, 153, 154, 156, *158*, *159*, *160*, *161*
  in notes to published balance sheet   *276*, *279*, *285*
  in published accounts   257, 261, 266, *273*, *275*
  see also SSAP 12
Directors' remuneration   266, 267, *275*, *277*, *279*
  in notes to published accounts   **257,** 266, *275*, *283*
Discounted cash flow   **322-4,** *351*
Discounted cash flow yield   **321, 323-4**
Dividend cover   45
Dividend yield   **45,** 163, 166, 167, 169, 171, 173, *175*, *176-7*, *178*, *180*, *181*, *183*

Dividends
    additional sales to cover   126, *138*
    and ACT   **243**, *249, 251, 253*
    appropriated from subsidiary account   *237*
    in notes to published account   *277*
    out of pre-acquisition profit   *235*
    proposed, is current liability   *237*
    tax credit on   *250*
Double entry system   *15, 16, 38, 82*
Doubtful debts and working capital   **151**, *159*
Drawings   *12*

Earnings   *49, 56-8*
Earnings per share   **306**
Earnings yield   **45, 163,** 165-6, 171, *175, 176-7, 180*
EEC's Fourth Directive on Company Law   **255**
Equity
    return on   *59-60*
Equity accounting   **218,** *241*
    see also SSAP 1
Exceptional items   **313,** *318*
Expansion proposals   **72,** *98-9*
Exposure documents
    ED 30   *285*
        see also SSAP 22
    ED 31   *239,* **309**
    ED 33   **244**
External capital   **217**
Extraordinary items   **307,** 313, *318, 319*
    in profit and loss account   *248, 249*
    in published accounts   *280*
    see also SSAP 6

Final balance   *7, 8, 15, 17*
Finance Act 1984   **244**
Financial implications   **74-6,** *102-6, 106-8*
Financial leases   **309**
Financing, short term   118, *135*
Fixed assets in balance sheet   **2**
Fixed costs   **61**
Flow of funds statement   24, *31*
    see also Source and application of funds
Foreign currency transactions   **309**
Franked investment income   **243,** 246, *248, 250*
    tax credit on   266, *275*
Freehold property
    in consolidated balance sheet   227, *231, 239*
    in published accounts   263, *273*
    in published balance sheet   268, *278, 281*
    sale of   *270*

Gearing   **44,** *52-3, 58-9, 135*
Gearing adjustment   **287, 290,** 296, *300, 303*
Gearing ratio   **44,** *59-60*

Going concern   **305, 306**
Goodwill   **272,** *284, 285,* **309**
    calculation   **219,** *228, 230, 231, 233, 234, 235, 237, 238, 241*
    negative   *181,* **309**
    written-off   28, *35*
Government grants   **306**
Gross profit   **42**
Group accounts   **217-19,** 220-7, *228-41,* **308**
Group reserves   **229,** *230, 232, 236, 240*
Growth   **44-5**

Hire purchase   **309,** 332, *344, 345*
Holding companies   **217,** *237*

Immediate finance   *107*
Imputation tax   **243, 307**
Inflation   **325**
    see also Current cost accounting
Instalment credit sales   117-18, 131
Interest
    accrued debenture   222
    in published accounts   **257,** 262, 264, *273, 274, 277, 280*
Internal indebtedness   **217,** 219
Internal rate of return (IRR)   **321, 323-4,** 337, *349-50*
Interpretation of accounts   **41-5, 46-51,** *52-60*
Investment
    in associated company   **218,** *240, 241*
    in subsidiary, cost of   *229*
Investment appraisal   **321-5, 326-39,** *340-54*
Investment income
    franked   **243,** 246, *248, 250*
        tax credit   266, *275*
    in published accounts   **257,** *274, 275, 281*
Investment options   78-9, *108-9*
Investment properties   **308**
    see also SSAP 19
Investment ratios   **44-5**

Leasehold property in published accounts   261, *273*
Leasing   **309,** 326, 332, 333, 334-5, *340, 344, 345, 346-7, 347-8*
Ledger accounts   *7, 13*
Leverage see Gearing
Liquidation   **183-4,** 185-95, *196-205*
    immediate   188, 189, 191, 193, 194, *198, 200, 201, 202, 204-5*
    local government authority offer   193, *203*
    order of priority of repayment   **183-4,** 185-6, *196-7, 198, 200, 201, 203, 204*
    piecemeal   186, *197*
    sale as going concern   187, 188, *198, 199*
    value   **164,** 165-6, 169, 171, 173, *175, 176-7, 180, 181*

357

Liquidity ratio 43, 49, *56, 57, 58-9, 59-60,*
   68, *90, 98*
Loan capital **3**
   preference shares included *59*
Loan finance 121, *140*
Loans
   notes to published balance sheet **259**
   see also Capital injection
London Stock Exchange 165, 166
Long-term capital
   employed 49, *56-8*
   return on *59-60*
Long-term liabilities in balance sheet **3**
Long-term work in progress 310, 311, *314-15*

Machinery disposal account *39*
Maintainable earnings 169, *177-8*
Maintenance costs in investment appraisal 334, 335, *345, 346, 347*
Manufacturing account **4, 9,** *19*
   budgeted 125, *147*
Margin of error in investment appraisal 339, *351, 352-4*
Margin of safety 102, 105
Mark-up 117, *127*
Medium-term liabilities *93*
Merger accounting *239*
   pooling **309**
Minority interests **217, 219,** *228-33, 235-8,* **240**
Monetary working capital adjustment **287, 290**
Mortgage loan in published account 267, *277*

Negative goodwill *181,* **309**
Net assets valuation **164,** 166, *175, 176, 178, 181*
   at liquidation 185, *196*
Net present value (NPV) **321, 323,** 336, 337, 338, *340, 342, 343, 348-49, 349-50, 350-1*
Net profit 49, *56-8*
Net profit margin **42**
Notes to published accounts **256-7**
   to balance sheet **259,** 266, *276,* 284
   to profit and loss account 266, 270, *274-5, 277,* 280

Operating costs *82*
Operating expenditure **257**
Operating profit 262, 263, *273, 274*
Operational leases **309**
Overdrafts 29, 65, 68, 72, 87, 97-9, 122, *141-2, 144*
   balancing item in balance sheet *84*
   compared with loan finance 121, *140*
   in published accounts 263, 267, *273, 277*
   maximum 117-18, 120, *131-2, 136*

Patents, exploitation of 328-9, 329-30, *341-2, 342-3*
Pay-back appraisal 336, *344, 348-9*
Pay-back period **321, 322**
Performance comparisons 47, *55-6*
Performance ratios **41**
Period of credit *see* Credit periods
Plant and machinery in published accounts 261, 266, 270, *273,* 276, 285
Pooling **309**
Post-acquisition losses *237*
Post-acquisition profits **219,** *233, 236, 239*
Post-acquisition reserves **218,** *229*
Post-balance sheet events **308**
Pre-acquisition profit **219**
   dividends out of *235*
Pre-consolidation procedure for cancelling internal indebtedness **219**
Present value *351*
Present value cost *346*
Price/earnings ratio **45,** 167, 173, *177, 180*
Price indices 293, 294, 296
Prior year adjustments **306-7,** *319*
   see also SSAP 6
Priority of repayment at liquidation **183-4,** 185-6, *196-7,* 198, 200, 201, 203, 204
Profit and loss account **3-4, 6-9,** *11-12, 14, 17, 18-19,* 61, *99,* 121, *140*
   budgeted 80, *109-12,* 116, 117, 119, 125, *126, 128, 134, 147*
   consolidated *218*
   current cost **287, 291,** 293, 296, *297, 299, 301*
   distributable reserve *233*
   estimated 118, 120, *132, 137*
   including tax 245, 246, 247, *248, 249, 252*
   of retained earnings 313, *318-19*
   published 262, 263-4, 266, 268, 270, 272, *274, 277, 280,* 283
      illustration of **256**
      summarised 77, *106*
Profit/earnings ratio **163**
Profit margin 56, *59*
Profit margin ratio **42**
Profit/volume ratio **42, 62,** *89, 105, 106*
Profitability **42,** *58-9*
   of options 74-5, *102-4*
Profits
   after tax 46, *52*
   calculation of 73, 74, *99-100, 100-1*
   post-acquisition **219**
   pre-acquisition **219**
   statement *87*
      estimated 124, *144*
   unrealised, elimination of **217**
Property valuation 168-9, *178*
   and working capital 151, 156, *159, 161*

358

Property valuation — *continued*
  at liquidation 185, *196-7*
Proprietorship ratio 44
Prudence basis 305, 306
Published accounts 255-60, 261-72, *273-86*
  extraordinary items *see* Extraordinary items
  illustration of balance sheet 258
  illustration of profit and loss account 256
  notes 256-7, 259
Purchases 62

Rate of collection of debtors 46, *54*
Rate of payment of creditors 46, *54*
Rate of return on total assets 47, *55-6*
Rate of stock turnover 46, *54*
Ratio analysis 41-5, 48-9, 51, *56-8, 59-60*
Reconstruction of capital *see* Capital reconstruction
Redemption of capital *see* Capital redemption
Reducing balance depreciation 312, *316-18*
Reduction of capital *see* Capital reduction
Registrar of Companies 255
Reorganisation of capital 207-8, 209-12, *213-15*
  see also Capital reconstruction
Replacement cost 164, 169, 173, *177, 180, 181, 182*
Required residual value *348*
Research and Development expenditure 308
  in published account 265, 272, *275, 284, 285*
  see also SSAP 13
Reserves 37
  apportionment of 219
  capital 240
  capital maintenance *see* Current cost
  capital redemption 37
  consolidated 218, 239
  current cost 290, 293, 296, *297, 298, 303*
  distributable *233*
  group 229, 230, 232
  in balance sheet 3, 4,
    forecast 30, *38-9*
  movement on, in published balance sheet 259
  post acquisition 218
Retained earnings 313, *318*
Return on assets 47, *55-6*
Return on assets ratio 41
Return on capital employed *58*
Return on equity *59-60*
Return on equity ratio 41
Return on long-term capital *59-60*
Return on long-term capital ratio 41
Returns to shareholders 46, *52-3*
Revaluation of freehold property 28, 30
Revaluation reserve *283, 285*

Royalties 247, *252,* 328, 329, *341, 342, 343*

SSAP *see* Statements of Standard Accounting Practice
Safety ratio *see* Solvency ratio
Sale of company as going concern 187, 188, *198, 199*
Sales
  additional
    break even point 77, *107-8*
    to cover dividend 126, *138*
  budgeted *102-4*
  calculation of 64, *82*
  instalment credit 117-18, *131*
  margin of safety *102, 105*
  required calculations 76, *104-5*
  required to achieve expected profit 65-6, 67, *84, 86-7, 87-8*
  required to give expected balance 66, 67, *86, 88*
Scrip issue 32, 154, 156, *161*
Secondary ratios 42
Sensitivity analysis 322, *351*
Share capital
  in balance sheet 3
    budgeted 68, *90*
  in group accounts 233
  notes to published balance sheet 259, *279*
  redemption *see* Capital redmeption
Share valuation 163-4, 165-74, *175-82*
Shareholders
  criticism of proposed amalgamation 211-12, *214-15*
  return on capital 46, *52-3, 58*
Shares
  cost of 234, 235, 237
  ordinary, in proposed reconstruction 209-11, *213-14*
  unquoted, in published accounts 261, *273*
Short-term financing 118, *135*
Solvency *58-9, 59-60*
Solvency ratios 43-4, 72, *97-9*
Source and application of funds 21-2, 23-30, *31-9*, 307
  ASC format 21-2
  budgeted 65, *83-5*
  statement 4
  see also Flow of funds
Stability 43-4, 50, *58-9*
Statements of Standard Accounting Practice 305-9, 310-13, *314-9*
  SSAP 1 218, 227, *241,* 305
  SSAP 2 305-6
  SSAP 3, 4 and 5 306
  SSAP 6 305, 306-7, 313, *318, 319*
  SSAP 7 (provisional) 307
  SSAP 8 243, 307
  SSAP 9 *100,* 305, 307, 310, 311, *314, 315*

359

Statements of Standard Accounting Practice
— *continued*
  SSAP 10   307
  SSAP 11 *see* SSAP 15
  SSAP 12   *285*, **305, 308,** *317*
  SSAP 13   **305, 308**
  SSAP 14   **217, 227, 308**
  SSAP 15   **243, 244, 247, 308**
  SSAP 16   **287, 294, 295, 308**
  SSAP 17 and 18   **308**
  SSAP 19   **305, 308**
  SSAP 20, 21 and 22   **309**
Stock figures   68, *90-1*
Stock in working capital   **149,** 156, *161*
Stock turnover   *59,* **62,** 68, 71, *91*
Stock turnover rate   46, 49, *54, 56-8*
Stock valuation   *100, 101,* 171, *179,* **307,** *315*
  at liquidation   185, *196*
  in published balance sheet   259, 268, 272, *276,* 279, 285
Strength   **44-5**
Subsidiary company   **217**
  cost of investments in   *229*
  dividend appropriated from   *237*

Takeover   190, 193, *200, 202, 204*
Target rate of return   **339**
Tax rate, effective   *59-60*
Taxation
  dates liabilities payable   246, *250, 251*

Taxation — *continued*
  in company accounts   **243-4,** 245-7, *248-54*
  in published accounts   264, 270, *274,* 275, 277, *280*
Timing differences   **244,** 247
Total bank account   80, *84, 110-12*
Trading account   **3,** 6-9, *11-12,* 14, 17, *18-19,* 99, 121, *140*
  budgeted   80, *109-12,* 116, 125, *126, 147*
  forecast   117, 118, 119, 120, *128, 132, 134, 137*
Turnover in notes to published accounts   257, *274,* 277, *280*

Utilisation ratio   **43**

Valuation   **163-4,** 165-74, *175-82*
Value added tax (VAT)   **306**
Variable costs   **61,** *89, 100, 106,* 338, *350*

Wage costs   *106*
Weighted average cost of capital   **324**
Work in progress *see* Contracts in progress *and* Long-term work in progress
Working capital   **3,** 47, *54,* **149-50,** 151-7, *158-61*
Working capital ratio *see* Current ratio

Yield valuation   **163-4**
Yields   **45**